"You'll like it here."

Ed Orzechowski

"You'll like it here."

The Story of Donald Viktus
—Belchertown Patient #3394

Ed Orzechowski

Copyright © 2016 Ed Orzechowski
All rights reserved including the right of
reproduction in whole or in part in any form.

Published by *Levellers Press*, Amherst, Massachusetts

Printed in the United States of America

ISBN: 978-1-945473-10-4

Dedication

*T*his book is dedicated to all former residents of Belchertown State School living and deceased, and in particular to Carol Chunglo, Al and Agnes Warner, Russel Daniels, Bobby Ricci, and his parents, the late Virginia and Ben Ricci.

Acknowledgements

Writing a book is not a solo project, and I am grateful for the many who helped make this book a reality. I thank my friends Tommy Shea and Suzanne Strempek-Shea, who inspired me from the beginning, Sandy Kaye and Allan Hunter who told me to start with a scene, and my book doctor Mary Carroll Moore, who guided me through the long process. I thank Clare Ansberry of The Wall Street Journal for her interest and support, Denise Fontaine-Pincince and Kevin O'Hara for their friendship and encouragement, James Heflin for his critical eye, and Jacqueline Sheehan for welcoming me into Straw Dog Writers, a wonderful community of talented writers.

I have enjoyed the huge benefit of membership in three writing groups—Carpe Stylum, the Blue Hills Writers, and the writers of the Northampton Senior Center. I am indebted to all who offered suggestions along the way, including LuWanda Cheney, Joy Hibsher, Martha Shea, and Melissa Weise; Chuck Latovich, Vivian Brock, Madeleine Biondolillo, Lyn Brakeman, Irene Buchine, Patricia Horwitz, Marilyn Morrissey, Jean Mudge, Jane Perkins, Mary Lou Shields, Alissa Newton, Holly Pappas, Lee Varon, and Miriam Stein; Candy Carlisle, Lucy Greenburg, Peggy Winnett, Jillian Hensley, Sasha Berman, Cie Simurro, Billy Lynch, and Fred Shea.

My special thanks to Jim P. Spencer for his able and generous guidance, to Steve Strimer of Levellers Press for accepting my manuscript, and in particular to Cheryl Suchors for her unending support, her keen reading, and her faith in my writing.

Author's Note

This is the true story of the life of Donald Vitkus, as he told it to me. It is a story of the resiliency of the human spirit. The result of more than 40 hours of interview, this is Donald's recollection of growing up at Belchertown State School, how that experience shaped the rest of his life, and his passionate desire that we never return to those days. In reconstructing conversations, scenes, and events, I have made every effort to remain as accurate and faithful as possible to his account. In the interest of privacy, names of some individuals have been changed.

In 2005, I assisted Benjamin Ricci, a retired professor from the University of Massachusetts in Amherst, at a book signing at nearby Holyoke Community College. Ben was the founder and tenacious heart of Advocacy Network, Inc., a nonprofit that advocates for the rights and care of the developmentally disabled, and I was editor of the organization's newsletter. My wife Gail and I are co-guardians for her sister Carol Chunglo, who is severely autistic, and we both serve on the Advocacy Network board of directors.

Ben was at HCC to discuss his new book, Crimes Against Humanity (iUniverse 2004), a chronicle of Ricci v. Greenblatt, a 1973 federal class action lawsuit against the Massachusetts Department of Mental Retardation. The book is an unflinching account of the horrific conditions that existed at Belchertown State School, a nearby institution for people who were referred to as mentally retarded, including Ben's son Bobby and my sister-in-law Carol.

Following the presentation, a member of the audience approached me. Donald Vitkus, a soft-spoken man in a tan leather jacket, was then a 62-year-old student at HCC. I didn't know it at the time, but he was president of the school's Human Services Club and had been responsible for arranging Ben's talk. Donald told me he had grown up at Belchertown, and was looking for someone to help him write his life story. That conversation evolved into this book.

Donald's voice is the voice of Bobby Ricci, Carol Chunglo and the thousands of others who lived at Belchertown and similar institutions across the country in the mid-1900s. Their experiences vary, but what they endured they hold in common.

Thank you, Donald, for trusting me with your remarkable story.
—Ed Orzechowski

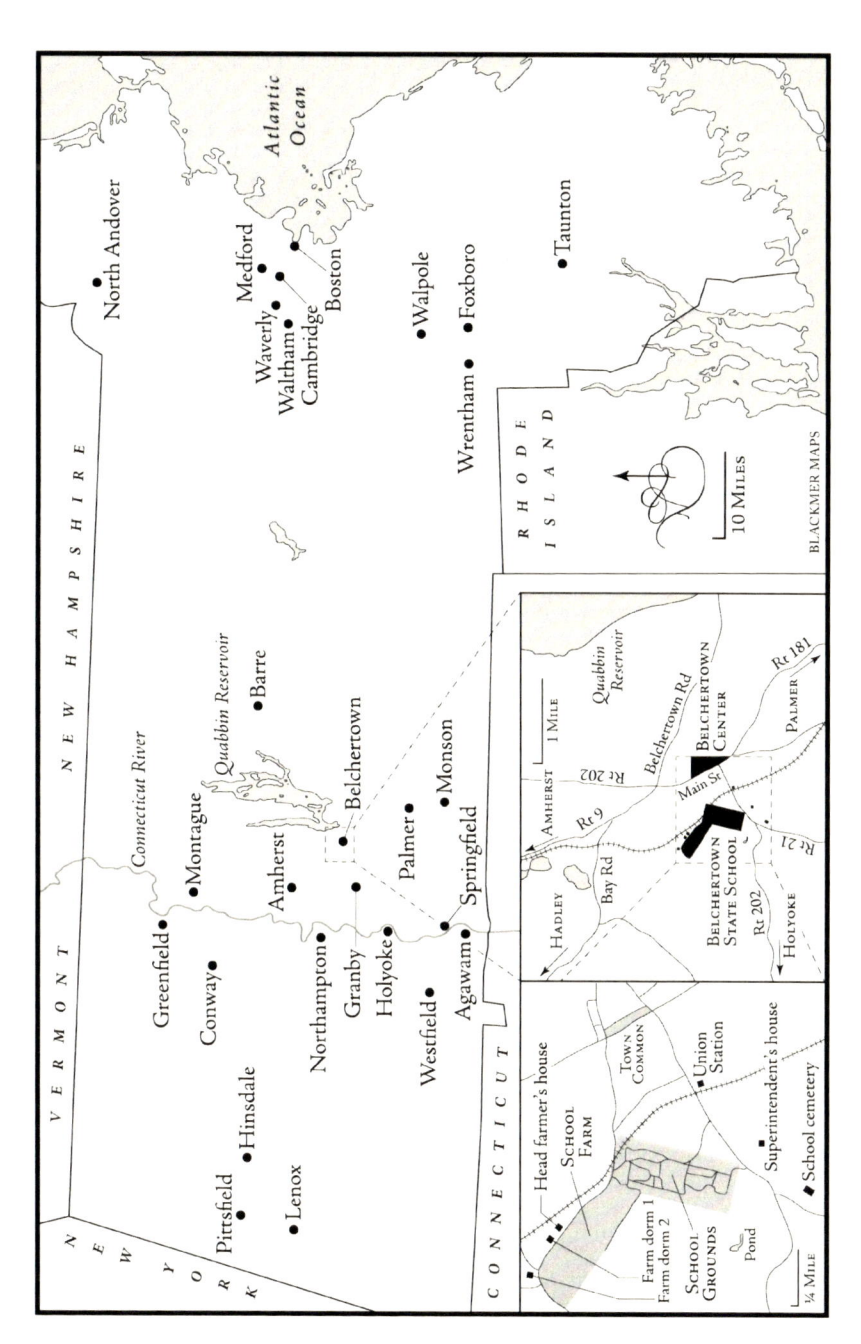

Courtesy Blackmer Maps and University of Massachusetts Press

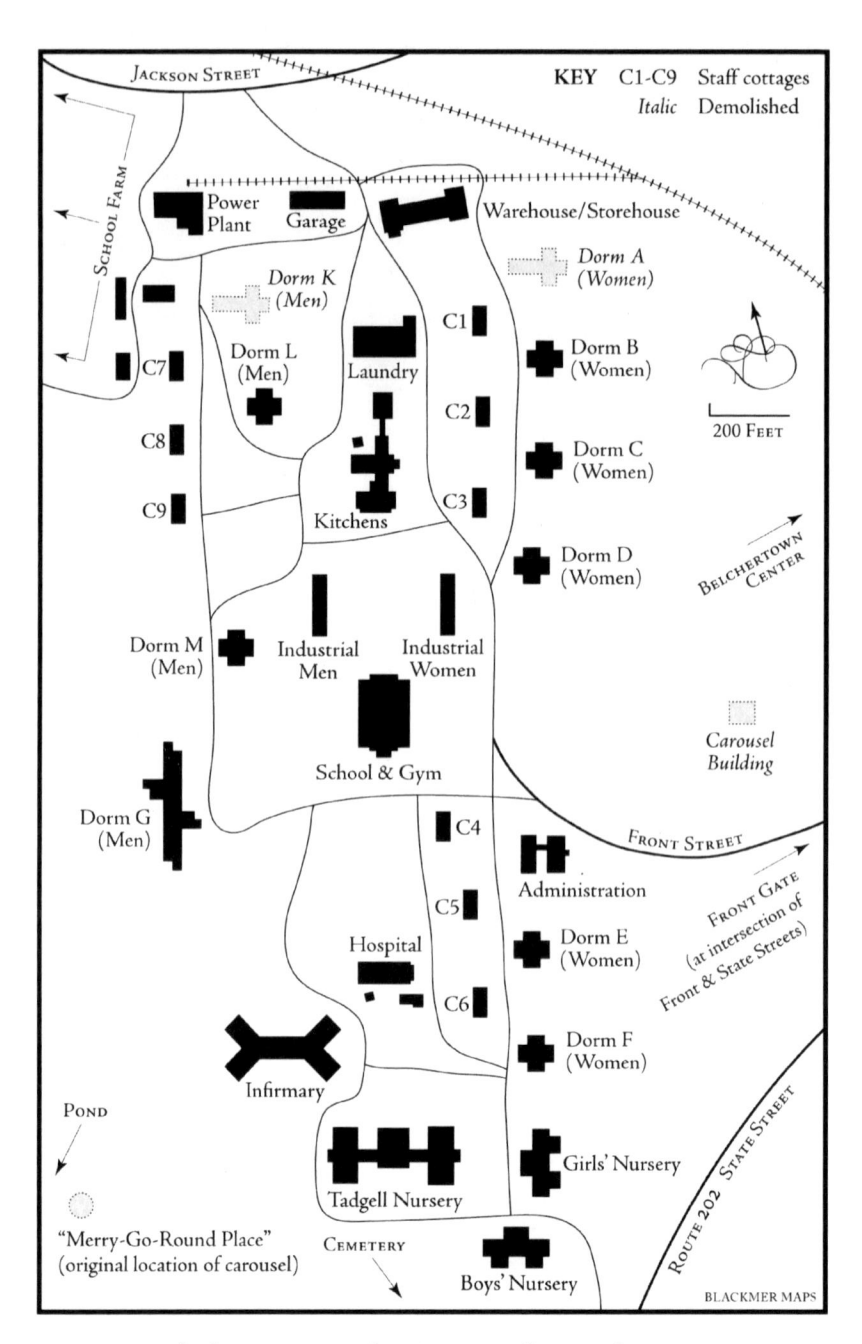

Courtesy Blackmer Maps and University of Massachusetts Press

Number 3394

Donald was brought for admission by Miss Craig of D.C.G. and was sent to Nursery I. He is 6 yrs. old. I.Q. 41, Maternal grandfather said to be below par mentally and alcoholic. Mother committed to Lancaster.

- July 13, 1949.
Information for Case Record Folder

"Okay, now are you happy?" The woman shut off the car and glared at me in her rearview mirror. I didn't answer. I was sweaty and felt like I was gonna puke. When you're six years old, every trip is long, but it's even longer when you can't roll down the window in the middle of summer. She wouldn't even stop to let me pee.

"That must be it," she said to the man beside her, pointing to a brick building with a clock at the top. The lady wore a dark blue dress and hat with a kind of veil thing on it, and he was in a brown suit. This must have been an important day.

They got out and the man came around to my side, holding a big tan envelope. "Let's go," he said, grabbing my arm. He pulled me along the sidewalk toward a set of granite stairs, while the woman gripped her pocketbook with both hands, like she thought I was gonna steal it or something. I had to walk fast to keep up.

At the top of the stairs, the man pushed a button at the entrance of the building and I heard a bell ring inside. "You'll be happy here," he said, looking down at me. "That's right," the woman added. "You'll be with a lot of other kids like yourself. You'll like it here."

When the door opened, another lady led us down a long hall, the hard heels of her shoes echoing off the walls. She took us into a room where a woman sat at a desk behind stacks of paper, folders, and a typewriter. The place smelled like stinky flowers, but I couldn't see any. To one side was a row of dark wood cabinets, each with a bunch of drawers with little signs on them. Near the window a fan turned slowly back and forth. The window was shut tight.

"Here they are," the door lady said, and left.

"You must be tired," the desk lady said to the man and woman, standing to shake their hands. "We're a long way from Boston." She was big like her desk, and she had on a dress with big flowers all over it. The three of them put on smiles, told each other their names, and she extended her hand toward chairs by her desk. Then she turned to me. "You sit over there." The smile had vanished from her voice. She pointed toward a bench on the side of the room, away from the fan.

The man handed her the envelope. She unwound a red string at the top and took out a bunch of papers. I knew they were about me.

"So, this is Donald." The desk lady picked up a pencil and scanned the first page through a pair of glasses that looked like someone had cut them in half. They were attached to a cord that dangled from her neck.

"'Born 1943 in Waltham, Massachusetts,'" she read out loud. "'IQ of 41. Moron.'"

She leaned toward me, tilted her head and examined me over those glasses—I didn't like the way she did that—and the stinky flower smell got even stronger. "You wouldn't guess, would you?" She scanned me up and down. "Look at that blond hair and those bright hazel eyes. He looks normal enough."

I gazed through the closed window at a building in the distance. It had bars on the windows.

"Some of them just don't show it," she said, and resumed reading. "'Grandfather below par mentally, alcoholic.' That's a great combination, isn't it? I see at least he doesn't mess his pants or bed, and he knows how to feed himself and get dressed." She stared at me again. "That's better than a lot of 'em in here." She tapped her pencil on the desktop while her eyes moved down the page.

"God, can you believe this!" she said, without looking up. "'On day child was born, mother had worked all day...returned to rooming house...delivered self of child...walked down two flights of stairs to telephone former foster mother, who called ambulance. Mother committed to Lancaster.'"

"Well, at least she won't be putting out any more like this one while she's locked up. And who knows where the father is." She glanced up. "Any clothes with him?"

"Just what he's got on," the man said.

"Stop squirming, young man!" The desk lady glared at me over her glasses. I still had to pee. She handed a pen to the man and woman, and they wrote something on a couple of papers while she picked up her phone.

"Elizabeth, tell Nursery One that we're bringing another one over. Right, Number 3394," she said, and hung up. "Okay. I'll take it from here," she told the man and woman, and led us out the door.

The driver lady and man headed back to their car while the desk lady took me up a sidewalk toward another brick building, not far away. There was a set of swings beside it, but no kids on them. In the distance, I heard screaming. No words, just screaming. The voice sounded young, but I couldn't tell if it was a boy's or girl's.

Inside was a woman dressed all in white. She had a funny pointed hat on the top of her hair, and a ring of keys on a chain thing hooked to her waist. I never saw so many keys. She bent over close to my face and put on a fake grin. A little too loud and a little too slow, she said in a singsong voice, "How would you like to wear a monkey suit?" Her head bobbed back and forth to the rhythm of her words.

"Sure." I held my crotch. "Is there a toilet here?"

The pointy hat took me inside, stretched out her keys, locked the door, and led me straight to a bathroom. She watched while I peed. When I zipped up, she brought me to a bench down the hall. "Sit here," she said, and walked away.

A kid about my age was on the other end, rocking back and forth. With each repetition, he struck his head against the wall behind him. A few other boys wandered the hall, dressed in gray one-piece outfits, buttoned up the back. Monkey suits, I guessed. In a nearby room, smaller kids sat in cribs with tops across them, padlocked like cages. Some wore diapers, others were naked. A few were tied down with leather straps, their wrists and ankles rubbed raw. Some cried, moaned, or laughed for no apparent reason. Others looked normal.

This was Nursery 1, my first stop at Belchertown State School.

Pecking Order

In our mental examination Donald scored a mental age of 1 year and 3 months which gave him an I.Q. of .41. It is impossible to predict whether the boy is slow in starting because of some early nutritional deficiency and may pick up in later years, or whether the boy will remain on a rather low mental level with his I.Q. probably dropping still further.

—June 6, 1946
C. Stanley Raymond
Superintendent of Wrentham State School

I was three years old, living in a foster home in eastern Massachusetts, when it occurred to someone in the system that I needed my head examined. Literally. My guess is that I was slow in developing. The finding that I had an I.Q. of 41, three years later became my ticket to Belchertown.

It was standard practice to discourage or even prevent family from visiting in the first month after their child was admitted, sometimes committed, to the state school. The child needed time to adjust, the belief was, and seeing parents during those early weeks would only delay his or her adaptation. Once a month had passed, parents were allowed to wait downstairs in the tiny visitors' room across from the matron's office for an attendant to deliver their son or daughter. They were forbidden to enter the wards where their child slept.

In my case, there was no need for concern. October 13, 1949: Donald lives in "F" Building. He is well behaved, quiet, and clean. Occasionally he has temper fits ... He receives no mail and has no visitors. Three months after my arrival, no one had come to see me. I was six years old, had bounced around six different homes, my last set of foster parents made no attempt to visit, and I didn't know who my real parents were.

The format of these periodic entries in my file was consistent—a comment filed by an attendant or administrator about my behavior, my hygiene, and my contact with the outside world. Three months later, little had changed: January 13, 1950. Donald has adjusted well in "F" Building. He is clean, quiet, and nice. He has had no visitors. And a half year later: July 20, 1950. Donald is well nourished and cooperative. He is tidy. Receives no mail or visitors.

By then, I was seven years old, and "no mail or visitors" had become a continuing refrain in my record. They could've made a rubber stamp and saved themselves some time.

In the early 1900s, Massachusetts institutions for the "feebleminded" were regulated by the State Board of Insanity, which later became the Department of Mental Diseases. By the time I arrived, Belchertown State School was part of the Department of Mental Health. Twenty years after I was released from the system, a separate Department of Mental Retardation was created. Now it's called the Department of Developmental Services.

When I was admitted in the summer of 1949, the population of Belchertown State School was about 1,300 residents, from preschool to elderly. Set well back on 860 acres of former farmland off Route 202 in western Massachusetts, it appeared to be a scenic New England campus of brick buildings, cottages, trees, grass, and fields. Complete with its own utilities and infrastructure, it was a town within a town. There were residence halls, a school building and nursery, industrial building, an infirmary with full operating room, dentistry, and pharmacy. A coal-fired plant and towering smokestack that supplied steam heat to every building through a maze of underground tunnels. A dairy farm, acres of crops, a cannery, warehouse, laundry, bakery, broom factory, print shop, barber shop, shoe repair, and a sawmill. A sewerage plant, a rail spur for coal and freight delivery, a trash dump. Even a burial ground.

Many of the attendants and staff resided in cottages on the property, with free housekeeping supplied by the girl patients who made their beds, mopped their floors, and cleaned their toilets. The head of the operation, the superintendent, also lived on the grounds, but on the opposite side of Route 202 in a large white house set on a hill among trees, where he and his visitors wouldn't have much contact with us retards. A patient named Al Warner painted that house. He told me he peed in the paint.

No matter how mentally challenged, injured, sick or healthy, residents were all "patients," segregated by sex and grouped by age, a captive population that was a convenient target for medical experimentation from fluoride to radiation, electric shock to lobotomy.

In some cases, the population included entire families, but the mother lived in one building, the father in another, sons and daughters in others. The only time these parents were together with their children was for a few hours on Mother's Day and Father's Day.

A group called the "farm boys"—many were actually in their 30s and 40s—had the most freedom and privileges. They lived in a separate farmhouse that produced our food, tending chickens and pigs, milking cows, plowing fields, and raising vegetables that were canned right at the institution.

A pecking order divided us into three clinically labeled categories. "Idiots," otherwise known as "Low Grades," were at the bottom. Then came "Imbeciles." At the top of the I.Q. heap were "Morons." Like me.

The most seriously handicapped and medically fragile were confined to the infirmary, while the rest of us lived in ward buildings identified by a single black capital letter, about the size of a hand, nailed above the entrance. I spent the bulk of my eleven years with other school age kids in "D," "F," and "M." Each building had the same institutional layout—a dining area in the basement, day hall on the first floor, barracks-like sleeping quarters on the second, and bars on the windows.

Getting the Hang of Things

```
Donald is being cared for in "F" Building and
attends school classes. Hygiene-clean. Conduct-
he is one of Peck's bad boys, sometimes good,
sometimes bad. Does not receive mail or visitors
and does not go on vacation.
```

– August 22, 1951
Yearly Physical Examination

"Rise and shine, you retards! Think you're gonna sleep all day? You got work to do. Get a move on!"
Jones had an oddly high-pitched voice for such a big man. From under my blanket, I could hear him banging on metal bed rails with his sawed-off broomstick as he worked his way down the rows. I had been at Belchertown for two years now, and had learned a couple of things. One of them was to sleep with the covers pulled over my head, a behavior that would stay with me for life. Even now in late summer, it seemed safer that way.

The sun wasn't up yet but the room was bright because the attendants never turned the lights off. When I lifted the blanket, I watched Jones jabbing at guys, pulling the sheets off some, smacking others with the broom handle because they didn't move right away. The lights shined off his bald head.

This was how every day started, crammed into a ward with thirty other young boys, with Jones bellowing at 5:30 in the morning, preparing us for all the hollering we'd hear the rest of the day. I was eight years old, and still had "received no mail or visitors." F Building was now my home.

I had gotten into trouble the day before for chasing Edward down the hall. He slammed the door on my finger and I had to get stitches, but I was the one who got yelled at for bothering the doctor. I was jealous of kids like Edward, who had visits from family, and I ached for attention. Sometimes I went after another kid, especially if he had ratted on me. "Donald peed on the floor!" "Donald stole my shoelaces!" There was a lot of that—boys snitching on each other, trying to get on an attendant's good side. Sometimes, though, my outbursts were merely to demonstrate that I existed. *Hey, I'm here. I'm a human being, not a piece of furniture!*

Negative notice was better than none, but I chose my spots. If I laid low today, maybe I could still make it to the movie. It was Monday and tonight we'd be marched to the school auditorium to watch a movie, a reward for good behavior. Boys always sat in the front, girls in back—the girls probably thought that was unfair, but up front the attendants could keep a better eye on us—while a 16-millimeter projector flickered images onto a small portable screen.

I rolled out of bed, my eyes half-closed, and walked across the room to a line forming at the door. Dressed in a long shirt made of drab scratchy material, I felt like a girl in a nightgown. On the other hand, the gray stripes made us look more like little prisoners.

Everything here, even peeing, was done on schedule and in alphabetical order. With a name like Vitkus, I was doomed to be near the end of every line for food, clothes, and the bathroom. We followed Jones as he lumbered across the hall, swinging one arm to haul one side of his ass, then the other. He was breathing hard, his face as shiny as his head, only redder. At the bathroom, we waited while he unlocked the door.

All the attendants had big key rings on a chain. Keys meant authority. The more keys, the more authority. They had 'em, we didn't, and they knew it pissed us off that they controlled our lives at the end of that chain. To this day, I hate people with a bunch of keys hanging from their belt, even if they're maintenance workers at the mall.

"Get in there, and get out!" Jones barked.

Along one wall of the bathroom stood an open row of toilets, half-a-dozen of them, each about a foot apart, with no partitions or doors. Privacy was non-existent at Belchertown State School. We dressed together, slept together, ate together, and shit together. There were also no lids or seats, just naked bowls. If you had to take a crap, you sat there right on the porcelain beside the next guy. And forget about wiping—there was also no toilet paper. Nor were there any urinals. Toilets *plus* urinals would've cost more.

I aimed for the center of the bowl as I peed because I knew I'd be back later to clean the bathroom after breakfast. I didn't have to worry about washing my hands. On the opposite wall was a row of sinks, but the faucets were shut off.

When we were finished, "Chrome Dome" got us back in line to move down the hall, where a kid in the clothes room reached into a cubby with my name on it, and handed me the jersey, pants, socks and underwear I had turned in the night before, all rolled up in my belt. These were the same clothes I had gotten five days earlier after our weekly shower. The jersey smelled sweaty and the underwear was soiled, but this outfit had to last two more days before I'd get another set. I got dressed, stuck my nightshirt under my mattress and made my bed. We lined up again, and Jones led us downstairs.

Against the walls of the dining hall, arranged in close rows like our beds, were sturdy wooden tables, four chairs on a side. Each table had eight tablespoons already laid out, each engraved "Property of BSS." I went to my place, always the same table, stood by my chair, and waited.

"Okay, sit down, and be quiet!" a female voice commanded. Jones had passed us off to a woman we knew as Ol' Lady Howard, an intimidating battle-ax in a white tent of a dress. She maneuvered her hulk like an ocean liner, but was deceptively fast. I had seen her knock a kid on his ass with a quick backhand.

Other boys on duty that morning brought us each a bowl of corn flakes and a glass of milk. In winter, the menu was lumpy oatmeal or cream of wheat, with no sugar or salt. If you were lucky, it was hot. I poured my milk over the cornflakes and checked my bowl. That wasn't a stray raisin floating on top. Flies were everywhere. Spiral strips of sticky brown paper hung from the ceiling, dotted with black bumps.

"Eat," Ol' Lady Howard grunted, and the room rattled with spoons striking bowls. Spoons were our only utensils. Knives or forks could become weapons. Then again, all our food was served smooshed together, so a knife or fork would've been pointless. Breakfast, lunch and supper were served in the same thick plastic bowls, a puke green that matched the walls. They had numbers molded into their bottoms, and I liked to see if I ever got the same one, a little game I played with myself.

Ol' Lady Howard loomed over us while we ate. She looked like she had just smelled something bad, but that was nothing new. She couldn't wait to holler at us. If you talked, she'd yank you out of your chair and make you stand in the next room till everyone else was done. I didn't feel like talking that morning anyway. I was hungry, ate fast, and turned my bowl over for a peek. No luck today.

After breakfast a few others stayed behind to clean up. My job was the bathroom back upstairs. I had a broom, bucket, detergent, and a towel—no gloves or mop. Jones waddled in to turn on a faucet at the base of the wall. It didn't have any handle so he used a key from his ring. When I filled the bucket, he twisted the faucet shut again and left. I wiped down the sinks and faucets first, then the toilets. With no seats or stalls, that didn't take long. I dumped the rest of the soapy water onto the floor and scrubbed it with the broom. Then on my hands and knees, I bunched up the towel to push the water toward the drain in the middle of the bathroom. The cement scraped my knees and snagged the towel. When I reached the center, I wrung out the towel, went to another side, and repeated the process. I had this job down pretty well.

When I was done, I went downstairs to the day hall, where a few of the other kids were already sitting on benches. Sometimes they'd let us outside to play, or an attendant might take us on a walk, and we'd get, "Stay in line. Pick up your feet, you're gonna ruin those shoes!" But this morning, the schedule called for sitting. We did a lot of that, a hundred of us planted on benches along each wall of the day hall, sometimes for hours. That was asking a lot of a bunch of young boys.

"Hey, I told you, no talking!" Ol' Lady Howard had plunked herself into a chair in the day hall. Her mouth was permanently set in one of those upside-down smiles, like she practiced till she got it right. All she needed was a broom to ride. There was a radio on a shelf beside her and a newspaper in her lap, folded to the crossword page. She was ready for sitting.

"Knock it off! Just sit there and shut up, like you're supposed to."

So we sat.

She pulled a pencil from her hair and turned on the radio, a dark plastic box with a red pointer on the dial. I liked when it was tuned to "56," WHYN, a Springfield station that was beginning to play rock 'n' roll. But today she was listening to WBZ-A, which carried a lot of news from Boston, of no interest to me. At least it was background noise.

Since we couldn't talk, it was better not to make eye contact with anyone, so I sat and stared at the floor. A cockroach skittered by, then a couple more. That was nothing unusual, even in daylight. Like the mice and rats, they were attracted by food in the dining hall. Every now and then, maintenance would put down poison and traps, but it was a losing battle.

Cockroach watching could help pass the time, even be a source of entertainment. How long would it take that fat one to get to the other side of the room? Would that small one get there first? Would it crawl across the crack in the floor when it got there, or turn in another direction? If I concentrated hard enough, could I use my mind to make it go that way? Better yet, could I make it crawl up Ol' Lady Howard's leg and bite her? I tried for a while, but the cockroaches had minds of their own.

There was no clock in the day hall—I couldn't read one anyway—but time dragged. I shifted back and forth. Roger, an imp with a faceful of freckles, sat next to me on the end of the bench. I glanced at Ol' Lady Howard. She was deep into her crossword, so for the hell of it, I slugged Roger on the arm. With the radio on, the old bat didn't hear it and Roger didn't peep. He just slugged me back, harder. Game on! Without hesitation, I returned the favor, even harder. This time I knocked him right off the bench, and a couple of other boys burst out laughing.

"All right, that's enough, you two!" Ol' Lady Howard yelled. "Get back up, Mr. Whitney. And Vitkus, you go sit over there." She pointed with her pencil to an empty space on the next bench.

We did as we were told, but now the pattern was set. In a minute or so, someone—I couldn't tell who—farted. Just loud enough to be heard over the radio. Quiet snickers.

"We don't need any of that, either. I'm not impressed," the ol' lady said.

Harry held his nose, and seconds later Roger leaned to one side, let a big one rip, and everybody cracked up again.

This time Ol' Lady Howard *was* impressed. "You're askin' for it." She put down her newspaper. "Maybe the whole bunch of you would like to go without supper tonight? One more sound out of anyone, and I'll make it happen."

She could do better than that, I thought. Punishment here was usually fitted to the individual attendant, not to the crime. Ol' Lady Howard stood up, shut off the radio, and glared at us in the quiet. Some of the others looked back and forth between Roger and me. Not to be outdone, I stood up, turned my butt toward the old lady, and pulled down my pants, underwear and all. The place erupted.

"That does it!" She grabbed me by the arm, pinching hard. "Pull those britches up, mister, we're gonna put 'em to good use."

She dragged me across the room to a wall with coat hooks on it, picked me up by my belt at the back of my pants, and hung me from one of the hooks. Doubled over, my arms and feet dangling, immediately all my weight was on my crotch.

"So how do you like your pants now, smartass? Are they up high enough for you?"

I scrambled to press my feet against the wall to relieve the weight, but my socks slipped. Everyone watched me squirm. The pain in my groin was bad, but I wasn't gonna give that bitch the satisfaction of hollering or crying.

"Mr. Vitkus is going to hang around for a while, till he decides to start behaving himself," Ol' Lady Howard said to the others, now silent on their benches. No one moved. She went back to her chair, and turned on the radio. "And he can forget about the movies tonight."

Fine, I thought. *Who needs Shirley Temple?*

School Days

Donald has done exceptionally well in Grade 1. He gets very tense over his work if it is not right the first time.

-1952 Yearly School Report

"Today you'll be practicing your names again from the letters I've put on the board," Miss Thompson said, handing out our pencils. I liked our teacher. She was young, wore pretty dresses, and smelled like flowers, even now at the end of September.

"Remember to take care of your pencil, because you won't get another one," Miss Thompson cautioned the class, setting mine into the groove on my desk. She must have noticed the teeth marks. At the beginning of the year, she had etched our initials into a shaved flat spot beneath the eraser on each of our pencils so we'd always get the same one. I picked mine up, clicked my thumbnail across the letters, and tapped my finger on the lead. Miss Thompson had sharpened them overnight.

At nine years old, and in my second year of first grade, I was learning to write my name in longhand. I wanted it to look good at the top of my papers. I wanted to be Donald Vitkus, not #3394, or "you retard."

I bore down on my pencil, repeating a string of capital D's on the lined yellow paper at my desk, concentrating to reproduce the loops and slant of the model letters on the green cards that stretched across the top of the blackboard. If one of my D's dropped below the line or floated above it, I scrubbed it out and tried again. The eraser at the top of my pencil was already wearing out, and I had to bite the metal band around it to squeeze out a bit more rubber. I had to make it last.

Though the whole institution was called Belchertown State School, the building where we studied the three R's was on a small hill behind the administration office. It was a two-story brick structure with no bars on the windows. It looked like a regular school with regular classrooms. The desks and chairs were smooth and shiny with a buildup of yellow-orange varnish, the same stuff the janitors used on the floors. You could smell it every September.

Boys and girls were divided into separate classrooms, seated alphabetically, so I was always near the back of a side row. Desks and chairs faced the blackboard in rigid straight rows, their black steel legs screwed to the floor. Our desktops didn't lift up to put stuff in, because we didn't have any stuff. Each day teachers like Miss Thompson passed out books, paper and pencils, then collected them when our lesson was over.

The school auditorium, where our church services were held, doubled as a gymnasium. Once a week we participated in "physical therapy," which consisted primarily of marching around the perimeter of the gym to the tune of The Star Spangled Banner blaring from a record player. It was important to turn sharp corners.

The patients who attended school were higher functioning, but we spent two years in each grade. After all, we were retards. So I would be 17 by the time I finished fourth grade. That was okay by me because I loved school. It was a safe haven. The teachers never struck us or swore at us like the attendants, and I liked learning.

We were graded in Reading, Articulation, Spelling, Language, Writing, Geography, Time-telling, and something called Number. I guess "math" or even "numbers" would be too advanced. I often finished my work early and had to wait for the others, so I had a lot of time staring out the window or at the clock. I aced Time-telling! My record shows that overall, I got mostly B's and C's.

On the ward, I got mixed written reviews from building attendants:

> Hygiene, clean. Conduct is sometimes good, sometimes very naughty; in need of constant supervision.

But my school reports were primarily positive.

> Donald has done exceptionally well in grade I. He gets very tense over his work if it is not right the first time.

If they had been smart, guys like Jones would've realized my worst punishment wouldn't be whipping, straitjackets, or solitary, but preventing me from going to school.

By second grade, I was honor roll material:

> Donald's attitude and interest in class are both commendable. His reading and spelling are excellent and other work is very good, including handwriting. He has a very good singing voice and does excellent work in singing. His conduct is always excellent.

Not bad for a moron. Of course, I never saw these statements till years later because the state perceived us as patients, not students. We never got report cards. Who would sign mine, anyway?

That's a State Issue

```
We have no copy of the Baptismal Record but in the
family sheets it states that Donald was baptized
at St. Joseph's Church, Boston, June 8, 1943.
```

> –May 25, 1962
> Department of Public Welfare
> Division of Child Guardianship

When I turned nine, I decided to become an altar boy. I had been baptized before arriving at Belchertown, but the records were lost somewhere. When my mother gave me up to the state, she insisted that I be raised a Catholic, so I was re-baptized in the institution. That put me on track to serving at the altar. "So, Vitkus, you're Catholic? Wanna be an altar boy?" an attendant asked.

The attendants made us get on our knees every night for bedtime prayers, but I didn't care much about God" On the other hand, I knew how to be a brown nose if a situation called for it" In a hell-hole like Belchertown, there was a certain status to being an altar boy, and I could use some of that prestige. Who knows? Being an altar boy might even save me some abuse.

There weren't any regular Sunday school classes, but we needed at least some instruction about how to serve Mass. Once a week, a priest named Father Dudley gave lessons to half a dozen of us F Building boys in the school auditorium. With no chapel, this is where services were conducted, the same place we watched movies the night before. King Kong at night, God in the morning. Catholics first, then Protestants in the afternoon.

Father Dudley told us it was important to serve Christ. Maybe the others were there to serve the Lord, but I was serving myself.

I wasn't sure what to make of this guy, but I could see he was aware of his appearance. He kept his hair slicked back, black and shiny so it matched his black suit. There was always a sharp crease in his pants. I wondered why he had that white notch in his collar, but I never felt comfortable asking. He was a Yankees fan, talked baseball, and I liked that. On the other hand, he wasn't the most patient instructor. He'd cuff you on the back of the head if you messed up.

Even though it was still the days of the Latin Mass, we never had to learn the responses. After all, we *were* retards. Father Dudley showed us how to wear our cassocks, how to hold the big book for him to read from, how to handle the cup of wine and water that he drank and the huge white wafer that he ate, when to kneel, when to stand, when to sit.

"Hold the missal a little higher, Harry. There, nice and steady. Excellent. Tim, good posture. Don't tip that chalice, Donald, or you'll spill everything. And stand up straight."

Even among the altar boys, there was a pecking order, and I wasn't high on Father Dudley's list. Harry, with his blue eyes and curly blond hair, was at the top. He at least looked like an angel. Then came Tim and a couple of others, then me. Maybe it was all a matter of holiness, but that didn't bother me. I felt special just being an altar boy.

I yearned for any sense of identity, any bit of recognition. I envied kids on the ward who had family—no, I hated them—kids with parents. I'd see them leave the building on holidays, and watch as they walked together out to their car. When they returned at the end of the day, the boy might be wearing new clothes, chewing gum or sucking on a lollipop.

On Thanksgiving weekend that year a kid named Bobby Ricci left and returned with a shiny black toy telephone. It had a dial like a real phone, and I watched him make pretend calls. He held the receiver to his ear, put his finger into one of the holes in the dial, turned it, and let it click back, again and again. He'd wait a few seconds, then say, "Hello, Mom, how are you?" or "Hi, Dad. It's me, Bobby."

Jealousy got the best of me. There usually wasn't anything lying around worth stealing, but when there was, it was easy because the only things that ever got locked up was us. After supper the next night, when I was sure no one was watching, I snuck upstairs, found the phone by Bobby's bed, took it to my bed, and hid it beneath my mattress. I didn't have parents, and I didn't have visitors. But now I had Bobby Ricci's phone.

In December, Tim, Harry, and I gathered in the little room at the rear of the school auditorium, where Father Dudley was getting ready for morning Mass. It was the third Sunday of Advent, and we'd have to put on a good show. "Okay, boys, get dressed. Look sharp," he said, unlocking the closet where he kept the church stuff. Inside was a cross mounted on a pole, a little silver bell, and our outfits—black robes for us with white tops long enough to cover our state boy clothes, everything but our state boy shoes—and a bunch of fancy colored robes and scarf things for Father Dudley. Today he picked out the purple one.

Then he flipped open a little suitcase that he always carried with him. The inside was lined with cushiony, bright red cloth that had indentations shaped like the stuff they held—a cross with Jesus on it, a shiny gold cup, a gold disc that held his communion wafer, a small bottle of red wine and another with water. He put the bottles on a tray. "Here, Tim, you take these. Harry, you carry the big cross," he said, and we moved to the back of the hall.

With Christmas on the way, attending Mass was even more important than usual. The place was packed with kids from all the buildings, boys on the left of the aisle, girls on the right. Seated at an upright piano at the front of the hall was Russell, a black kid from F Building, who often played the piano in our visitors' room.

"Okay, line up," Father Dudley said, and he gave Russell the high sign. When the music started, everyone stood up, and we marched down the aisle.

Kids on both sides turned to watch. Harry looked cool at the head of the line, carrying that big cross, and he knew it. Everyone had their eyes on Holy Harry, the leader, walking slowly down the aisle, while Russell played some hymn. Next came Tim with the tray, beside another altar boy holding the cup that Father Dudley used to drink out of and the dish he washed his hands in, then me and some other kid with our hands pressed together like we were praying. At the end of the parade came Father Dudley, his hands together, too, gliding slowly up the aisle, his purple and gold-trimmed vestments swaying.

The altar was just a table pushed up against the front of the stage with a white cloth and a couple of candles on it. In those days, the priest and altar boys faced the altar, their backs to the people. There was no rail to kneel at, but we didn't need one, anyway. The only one who would get communion was Father Dudley, who would give it to himself while we all watched. We were never allowed to receive, I guess because we never had confession. I think they figured us morons wouldn't know when we were sinning, anyway.

Father Dudley made the Sign of the Cross on his forehead, stomach and shoulders, began his mumbling and droned on. It always seemed like Mass took forever, and today was longer than usual. When the time finally came for Father to feed himself, Harry rang the bell that was our signal to kneel. The soles of my shoes had holes in them, so I covered them up with the bottom of my robe. But when it was time to stand again, I forgot to lift the robe, my heels got caught in the hem, and over I went. I could hear chuckling behind me. Father Dudley gave me the eye as I got back up. I couldn't wait to get out of there.

When Mass was finally over, I waited till everyone else was gone to turn in my robe. "Father, can I tell you something?"

I needed to talk. I had always thought that priests were something special, that they had special powers and the ability to change things, that they had this connection to somebody who could make it all happen, somebody called God.

"You don't have to apologize, Donald. Just don't do that again next week."

He pulled his cape over his head and hung it in the closet.

"No, Father, it's something else."

He checked his watch. "Okay, but make it quick. I have to get back to St. Martin's for real church at 9:30. What is it?"

"You won't get mad?"

He finally turned to look at me. "How can I know if I'll be mad till you tell me? What *is* it?"

"Well, something happened to one of my friends this week. He got hurt pretty bad."

"Oh. How'd that happen?"

"You know those windows in the basement where the dining hall is? The ones that are really high up?"

"No, I've never been in your dining hall, Donald, but I suppose everything looks high when you're a kid." He put Jesus and the other stuff back in his case and snapped the lid shut.

"Well, anyway, Ronnie had climbed up there onto the window sill, and wouldn't get down. He was just sittin' there, starin' down, with his arms around his knees. The attendants were hollerin' up at him, but he wouldn't come down."

Father Dudley sighed. "Get to the point, Donald."

"Ronnie just stayed there till one of 'em got really mad and reached up, yanked him down, and started beatin' on him."

"Why would they beat on him?"

"I just told you, 'cause he was up on the damn window, and he wouldn't get down when they told him to get down!"

I expected a backhand across my mouth, but Father Dudley just looked at me.

"When they grabbed Ronnie, he fell on the cement floor and I heard his arm crack. I could hear it crack! The bone was stickin' out of his sleeve, and blood was comin' out, and they were still beatin' on him and hollerin'." Now I was crying and I fought to get the rest of my story out between sobs. "I ran over to help him ... and I got Ronnie's blood all over me ... and they started beatin' on me, too."

Father Dudley looked at me with a blank expression. "Are you sure that's what happened? Maybe they were just trying to restrain him so he wouldn't hurt himself more." He glanced at his watch again and picked up his bag. "I don't know, I wasn't there. Besides, what you're telling me is a state issue, not a church issue. That has to be addressed by the state. Sorry. I've got to go."

I opened my mouth to say something, but nothing came out. In his sermons, Father Dudley had always preached that if you prayed enough, whatever you prayed for would come true. I had prayed to see my family, prayed that my mother would come and get me, prayed that I'd be let out of this place. But none of that happened. Now this. How could God allow Ronnie to be treated like that? How could God even allow this place to exist?

As I walked back to my building, I wiped my eyes and thought about how unfair everything was. Weren't priests supposed to stand up against sin? If breaking a kid's arm wasn't a sin, what was? I didn't realize it at the time, but that day, when I had handed in my gown to Father Dudley, I also handed in my religion.

When I came in, Jones was plopped in front of the day hall TV, arms crossed, resting them on his gut. Nothing much ever happened on Sundays, especially in winter, and for the most part, the attendants didn't bug us. Jones would be the last person I could tell about Father Dudley, so I headed upstairs, sat down on my bed and stared through the bars on the window.

I had a pretty good view of the parking lot down below, the baseball field covered with snow, and the still woods beyond. A few random cars came up the long entrance road. I knew they had already passed the big wooden Merry Christmas sign out by Route 202, and the tree all lit up beside the administration building. Inside those cars were mothers and fathers coming to pick up their kids for a few hours, maybe take them home for Sunday dinner, maybe give them a toy to bring back. I had watched so many times that I knew every car by heart. They stopped in the parking lot, a grownup would get out, slam the door shut and come up the walk to the front entrance downstairs. A few minutes later, they'd walk back out to the car, this time holding some boy by the hand, some lucky kid like Bobby Ricci.

Maybe my mother will come today, I thought. *I'll see a woman I don't know, and it'll be her.* A few more cars than usual arrived, and I watched a little longer. Maybe my mother would drive from wherever she was, and come to take me out for Christmas. I waited, hoping to see a car I didn't recognize.

But I knew them all.

It was a cold and windy night, less than a week before Christmas. We could see our breath as we marched single file under the streetlight from F Building to the school auditorium. When we arrived, radiators along the wall hissed and banged as the place filled with kids from other buildings. Attendants sat us facing the stage in rows of wooden folding chairs marked Property of BSS, girls across the aisle.

When we settled down, the curtain parted to reveal half a dozen men, one seated at a piano with the others standing around it, singing "Jingle Bells." Off to the side, a sign on a tripod said, *The 40 & 8*. They wore khaki hats, pointed in the front like little boats. I would later learn that these were army veterans who named their club after World War I railroad cars in France that were stenciled with those numbers. Each box car could hold either 40 men or eight horses or mules. They had come to the state school to put on their annual Christmas show for us.

Waving their hands, they got us to join in. "Frosty the Snowman," "Rudolph the Red-Nosed Reindeer," "Silent Night," and more. It was fun and took my mind off things. When they broke into "Santa Claus is Coming to Town," Santa himself stepped from behind the curtain carrying a sack over his shoulder. We cheered as he crossed the stage, waving a white glove and shouting, "Ho, Ho, Ho!" Anyone with half a brain could tell this wasn't the real Santa. It was the same guy as last year with a fake beard and not very fat. But that was okay. The real one would probably never come here anyway.

The attendants lined us up in the aisles.

"Santa has stockings for everyone," one of the khaki hats yelled over the music, directing us up the side. "But don't open them till you get back, or you'll get stuff all over the place and lose it."

When it was my turn to meet him, 'Santa' patted me on the head, gave me a "Merry Christmas, son!" in that big phony voice, and reached into his bag. He handed me a stocking of presents. The top was stitched shut but it was made out of red mesh, so I could see what was inside—a little blue plastic car with rubber wheels, a candy cane, a Hershey bar, an orange—all good stuff.

When the show was over, I carried what would be my only Christmas gift back to F Building, staring at that stocking, hoping this year would be different. I couldn't wait to get back to eat the candy and play with that car. It had started to snow, and really felt like Christmas. Inside we hung up our coats, took off our shoes, and lined up for head count.

Jones waited for us at the bottom of the stairs. His gut hanging over his belt, fatter than Santa Claus, he looked anything but jolly. "Okay, hand them over. You can't sleep with that stuff," he said.

There it was. As we filed by, he grabbed each of our stockings and dropped them to the floor, thirty of them thumping into a pile at his feet.

"All right, get to bed. You've had your fun for today."

I was crushed, but there was no use complaining. We were all quiet. Who wants to get beaten, especially around Christmas? I trudged upstairs, undressed, rolled my clothes into a ball, wrapped my belt around them, handed them to the kid in the clothes room in exchange for a wrinkled night shirt, then crawled into bed and pulled the covers over my head. Silent night.

I thought about Father Dudley and Ronnie's broken arm. I thought about staring at the parking lot for my mother's car, the loneliness, the crap that happened here today and every other day of the year. I wondered what became of our stockings. I knew we'd never see those toys and candy again, or the fruit on the table. Maybe Jones and the others gave them to their own kids at home. What would it be like to see presents, one with my name on it, under a tree decorated with colored lights and tinsel? Or to be in a real home around Christmas, even just for a visit?

Then I remembered. I reached under the mattress and took out Bobby Ricci's telephone. With the blankets still over my head, I dialed a number, any number, for someone to come and get me.

The Lone Ranger

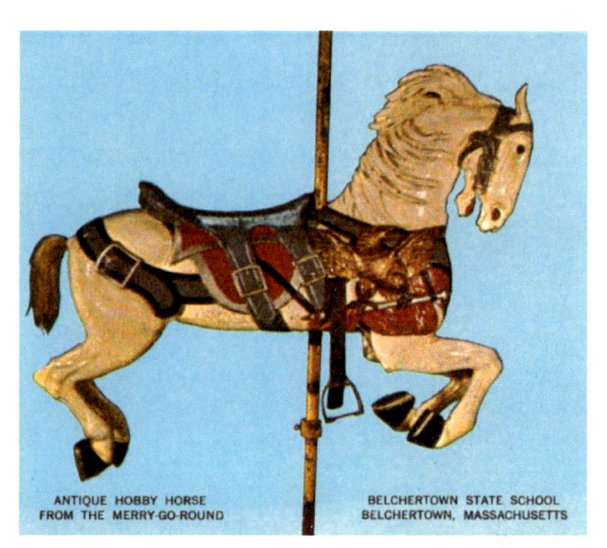

ANTIQUE HOBBY HORSE FROM THE MERRY-GO-ROUND
BELCHERTOWN STATE SCHOOL BELCHERTOWN, MASSACHUSETTS

"Hey, Donald, today we get to ride the merry-go-round!" Timmy jumped up and down as he handed me my clothes, a striped short-sleeve jersey and dungarees, from the cubby. School was out and summer had arrived, a time for ten-year-olds to celebrate.

"That's right, I almost forgot, today's the Fourth of July! There'll be games and stuff, and we get to ride the merry-go-round. Wait up for me after chores."

Set back against a grove of pine trees, apart from the brick ward buildings and the barred windows, the carousel was one of the bright spots at Belchertown State School. It was also one of the oddest. A full-sized, brightly colored merry-go-round that stood there in the open, like a carnival had stopped in this spot, packed up for the next town, and forgotten to take the merry-go-round. As an adult, I learned that it had been moved from Forest Lake Amusement Park in nearby Palmer in 1948, the year before I arrived. Its horses were handmade by two master carvers who also built carousels for Central Park in New York.

None of that mattered to Timmy and me. The ride had sat silent and stationary since last summer, but today they'd be cranking it up for a spin. I couldn't wait. I rushed through breakfast to get a quick start on cleaning the bathroom, skipped the toilets that didn't have skid marks, then ran outside where the attendants were lining us up. It was already hot and my jersey stuck to my back, but the walk to the carousel wouldn't be long. I could hear music playing, louder and louder as we approached. We didn't get many days like this.

As we turned the corner, I spotted it. Against a row of pine trees, the carousel was a whirl of color and sound, filled with girls on their horses, laughing, waving, and shouting as they spun by. In the center, a big machine with a rising row of shiny brass pipes cranked out happy music while a mechanical drumstick tapped and gold cymbals pumped up and down all by themselves, crashing to the beat. At the very top of it all was an American flag, waving in the breeze.

Standing in the center by the chugging motor was a stocky guy in bib overalls and a straw hat. With his shaggy beard and bulky arms, I recognized Buckie, the farm boy who was in charge of the horses down on the dairy farm. Like most of the farm boys, Buckie was actually a grown man who had been at Belchertown most of his life. I guess they figured if he could handle a team of real horses behind a plow, he could certainly handle fake ones going around in circles.

I got in line behind Timmy and other boys along a rope fence. Across from us in their own line, more girls waited their turn.

I jabbed Timmy in the back. "I'm gonna be The Lone Ranger and get a white horse like Silver."

"Neat! Then I'll be the bad guy, and you can chase me." He turned around and stuck his finger in my ribs like a gun.

With both arms, Buckie pulled against the big lever that braked the merry-go-round, and I scanned the horses while they coasted to a stop. Even motionless, they looked like they were still running. On the far side was a white one in full stride with all four hooves in the air. That was the one!

As soon as the girls got off, an attendant dropped the rope and a bunch of us boys raced for our mounts. No one wanted to settle for a ride on one of those bench things that didn't move. A little kid ahead of me eyed my target, but the horse had stopped too high for him to reach, so I got my mount. He had a dark saddle over a bright red blanket decorated with a gold eagle, its wings spread and a spear latched in its talons. His mane was carved like it was blowing in the wind, his ears were laid back, and his tail was made of real horse hair. I lifted my foot high into the stirrup, hoisted myself on, grabbed the reins in my hand, and leaned forward to get a close look at Silver's face. He had dark shiny eyes that said he was ready to run. His mouth open, he looked like he was smiling.

Timmy had picked a spotted brown horse in front of me, and was already twisting back at me, firing his imaginary pistol.

When everybody was saddled up, Buckie released the brake and the big wide belt on the motor began to turn. The merry-go-round started to move, slowly at first, then picked up speed. I glanced up and watched the rotating pipe joints that made the horses rise and fall. With the wind in my face, I shot back at Timmy while the music blared. I was the masked man, spurring Silver up and down the rocky trail, round and round, raising a cloud of dust at every turn—away from Jones, Ol' Lady Howard and the rest—far away from Belchertown.

Baby, Baby, Baby

"Face it, Vitkus, you're not smart enough to be on your own."

That summer I was put to work in the fields down at the farm, slinging bales of hay onto a horse-drawn wagon, where another kid stacked them for Buckie to deliver to the barn. It was heavy, dusty work. July wore into August, and then it was time to go back to school, where I'd be repeating third grade.

The buildings and grounds of Belchertown State School had become my world. For more than four years, since the day I was led up the steps of the administration building, I had no contact whatsoever with the outside. By now it was apparent to me that I wasn't wanted. No one visited, no one sent me mail.

I had often thought about running away, but never acted on it—until one night that fall. When we had all come in for supper, I hung up my jacket and took off my shoes as the others started upstairs. Then, on impulse, I bolted. In stocking feet and no plan about where to go, I ran straight for the woods, where I wouldn't be seen. When I got far enough in, I found a log to rest on. My heart was racing and my feet hurt from running across stones and sharp sticks. The bottom of one of my socks was bloody. I hadn't thought this through. It was a chilly October night and I was a runaway with no coat, no shoes, and no idea which way to turn. Where could I go now, what could I do? Jones's girly voice ran through my head, repeating what he and the others constantly drummed into us: *You'll never make it on the outside, Vitkus. You're not smart enough, you're a moron. Who would tell you what to do?*

What the hell did he know? Of course, I could make it. I could make it to that big brick building on the town common, the one with steps like a city hall. I'd get help there. On TV, the Lone Ranger always fought the bad guys for people in trouble. There might be somebody inside who I could tell about what went on at this place, somebody like the mayor or a cop would come to our rescue. Yeah, right, or maybe The Masked Man. Who was I kidding? The common was a mile away, and I'd probably get caught before I got there.

Face it, Vitkus, you're not smart enough to be on your own. Jones's voice again.

With my arms wrapped around me, I stared back at my building. At least I'd be warm there. The light was still on in Jones's crappy little office. *You're a retard, Vitkus. It's tough out there, you know.* Maybe he hadn't noticed I was gone. He'd be pissed when he found out because it happened on his watch and I'd pay for it eventually. Everyone knew the consequences, but running away always seemed worth the risk. After all, some boys had never come back.

An hour or more passed and the temperature was dropping. I began to shiver as a feeling of hopelessness settled over me. I'd never admit it to the guys, but I was scared. Maybe if I got to the road, I could hitch a ride. Forget it, I didn't know how to thumb. Finally, with no better idea, I decided to go back and face the music.

I ran back to the coatroom entrance. The door was still unlocked, so I snuck up to my ward, climbed into bed, and pulled my blanket over my head. My heart raced as I thought about what I had just done. Maybe Jones hadn't yet made his headcount.

"Where the hell have you been?" The sharp whisper made me jump. "I had to cover for you in the clothes room!" It was Roger in the next bed. He would never rat on me.

"What are you talkin' about? I been here all night." I giggled from under the covers.

"Right."

"Okay, everybody up!" Jones hollered at 5:30 the next morning, his gut crowding the doorway. He always waited till he saw us all out of bed. "And I mean right now. I ain't got all day, and you guys gotta get your asses to school!" I knew I should've taken off my clothes as soon as I had gotten under the blanket, but I had dozed off in the warmth.

"Get a move on!" Jones was swinging a strap with a big buckle on the end, itching for an excuse to use it. I crawled out of bed and stood behind Roy at the back of the ward, hoping Jones wouldn't notice me. But he did.

"Well, well, well. Look at this, boys," he said in that high mocking tone he always used when he was enjoying himself at our expense. "Would you look at Donald. He's so eager to get to school this morning, he's already dressed. He beat all of you guys. What do you think of that?"

Nobody responded. A few stared at me, then at Jones, who made his way past the first two rows of beds, and stopped.

"C'mere, Vitkus," he said. "What's the matter, boy? I'm not gonna hurt ya."

I stepped from behind Roy, and saw the strap dangling from Jones's meaty paw.

"What do you think, Vitkus, I'm gonna hit you or somethin'? Just cuz you're smart enough to be dressed before anyone else? No, I think that deserves a reward, don't you boys?"

Jones relished these moments, especially kicking off his day.

"Right up here, son," he beckoned. I moved up and stopped in front of him. He pulled out his key ring, unlocked a white cabinet on the wall, and removed a glass bottle and tablespoon. He unscrewed the cap and filled the spoon with liquid the color of weak piss. We all knew what it was—castor oil, a frequent treatment for misbehavior. "Here, Donald, I think you deserve this." I opened my mouth and Jones jammed in the spoon. It was foul smelling stuff, tasted worse, and made me gag. "Wow, I can tell how much you like it!" Jones said, refilling the spoon. "Here, have another." I forced down the second.

"I think you should also be the very first to use the bathroom this morning, Mr. Vitkus. " He yanked me by the arm toward the door. "The rest of you wait right where you are," Jones ordered. He shoved me into the bathroom across the hall, followed me in, and closed the door.

"All right, smartass, you were so quick to get dressed. I wanna see how you done it." His voice echoed off the tiles. "Take off those clothes. Everything."

I did as he said. Jones reached up to a shelf where a stack of laundered cloth diapers was kept for the little kids, grabbed one, and threw it in my face. I let it drop to the floor. "Put it on," he growled.

I had seen this act before, but it had never happened to me. I bent down and slowly picked up the diaper. A strong odor of bleach wafted up at me as I pulled it between my legs.

"But it won't stay on without these, widdle boy," Jones said, like he was talking to a baby. He tossed a couple of safety pins at my feet, his eyes twinkling.

I picked up the pins, fastened one side of my waist, then the other.

"Vewwy good!" Jones said softly. He sounded like a sick Elmer Fudd. "*Now*, you're all dwessed up for the day, and you won't be needing these dirty-wirty ones." He kicked my clothes aside, jabbed his thumb toward the door, and his voice returned to a shrill bark. "Get the fuck out there!"

The others were still by their beds, and Jones hollered for them to come out into the hall. They circled around me, a ten-year-old wearing a diaper. Everyone knew the routine.

"Lookit Baby Donald, boys." Back to the sing-song voice. "Ain't he cute? But you know what? Widdle Donald twied to run away last night, and thought I wouldn't notice. I don't wike that. He was a b-a-a-d boy! So now he's dressed the way he weewee should be. What do you say, boys?"

Silence. Jones swung his belt. Someone mumbled, "Baby, baby." Then another boy repeated, louder, "Baby, baby." And a memorized chant rose up. "Baby, baby, baby! Can't take it here? Run away, baby. Run away now!"

I stared at the floor. If I were them, I'd be saying *Baby, baby,* too, so I wouldn't get singled out. I'd go along. But I wasn't ashamed. I had earned that diaper. And a couple of hours later, I needed it. The castor oil started to work.

I was actually proud of being punished. To my way of thinking, any kid brave enough to try to get out of that place deserved a medal.

And, anyway, next time would be different.

The Summer of '55

```
I hereby request that you receive and provide for
my child, Donald Everett Vitkus, who is depen-
dent upon public charity in accordance with the
provisions of chapter 119, section 38, of the
General Laws.
```

–June 8, 1943
Veronica Vitkus

The summer of 1955 was my baseball summer. We didn't have an organized league, but we played a lot of pickup games on a ball field near the merry-go-round, a rough diamond with no bases or real pitcher's mound. An attendant would unlock the wooden box downstairs where the bats, balls, and gloves were kept, and count them out. There were two decent bats with black electrical tape on the handles and another with screws in the barrel where it had split. The gloves needed new rawhide stringing, and the balls were pretty well scuffed up.

After supper on Monday nights we played the farm boys, who had their own field, a much better one, down by the barn. They were intimidating opponents who usually beat the snot out of us. Many of the farm "boys" were shaving long before I was born. Some like Buckie, the guy in charge of the horses, were well into their thirties. Built low to the ground, he could control a couple of tons of animal from behind a plow, a job that gave him arms like a wrestler, and a sense of command. But he was a kind soul. I watched him as he cared for the horses, talking softly to them, feeding them, cooling them down with the spray from a hose after a long day in the fields.

Buckie wore long-sleeved flannel shirts even in summer, bib overalls, work boots, and a straw hat. That outfit was his baseball uniform, too. He was the farm boys' pitcher. On the mound Buckie was a competitor, and he could wing a baseball. When I faced him at the plate, I could hear the stitches whir by my face as his fastball smacked into the catcher's mitt. It scared the hell out of me.

In early June when I came in from the ball field one afternoon sweaty and dirty, one of the newer attendants took me aside in the day hall. Pete was younger than most, under thirty, with wavy black hair and an athletic frame. Like all the others, he wore a huge ring of keys on his belt, but he also wore a smile. I liked him.

He had a couple of rolled up magazines in his hand. I had long ago learned not to trust anybody in the institution, and even though this was Pete, he still wore an attendant's uniform. My first instinct was to duck.

"Take it easy, Donald. I'm not gonna hit you!" He put his free hand on my shoulder. "Here, you can take a look at these till supper," he said, "but before you go to bed, you gotta give 'em back. You know I can't let you keep 'em."

He handed me two issues of *Sports Illustrated*, one with Mickey Mantle, the other with Jackie Robinson on the cover.

"Did you know that I used to play ball, Donald?"

I stared at him, my mouth open.

"I never made the majors, but, yeah, I played a couple years on the Tigers double-A team near Detroit."

"No. Thanks," was all I could say. "I mean, no, I didn't know you were a ballplayer. But thank you." And I sat right down on one of the benches to look at the magazines. Two *Sports Illustrated*—from a guy who played on a real baseball team!

After school the next day, Pete unlocked the equipment box and I picked out a glove. I'm left-handed, but there were no gloves for lefties, so I had to use a right-hander's. With the fingers all backwards, catching the ball was more like using a basket than a glove, but it was better than nothing.

Pete walked us down to the field. "Donald," he said, "we need a left-handed pitcher for the game against Westover." Every year on the Fourth of July, one of the few real holidays we had, there was an organized ballgame at the state school. The little kids got to ride the merry-go-round, there was a parade in the morning, and the game that afternoon was a big deal. "Buckie will be there," Pete said, "but he's a rightie. I've been watching you throw out here, and you're not bad. You're the only leftie we've got, so I'm gonna show you how to pitch."

"Okay," I said to Pete. "Teach me."

While the rest of the boys were hitting flies to each other, Pete brought me to the side of our building. He took a piece of chalk from his pocket and drew a box about waist high on the brick wall. Then he paced off steps to a spot beyond the sidewalk, and dug a rectangle in the dirt with his heel.

"This is your pitcher's mound, Donald. I want you to practice hitting that strike zone." Pete dropped three hard rubber balls into my glove and stepped aside. "Let's see your stuff!"

I placed my right foot inside the 'mound,' stared at the chalk outline, leaned back and threw one of the balls. It struck a good two feet above the box. "That's okay, try again," Pete said. The next one glanced off the dirt in front of the wall. "Don't worry about it, Donald. Just keep throwin'." I wanted to hit that damn target bad. My third attempt landed a little closer, but would've nailed a right-handed batter.

"Here, watch me." Pete picked up a ball, wound up and threw, nailing the center of the rectangle with a loud smack. The ball hit so hard it bounced all the way back to him. My jaw dropped.

"All right, look," Pete said. He showed me how to grip the ball with two fingers and my thumb, and took me step by step through a windup and delivery. "Now you try."

Pete was right-handed. I tried to mirror his motion, but I let go of the ball too soon and it sailed high off the wall. "That's okay. You're tryin' too hard, you're over-throwing," Pete coached from behind me. "Ease off a little."

My next pitch bounced back with a chalk mark on it, and I grinned. "That's it," Pete yelled with a thumb's up. "Now keep at it! Hit that target as many times as you can, every afternoon from now till the Fourth."

Each day after school when Pete was on duty, I threw against the wall for an hour or so. When school ended, I practiced longer, concentrating on my delivery. Little by little, as my control improved, so did my confidence. Other boys began watching. "Hey, Vitkus," Roger hollered one afternoon. "You oughta draw Jones's fat kisser inside that box! That'd make ya focus!" He was right. Just imagining that bastard's face in the outline was enough to make me throw harder and with more accuracy. I started hitting the zone nearly two out of three times.

The afternoon of the Fourth was sunny and hot, a great day for baseball. A dark blue bus pulled up near the backstop at the edge of the field, and a stream of matching blue uniforms stepped off, airmen from Westover Air Force Base in Chicopee, about 15 miles away. They had trim waists and short haircuts. One of them unzipped a duffel bag and dumped out a bunch of bats, balls and gloves. We watched as the blue uniforms took batting practice and zipped the ball around the infield. These guys weren't morons.

As visitors, they would bat first, so when they were done with practice, we took the field. I walked to the mound, with that backwards glove on my right hand, and looked around. Even though there were no spectators, I felt like I was being watched. I tossed a few warm-ups to Johnnie, my catcher, and an attendant stepped behind him to be our umpire. The first blue batter, a righty, came to the plate and dug in for his practice swings. He was wearing cleats.

"Play ball!" the attendant yelled, and pointed in my direction. This was it. I stared in at Johnnie's glove, wound up, and threw. Right down the middle! "Stee-rike!" from the ump. That felt good. My second pitch sailed a little high and outside, but the batter swung and missed. "Strike two!"

"All right, Donald! Way to go!" Pete yelled from the bench. "That's it, keep 'em comin'!" I took a deep breath, wound up and threw as hard as I could. I grooved another one, but this time the batter laced a line drive into left for a double. The next guy up drove a fly ball high over our right fielder, and with no fence to stop it, the ball rolled and rolled. By the time he threw it back in, two blue uniforms had crossed the plate.

Roger looked at me from first base. "Jesus, Vitkus! A home run!"

It didn't get better. By the time the inning was over it was four-nothing. My pitching debut was a disaster. I trudged to the bench, threw my glove down, and stared at the ground. As our leadoff batter headed to the plate, I felt Pete's hand on my shoulder. "Don't worry about it, Donald. You did fine!"

The next inning Buckie took over and mowed 'em down. We eventually scored runs of our own, and even with that lousy start, actually won the game. In fact, now when I think back, we never lost on the Fourth of July. Somehow every year us Belchertown boys beat those Westover fly boys. It never occurred to me to wonder why.

That July it stayed hot for days. Each morning the weatherman on Ol' Lady Howard's radio gave us cheery updates on a building heat wave with "temps in the mid-90s, another triple-H day— hazy, hot, and humid." The brick buildings soaked up the heat and retained it. At night, even with the windows open, the bars seemed to block what little air there was from entering. Fans were unheard of, and I didn't know that air conditioning even existed. Each morning, my pillow was soaked in sweat.

With no relief from the heat, both patients and attendants grew cranky. Under Pete's wing, and with baseball as my incentive, I kept myself under control, but that wasn't the case for Harry, Johnnie, and Roger. Not long after the big game, the three of them got caught trying to escape, and were confined to a separate room on the second floor. They would have to spend a week there, isolated from everyone else, both to teach them a lesson and to send a message to the rest of us. It wouldn't be pleasant in that closed space.

I was wiping down the dining hall when Jones said, "Vitkus, take supper upstairs to your pals in the Strong Room. I'm sure they'll be thrilled to see you. Higgins will let you in." Strong Room was the official term for isolation. We called it the Dog House. Often, being sent to the Dog House meant solitary confinement.

All our food was prepared in a central kitchen, then delivered to steam tables in each building. It arrived in military surplus canisters stenciled "U.S. Army" on the side. I grabbed three bowls and scooped hamburg, a glob of mashed potatoes, and a few soggy beans into each one. "Whoa, way too much!" Jones barked. "This ain't Christmas. Those guys were runaways." I scraped half back into the containers, then poured water into three plastic glasses on a tray, careful not to fill them more than halfway.

Higgins was waiting for me at the Strong Room door. He wasn't as big as Jones and he had a normal voice, but as keeper of the keys, Higgins was cast from the same ugly mold. "Put it on the floor," he said. I set the bowls in front of the door, hoping the cockroaches wouldn't get at them. Higgins unlocked the door, opened it part way, and pushed the bowls inside with his foot. "Those, too," he ordered. I picked up the glasses, and set them inside. Before the door closed, I saw three hands reach for the bowls.

The next day as I prepared my delivery, I stuffed three slices of bread inside my shirt. When I stooped outside the door to put down the last bowl and glass, Higgins yanked me up by my collar.

"Why is your shirt so tight, Vitkus?" He poked at the bulges above my belt. "You puttin' on weight with all this good food?" He pulled up my shirt, and the bread fell to the floor. "Wow, smuggling food to the rats! You must really care about these guys. Maybe this time you'd like to stay and visit a while?"

With deliberation, he crushed each slice of bread like he was putting out a cigarette under his foot, unlocked the door, and pushed me inside. "Cheer up, you guys got company!" he said. Then, leaving the bowls and glasses outside, he kicked the flattened bread through the doorway and slammed it shut. I heard his key turn in the lock.

"Welcome to the Dog House," Johnnie said.

I looked around. Except for a radiator, a bare mattress on the floor and a bucket in the corner of the room, it was empty. A tiny airless cell with the same puke-green walls as the rest of the place, secured by a barred window and a gray steel door. Embedded in the top of the door was a four-inch-square, wire-reinforced window. You could almost touch opposite walls if you stretched out your arms. With four of us jammed in there, it was more than cozy.

"Jesus, you guys stink," I said.

"Yeah, well you ain't no rosebud yourself," Roger said, and farted in my direction, drawing laughs from the others.

The following afternoon Harry, Johnnie, and Roger were released, but not me—I had aided and abetted escapees. Twice a day, the door was unlocked only to slide in my food or take me to the bathroom, on Higgins' schedule. If he didn't respond when I hammered on the door, I had to use the bucket. Except for the shadows cast through the bars, I had no way to judge the time. I spent the days pacing, sleeping, sitting, and thinking.

Why was I being treated like this? Why was I in this place? Was there a family in my past? Not knowing who my mother or father was gnawed at me. Why did they give me up? How come no one ever visited or even wrote letters? Was there something I couldn't remember, an unforgivable offense, some terrible act I had committed in a wild rage? Had I set fire to their house? Did I attack my mother? Try to kill her?

My mind raced. What would it be like to live on the outside? What could my future hold with this kind of present? The frustration in my gut was growing. I banged my head on the floor, and sensed this would not be my last time in solitary.

At the end of day three I was released, and resumed the summer routine. With school not in session, our jobs became fulltime. We were the ones who kept the place running. Who else would sew all the clothes, scrub the floors, wash the laundry, shower the little kids, or change the crappy diapers of both kids and adults? Who else would do the canning and feed the cows? They couldn't do it without us.

If you were able-bodied, you were assigned a job. Sometimes I resisted because I thought we should be paid to work. "Who the hell do you think you are, Vitkus?" the attendant would say, "You think you're better than everyone else, is that it? Well, today at supper suppose you just stand in the dining hall and watch the others eat. Breakfast and lunch tomorrow, too. Maybe by afternoon you'll feel like working." That usually did the trick.

Over the years, I had a number of jobs. One summer I operated a dough machine in the bakery, setting bread loaves on racks to push into the steam room where they would rise before baking.

My shift ran from four in the morning till two in the afternoon when the ovens made it unbearable to continue. Tempted by the irresistible aroma, I snitched an occasional slice still hot from the oven, spread it with butter, and enjoyed my little crime.

Another job carried a distinctly different scent. I shoveled shit at the sewerage plant. The filter beds were huge round pits that required periodic draining. When the water was lowered, I donned a black rubber outfit and boots that reached to my thighs, climbed down inside with a couple of other boys, and shoveled the soupy residue into buckets that were hauled up into a dump truck. We wore goggles but no masks. Although the stench was strong, I had become accustomed to it on the wards and in the infirmary. Even so, I was careful to keep my mouth shut. It was impossible not to splash.

Another summer I set type in the print shop, where we cranked out the institution's administrative and medical forms, like the ones in my own record. Working with my brain, reading and writing, made me feel a little smarter. A smarter retard.

In the summer of '55, I got assigned to the infirmary. There was both a hospital and an infirmary on the grounds, the hospital to treat injuries and brief illnesses, while the infirmary was for bedridden and wheelchair-bound patients disabled by both mental and physical ailments from which they would never recover. Some were teenagers, others young adults, some older.

One of the men I cared for was a guy named Benjamin. In his mid-40s, Benjamin was ambulatory and functioned well enough to dress and feed himself, but he required constant attention. He was obese, blind, and mentally handicapped. But he was also a human being.

He would often hide on me, and I'd play along. "Benjie, where are you?" First I'd hear nothing, but soon there'd be a stifled laugh around the corner. He couldn't help giving himself away. Then it would be my turn, a game of hide-and-seek, a moron hiding on a retarded blind guy. Benjie couldn't count to three, never mind to 100, so when I was ready, I'd holler to him. Once I hid behind a door and scared the hell out of him when he came by. He got even by pinning me to the cement floor of the outdoor patio. "I ain't lettin' you up!" he said, teasing. The sun had baked the cement like a kiln and I ended up with burns on the side of my cheek.

Some of us were assigned to move wheelchair patients from room to room, and when the attendants went on break, we took advantage of the unsupervised time. The building was V-shaped, with one whole wing unoccupied at that time. Because it was vacant, the lights were never turned on, and the long dark hallways were perfect for racing. Two of us would hop into wheelchairs, and a couple other boys would run behind and push us off. It's tough to keep a wheelchair in a straight line when you're careening through the darkness, popping wheelies, pumping as fast as you can, crashing into your competition, smacking off walls and hurtling toward a stairwell at the end of the hall. It was our homemade amusement park ride.

Of course, the infirmary wasn't all fun and games. Like the other buildings, it smelled of pee and shit, but here it combined with industrial disinfectant—a nauseating combination. Many patients were sad cases with severe medical complications that offered no hope of improvement. The strange thing is, as sick and feeble as they were, no one ever died at Belchertown. They just disappeared, and were never mentioned again. If you questioned, an attendant might say, *Richard? Oh, he went to Turkey Hill.* And Richard became an unperson.

What the hell is Turkey Hill, I wondered. A place where they raise turkeys? Or was it like "the glue factory" I had heard the farm boys talk about, where they sent horses to die? It wasn't until years later that I learned about an isolated site off Turkey Hill Road, Route 21, less than a mile from the main grounds of the state school. Set well back in the woods, down a narrow, unmarked and unpaved road, was Pine Grove Cemetery, a hidden burial ground where people who had lived their lives hidden from the community came to rest. There was no monument that identified the area as a cemetery, and no fence around it.

The farm boys dug the graves. To my knowledge, there were no ceremonies. Some say the bodies were simply wrapped in blankets, lowered into the hole, and covered with dirt. When the hole was filled, it was marked by a flat cement bar with the patient's number pressed into it. No name, no date of birth or death—just "217" or "132."

After years of neglect, the place was eventually taken over by weeds. As the markers sank beneath the overgrowth, the numbers that once identified the deceased disappeared, and Pine Grove became a disposal site, a dumping ground for tin cans, broken bottles, and discarded souls.

One morning in the summer of '55, attendants told us some very important people were coming to visit, and we were to treat them as special guests. The staff was determined to put the best face possible on the institution. They decided to stage a little show to entertain these VIPs, and for days they made us rehearse skits and songs in the sweltering school auditorium.

When the curtain opened on the big night, I was center stage with two other boys, dripping in long-sleeved white shirts and neckties. We were the color guard, Harry in the middle carrying the American flag, Brian at one side with a snare drum strapped to his waist, and me on the other. Guests in the audience fanned themselves with programs the print shop boys had passed out. On cue, Brian tapped the drum and we marched to the front of the stage. The audience rose, placed their hands over their hearts, and we saluted. Everyone recited the Pledge of Allegiance, and we marched off to the same drum tap.

Later during the show, Harry, Brian and I returned to the stage, this time wearing cowboy hats, seated around a fake campfire lit by a flickering red bulb. Russell played the piano and we sang Red River Valley while a bunch of other boys with feathers on their heads lurked in the background. Other acts followed, and the show closed with a group of the more able girls tap dancing across the stage in top hats and white gloves. The guests clapped, the curtain closed, and we returned to our stifling wards.

The next morning, I reported to the infirmary. One of my duties was to feed the patients who couldn't feed themselves, which was most of them. Many lacked teeth and we spoon-fed them a watery gray mush. While I was getting ready, the VIPs came through, a dozen or so men in dark suits, shiny black shoes and neckties, despite the heat. I recognized a few from the night before. I sat down beside one patient, an old guy strapped into a chair behind a steel tray. What teeth he had were rotted, and he couldn't keep his tongue in his mouth, so a steady stream of saliva ran down his chin. He rocked from his waist. Forward and back, forward and back, drooling endlessly.

Two of the important men stopped to watch.

I tried spooning food into the patient's mouth. It's hard to hit a moving target, and most of the mush dribbled onto his johnny, then to the tray. When a few minutes had passed, his rocking stopped, and the expression on his face changed. I knew what he was doing.

I put down the spoon and waited. When it looked like he was finished, I undid his restraints and got him back into bed. I lifted his johnny. Disposable diapers didn't exist back then, nor did latex gloves. I used my bare hands to remove his cloth diaper. It was yellow and heavy. I held it over a bucket to let the shit fall out, then dropped it into a container for the laundry. The stench hung in the thick air. The suits gagged and put their hands over their faces.

When I had the man's diaper off, I lifted him onto a stainless steel gurney, and rolled him, naked, between the long aisle of beds, down the hallway into a large room with an overhead shower operated by a pull chain. I put on a heavy black rubber apron.

We didn't have wash cloths, so I used my hands to clean him with a cake of Octagon, a huge block of cheap lye soap, brown with sharp edges, meant for doing laundry. It's still advertised on the web today as great for cleaning stoves and paint brushes.

Some of the guests watched from the doorway, their foreheads glistening with perspiration. I didn't touch the guy's genitals, and I didn't roll him over to wash the crap out of his ass. I wasn't sure if that would make me a homosexual. When I finished soaping him up, I reached up and yanked the chain. The sudden flood of cold water made him wince, and soaked me despite the rubber apron. Then I rolled the man back down the hallway, with the visitors following. I lifted him onto the still-soiled sheets of his bed, and dried him off with a towel.

From a nearby shelf I picked up a couple of safety pins and a clean diaper. As I was pinning the diaper, the visitors went outside. I could see them through the bars on the window. One of them walked faster than the others, rushed to the edge of the sidewalk, bent over, and vomited in the parking lot.

That summer the Brooklyn Dodgers led the National League for the entire season. They won 22 of their first 24 games, never let up, and by the time we returned to school in September they ended up taking the pennant. Over in the American League the high and mighty Yankees, those "Bronx Bombers," were on top again.

The Dodgers were my favorite because until now they had always been losers. A retard like me could identify with a team that had earned the nickname the "Brooklyn Bums"—guys like Gill Hodges, Duke Snider, Pee Wee Reese, Roy Campanella, and, of course, Jackie Robinson, the underdog of underdogs.

Brooklyn had never won a World Series. In fact, the Yankees had beaten the crap out of them five times before with all-stars like Mickey Mantle, Yogi Berra, and Whitey Ford. And in 1955, it looked like it might happen all over again as the Bums faced the Bombers.

The Yankees took the first two games at home, but the Dodgers won the next three at Ebbets Field. Then it was back to The Bronx, where the Yankees won game six to knot the series at three games apiece. The World Series had edged into October, and all I could think of in school that morning was Game 7, the big showdown.

Back then all the World Series games were played in the daytime, and I looked forward to watching them on TV. In the upstairs day hall was a small black-and-white set mounted on the wall, inside a padlocked cage of chicken wire, about six feet off the floor. Like everything else, the attendants controlled the TV. They had the key to the cage. They could turn the TV on or off. They could turn the volume up or down. They could change the channel anytime they wanted, whether we were watching or not.

If Pete was working the afternoon shift today, the game would be on. The problem was that I hadn't finished cleaning the bathroom before school. Jones would be pissed when he checked at noontime, and there'd be no TV for me. So as soon as we were dismissed for lunch, I ran back to get it done.

As I threw a bucket of rinse water across the floor, I could hear keys jangling in the hall. The door opened and Jones glared down at me. "You shoulda finished this before school, Vitkus. You're done in here. The matron needs her office cleaned before the end of the day. It's unlocked. Get down there now."

The matron's office was on the first floor by the visitors' room, just inside the main entrance. We weren't allowed to use that door, and since I never had visitors, the only times I had been to the matron's office was to get my ass reamed when Jones or one the others reported me.

Her door was open, but I hesitated before stepping inside. Even at noontime it was dark, but I didn't want to turn the light on and get screamed at. The place wasn't fancy—a desk, couple of chairs, some shelves with books, and a wooden filing cabinet behind the door.

It was the filing cabinet that caught my eye. Each drawer had a little white card neatly labeled with letters of the alphabet. The bottom one said "U-Z." When I was let out of solitary, I had watched the matron take my file out of that drawer to record the incident.

This was my opportunity. If Jones was stupid enough to trust me in here, why shouldn't I take advantage of the chance to see my file? Maybe I could find out who I was, why I had been sent to this place. I glanced back. The opened door blocked my view of the hall, but also gave me cover. I took a second to listen…it was quiet out there.

I stooped down and tugged on the bottom drawer. Not locked. The drawer squeaked as I slowly pulled it all the way out. There, way in the back, was `Vitkus #23-3394.` I looked around again, then lifted out the folder. It was fatter than I expected. The first sheet inside was a form dated June 8, 1943. My eyes jumped straight to my name, handwritten, filling a space near the top:

```
I hereby request that you receive and pro-
vide for my child, Donald Everett Vitkus,
who is dependent upon public charity
```

in accordance with the provisions of chapter 119, section 38, of the General Laws.

"Everett," that sounded distinguished. I didn't even know I had a middle name. On a line below, the words `Guardian, Friend,` and `Board of Public Welfare` each had lines drawn through them, leaving a single word not crossed out—`Parent`. Beside an X, in the same handwriting, was *Veronica Vitkus.* My mother. For the first time in my life, my mother had a name. I whispered it—Veronica, Veronica Vitkus. It sounded nice.

"Tompkins, get your ass down to the lunchroom now, or you'll be late getting back to school!" Jones' was bellowing from the top of the stairs, and getting louder as he started down.

I didn't have much time. On another form I caught the phrase, `Her twin sister Alice.`

"Vitkus, for Chrisssake, ain't you done in there yet?" Jones had almost reached the bottom of the stairs. I shoved the folder back in the drawer, closed it, and picked up my mop as he came through the door.

"What the fuck is takin' you so long?"

"Nothing. I'm done."

He looked at me for a second, then pulled the ring of keys from his belt. "Then put that stuff away and get the hell out of here."

In the empty day hall I sat down on a bench and stared out through the bars.

Veronica … my mother's name is Veronica. And she has a twin sister, who would be my aunt. What does a woman named Veronica look like? Does she smile? What color are her eyes and hair? Do I resemble her?

When I returned to school that afternoon, my mind was on anything but spelling or math, or even the World Series. Veronica Vitkus, my mother. The same old questions ran through my head. Why didn't she keep me? How come she has never visited? How old is she? Is she even still alive? Will I ever see her? Where is she? Who is she? Who am I?

As the afternoon wore on and dismissal approached, Roy pointed at the clock, reminding me of the big game. When the bell finally rang, we ran to the day hall. Pete was there, and the game was already on. There was no score in the third inning, when I sat down beside Harry.

Every time one of the Bums got a hit or made a great play, I wanted to jump up and yell. But I had to stifle it because we weren't allowed to talk in the day hall, not even while watching the World Series. Not even with Pete on duty. On that October day in 1955, segregated from the rest of the world inside a building with bolted doors and barred windows, we sat in silent rows on wooden benches, staring up at snowy black-and-white images through the wire of a locked TV cage, watching the "Great American Pastime." The Bums won, 2-0.

Beyond the Bars

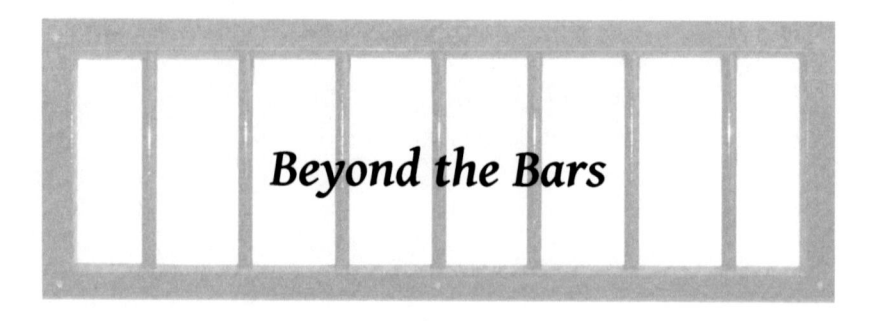

I was becoming a teenager, and that TV in the wire cage was making me think.

I didn't realize it at the time, but that TV had been bought by members of the Belchertown Friends Association, a group formed by parents of patients. Without them, we wouldn't have known what television was. I wouldn't have gotten to see the only World Series the Dodgers ever won in Brooklyn.

And I wouldn't have known about life on the outside. Television was my window on the world. Besides bringing me baseball, it made me begin to realize there was something better out there. I watched *The Howdy Doody Show*, where a bunch of screaming, happy kids in The Peanut Gallery laughed at the antics of Clarabelle the Clown, while we watched in silence. There was *Ding Dong School* with the kindly Miss Frances, who didn't yell, or call you stupid. My Saturday morning favorite was *The Lone Ranger*, the good guy on a white horse who rode into town and saved people. One day, maybe The Masked Man would show up at Belchertown and make everything right.

TV brought me commercials for Lucky Strikes and Camels. To me, a cigarette was just a butt on the sidewalk I picked up to smoke, but television showed me The Marlboro Man, master of his horse, free to ride the wide-open spaces.

TV also showed me disturbing news coverage about a Negro woman named Rosa Parks, who refused to move to the back of a bus in Alabama, and a young preacher named Martin Luther King whose house got bombed because he made powerful speeches about what he called civil rights. I watched as President

Eisenhower sent federal troops to protect colored students who were trying to enter a white school in Arkansas.

These images raised troubling questions. Why were colored people treated like that? Why was anyone treated like that? Why did places like Little Rock, Montgomery, and Belchertown exist? Where was justice?

I was becoming a teenager, and that TV in the wire cage was making me think.

Smoke 'em if Ya Got 'em

This "M" Building patient was caught smoking in bed. He refused to answer any questions where he got the match or cigarette.

−September 11, 1958

It turned out that the visiting VIPs were state legislators who had travelled from Boston to see firsthand what taxpayers were getting for their money in the DMR budget. Almost a year later, the place got a facelift of sorts. Maintenance started painting everything in sight. Even though it was still puke green, the day hall and wards at least looked cleaner, and we had hopes that conditions were finally going to improve.

They also began taking the bars off the windows. Apparently, the lawmakers had thought the place looked too much like a jail. The mounting brackets, though, were left in place—a reminder, I thought, that the bars could always be put back.

Of course, they still had to find a way to keep us in. Heavy-gauge screens were installed on the inside of every window. They told us the wire mesh was *so strong that you couldn't cut them with an axe.* Like we had access to axes. The frames were hinged on one side, with a lock on the opposite. I watched the attendants insert an ell-shaped key into a hexagonal hole in the frame, and that got me thinking.

"Get in there, piss, and get the hell out, goddammit!" Bill jerked his thumb toward the bathroom door. "I ain't got all day, my break is comin' up." He patted his shirt pocket to check his cigarettes, and twirled the ring of keys on his chain, winding them around his index finger till they stopped, then back in the other direction. He acted like he was doing us a favor, letting us take a leak before lunch, even though that's exactly what we did every day of every week. Bill wasn't as bad as Jones, but he was no friend. And he wasn't very smart.

Harry, Tim, Roger, Johnnie, and I walked in, and the boys room door swung shut behind us. It was a warm spring morning, but inside the radiators were still pumping. The heating system wasn't known for its efficiency, so the attendants' solution was to open windows. At the back of the bathroom, on the other side of the locked screen, the window had been cracked open a few inches.

"Hey, guys, look what I got!" I said in a hushed voice. I reached inside my sock and pulled out a flattened, inch-long cigarette butt. I had picked it up earlier when I pretended to tie my shoe on the sidewalk.

"Neat!" Harry said. "Smoke 'em if ya got 'em." He had heard that on some army movie on TV.

Attendants could smoke any time, anywhere they pleased, but cigarettes were forbidden to us. They were a sign of status. Among the patients, only the farm boys had smoking privileges. High on the pecking order, they worked with little oversight and were allowed to make unsupervised trips into town to pick up their Camels and Luckies, always unfiltered. The rest of us picked them up on the sidewalks, butts squashed under someone's shoe.

Attendants on bathroom duty, both men and women, often stepped inside to watch. But today, with break on his mind, Bill wouldn't be bothering us for a while. We were in the clear.

Along the left wall of the bathroom were the sinks. In the middle of the room was a single shower head where we lined up for gang showers on Saturdays. The tile floor sloped inward, toward a drain below the shower. Very utilitarian.

Even in the daytime, the dim overhead bulb was turned on. It had a white metal shade with a black stripe around the rim. "That bulb's gonna be hot," I said. "Tim, you douse the light." Behind the door was a pushbutton light switch—white for on, black for off.

The rest of us gathered beneath the light. Everyone knew the routine. I stuck the unburnt end of the butt between my lips, already tasting the tobacco. Roger stayed by the door to listen for footsteps and keys.

Like cigarettes, matches were forbidden because everyone was afraid we'd burn the place down. But we had that covered. Johnnie reached into his pocket and took out a steel wool pad he had stolen from the kitchen when he was scrubbing pots the night before. He stretched the end till he drew out a single strand about four inches long, broke it off and handed it to me.

Harry squatted next to a sink and grabbed the edge to steady himself. I stuck the butt between my teeth, used Harry's knee as a step, climbed onto his shoulders and hooked my feet behind his back, like a kid getting a piggyback ride. Harry gathered himself, pushed up, and carefully rose.

"Damn, Harry, you strong like bull!" Tim snickered, pronouncing it "bool." He and Johnnie stood on each side, their arms extended like spotters in a gym. "Shut the fuck up and just be ready to catch us!" Harry snapped, keeping his voice low.

Once he was upright, I pressed on the top of Harry's head with one hand, inched my other hand up the wall, and got to my feet on his shoulders. We were a small circus act with no audience to cheer, just Roger watching silently from the door.

Harry sidled toward the center of the room, clutching my feet while I teetered on top, the cigarette butt between my teeth. By the time he got to the sloping drain, I could just barely reach the overhead light fixture. Good thing I was tall for 13. I unscrewed the now cool bulb. "Okay, Roger. Now!" Roger snapped the switch and I stuck the thread of steel wool into the open socket. Within a second or two, the tip began to hiss and glow. Experience had taught us to use a single strand, stretched very thin. Too thick, and a sudden jolt would run down my arm, straight through Harry!

When the end was red hot, I touched it to the butt. I sucked in, while the others held their breath. The tobacco flickered, and soon smoke trickled from my nostrils. "Cool, or what?!" Tim said. I screwed the bulb back in and jumped to the floor while Johnnie flushed.

The four of us scrambled to the window and passed the cigarette among us, taking deep drags that brightened the tip as the butt shrank still more. "Save some for me!" Roger hissed from his post at the door. We exhaled through the screen and waved like we were fanning farts.

Roger could wait no longer. He ran toward us, but just as I was about to hand him what was left, a jingle of keys echoed down the hallway. I took one last pull at what was now no more than a pellet of tobacco, spit into my hand, dropped the nub into my palm and squeezed. The door opened and Bill stuck his ugly head in. "Hey! What's takin' you idiots so long?" He glanced up. "I've told you a million times, *leave-the-light-alone!*" He emphasized each syllable. "Which word is too hard for you retards?" Then he sniffed the air. "And you been smokin' in here!"

"We know you think we're stupid," Harry said, reaching for his fly. "Can't we just take a leak in here without you watchin'? You couldn't wait for your break and were smokin' yourself, I can smell it on your clothes. Besides—where would we get cigarettes and matches, anyway?"

Escape Committee

"What's your favorite kind of ice cream, Donald?"

The next evening the five of us gathered again in the coat room after supper. At thirteen, a year or two older than the others, I had called this meeting of the Escape Committee.

"Did you bring it?" I asked Tim.

"Yeah," he said in a hushed voice, "I took one from the visitors room this afternoon. Here." He pulled a wire coat hanger from beneath his shirt, and handed it to me.

"Great!" I began to untwist the hook, where it was welded together.

"What are you doin'?" Johnnie asked.

"You'll see."

When I got the hook untwisted, I bent the hanger back and forth until I broke off a straight piece about five inches long. Then I put it between my teeth, bit down hard, and bent the tip into a right angle. I had strong teeth, probably from fluoride. As a captive population, we were an easy target for medical experiments like fluoridating our water to a level many times beyond what is considered safe today.

I shaped the other end into a loop for a handle, then pushed the bent end into the key hole in the screen frame, and turned it. Nothing happened. I tried again. Still nothing.

"The hell with it! This ain't gonna work, and we're gonna get caught," Roger said, glancing back toward the hallway door.

"Be patient," I told him. I kept jiggling and after four or five tries, I could feel resistance. This time when I turned the wire, the lock clicked and the screen swung open.

"Jesus, Vitkus, you did it!" Johnnie blurted, and Harry covered Johnnie's mouth with his hand.

"Okay," I said. "Now when I get out, you guys close the screen, lock it up again, and hide the key somewhere good. And get rid of the rest of the hanger in the trash."

"Okay, but what about us?" Roger asked. He was still sore at not getting a drag on the cigarette in our previous caper.

"Don't worry, you'll get your turn," I said. I stepped onto the bench, climbed through the open window, and dropped to the ground outside. It was getting dark, and I made my way past the merry-go-round, through the woods and to the highway. This time I wasn't going to sit on a stump and stare back at the building. I was determined to make good. I decided not to try to find help up the road at that brick building on the common. No one would believe me, and they'd just report me for leaving, anyway. Instead, I turned right and started walking. The sign said Route 202, Holyoke, 15 miles. I had no idea what I'd find when I got there. I just kept walking toward this place called Holyoke.

I hadn't gotten far down the road when a dark-blue car pulled over ahead of me. The driver got out, waving a flashlight. It was a cop. We had a security guard on the grounds, an old codger who wore a badge, but I had never seen a real policeman.

He shined his light in my face. "Are you Donald Vitkus?"

I thought about telling him my name was something else, but this guy wore a badge and a uniform, and he carried a gun.

"Yes."

"Okay." He opened the rear door of the cruiser. "Get in. I'm taking you back."

He reached inside for his radio microphone. "Yeah, I got him," he said. Then he climbed in, spun a U-turn, and headed back to the state school. He knew exactly which building to take me to. He walked me up the big front steps, the ones that only visitors used. Jones let me in, and the cop left.

As soon as the door closed, I knew that was it. He brought me straight to the downstairs day hall, where all the other boys, including Harry, Tim and Johnnie, were sitting on the benches along the walls.

Jones stood me in the center of the room. "Take off your belt."

I did what he said.

"Give it to me."

I handed it to him.

Punishment—whether with a belt, broom handle, or bare fist—was always a public display. The attendants never tried to hide it, because there was *nothing wrong* with what they did.

"Turn around," Jones said. And there, in front of every boy in F Building, he used my own belt to give me a good whipping. He held onto the buckle, and swung the belt across my back. Each swing cracked like a whip when it struck. The pain was awful, but I refused to cry or scream.

Then, true to form, Jones made me put on a diaper and walk around the day room while everyone chanted *Baby, baby, baby, trying to escape* again. It didn't matter. Despite all the beatings and punishments, despite the warnings about "life on the outside," I had a growing sense that there had to be something better out there.

Later that year, when school had let for the summer, I resurrected my plan, again enlisting the Escape Committee. None of them had spilled the beans about how I got out the first time, so we went through exactly the same procedure—a rendezvous in the coat room and a coat hanger to unlock the screen. I climbed out and followed exactly the same route toward Holyoke. Again, a police car with a flashing blue light pulled up beside me. The window rolled down.

"You're Donald Vitkus, aren't you?" It was the same cop.

"Yes," I said.

"All right, get in."

He switched off the light, turned the cruiser around and headed back toward the state school. This time, though, he drove past the entrance and up the road toward the center of town. Was he taking me to the station or courthouse? Was I under arrest? I was even more scared than the last time.

He turned left at the common, and a half-mile down the road pulled into a parking lot. The building in front of us looked like a barn. Two big plastic cow heads stuck out from the roof below a sign that said Crystal Springs Dairy Bar. The cop took me inside, pointed to a stool at the counter, and pulled up another one beside me. The leather on his gun belt creaked as he sat, and a pair of handcuffs dangled at his waist.

He looked straight at me. "What's your favorite kind of ice cream, Donald?"

"Vanilla," I said.

"Helen, get this young man a vanilla ice cream sundae," he told the woman behind the counter, "with hot fudge, plenty of whipped cream, and a cherry on top." Then he turned back to me. "Look, kid," he said. "Next time, you gotta find yourself a different route."

Seeing Red

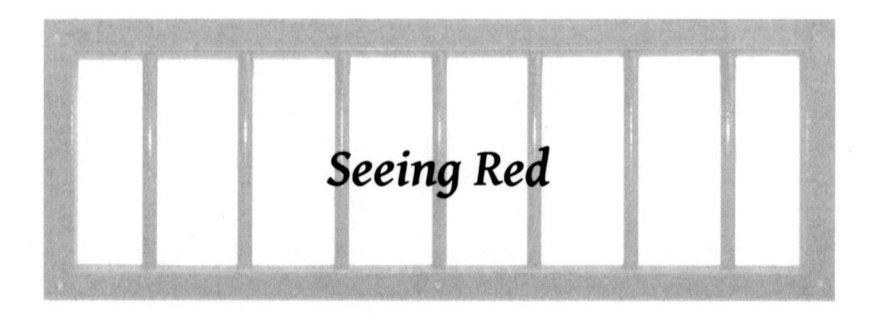

> Donald was transferred to "M" Building. He is a large boy, has temper tantrums, and female employees are afraid of him when he is disturbed.
>
> –*October 21, 1957*

"Hey, guys, c'mere! Quick, hurry up!"

Roger stood by the window, peering out into the night. A week into February, it was snowing again. We had just come up to our ward after supper, and it would be a while before Jones would order us into bed.

"Wow!" he said. "Look at that!"

Brian, Harry, and I joined him at the window.

"Yeah? So, it's snowing," Harry said. "Big deal."

"No, over there." Roger pointed across the way.

There, in the yellow light of a window about 75 feet away, the teenaged girls of G Building were getting ready for bed. Right before our eyes, three of them were undressing, and we could see everything. I wondered if they knew.

Girls were a great mystery to us. We were forbidden contact with these creatures. They were taught in separate classrooms, they were trained for separate jobs, and they ate and slept in separate buildings. Doing anything with them except staring from a distance was a challenge.

But some of the older boys were up to it. All the buildings at Belchertown were heated by a coal-fired plant on the edge of the property. Along with other utilities, steam pipes ran through underground tunnels in a miles-long network of arteries that serviced the entire facility. On winter days like this, you could see steam escaping from manhole covers, and from low cement structures that provided maintenance workers access to the tunnels. The tunnels themselves were about eight feet high and wide enough for four or five people to walk abreast. Older guys like Louie bragged about using them for dates.

"Hey, you know that girl with the red hair and the big ones? I had a date with her last night. After lights out, I snuck through the tunnel and met her in the gym."

For some reason, the gym seemed to be the place. Where else was there to go?

"Whoa! Did you kiss her and stuff?"

"Course I kissed her, you idiot! A whole bunch of times, what do you think? We did a lot more than that, too. We made out, and I got laid under the bleachers."

I was never quite sure what he meant, but from the tone of Louie's voice, it must've been fun. Sex education at Belchertown consisted of threats, punishments, jokes, and rumors—lots of stories about "doing stuff" with girls. Jones and other attendants were constantly warning us that if we ever got a girl pregnant, they'd cut off our balls. I knew what it was like to get kicked in the nuts, and I had a very strong interest in preserving those little round things.

"Holy jeez, what I couldn't do with *her* in the tunnel," Harry whispered now, like the girls could hear us as we stared through the window. He was trying to sound like he knew what he was talking about. All of us, Harry included, knew that staring out the window and talking was as close as he was gonna get, tunnel or no tunnel. Even so, it was fun to play the game.

"Which one?" Roger asked, his nose pressed against the glass, steaming up the window. He was hardly blinking.

"That one by the door. Check out those tits!"

"Right, Merullo. Like she even knows you exist," I said. "Or ever will."

"Oh, yeah, Vitkus?" Harry was no longer whispering. "Since when are you such an expert on girls? You spend too much time diddling with yourself to know what to do with a girl."

At 13 years old, we didn't understand much about hormones, but we were certainly feeling their effects. Masturbation was common practice. They moved us around from time to time, in case we formed "relationships" with the kid sleeping next to us. We were teenagers, after all, and even locked up in a hell hole, hormones still had their way. To prevent those ties, and to discourage talking or whispering, they also made us lie in opposite directions, so you faced the next guy's feet.

"Look who's talkin'," I said. "You're gonna wear your pecker out from beatin' on it."

"All right, all right, forget about it!" Harry turned back to the window and lowered his voice again. "Look, Valentine's Day is coming, remember? After that, she'll know who I am, all right."

"Yeah, the jerk-off next door."

For some strange reason, maybe as an exercise in socialization, each year the staff arranged a semi-formal Valentine's Day dance for us in the school auditorium. Besides Christmas and the Fourth of July, it was the only other celebration we ever had—no Halloween, no Thanksgiving, no New Year's Eve, no birthdays. I didn't even know when my own birthday was.

All the rest of the year, we were never allowed to talk to girls. Females were a no-no, plain and simple. You gotta stay away from them, they're not good for you. But you can dance with them for one hour on Valentine's Day. I didn't get it.

When the big day arrived, we had to dress up in borrowed suits. Mine had gray pinstripes. I don't know where it came from, but the pants didn't even cover my white socks, and the sleeves reached just below my elbows.

The wooden folding chairs in the auditorium were pushed back to form a couple of rows on opposite sides, girls on one, boys on the other. There were no red balloons, hearts, cupids, or refreshments. Just a record player on the stage.

All the attendants, including Jones, Pete, Bill, and Ol' Lady Howard were on hand, to make sure nothing happened that wasn't supposed to.

Pete stepped to the record player, dropped a stack of 45s onto the fat spindle, and pushed the button. The needle came down, Dean Martin broke into his rendition of *Volaré* in the Belchertown State School auditorium, and we were supposed to dance.

The attendants had nothing to worry about because, at first, nothing happened. The girls stared at the boys, the boys pretended not to notice, and stared at the floor. But in a few minutes, one brave kid crossed into No Man's Land. A few others followed his lead, and before long a bunch of boys were pushing girls around the floor, while the attendants circulated like referees at a basketball game.

"You already danced with her before, Russell. Ask someone else."

"Stop that talking, Jenkins. Just dance and go back to your own side."

Across the way was a girl I had noticed in school one day as we were passing from the gym to our classroom. She was pretty, with dark skin and black hair that shined under the auditorium lights. I wanted to ask her to dance, but I didn't know her name, and I was afraid she'd say no, anyway. I felt like girls were smarter than boys, and she wouldn't want anything to do with a retard like me. I waited. When a slow song started, I wiped my hands on my thighs, walked across the hall, and asked. She said yes.

I had watched a lot of Dick Clark's American Bandstand on that TV in the day hall, but this was the real thing. I led her out onto the floor, put my left hand in the air, and she took it in hers. It was soft and warm. I placed my other hand at her waist, and she did the same to me. I made sure nothing else touched. God forbid I should get a hard-on.

"Keep those hands loose, Mr. Vitkus. You're standing too close."

I stepped back, stared straight ahead, and shuffled my feet, trying not to step on her toes. I was too nervous to ask her name. That would've been useless information, anyway.

It would be another year before we'd be allowed any further contact with the opposite sex. In the meantime, we resumed our daily routines.

"All right, you guys, line up!" Jones ordered. We had just returned our bowls and spoons after supper. It was Saturday night, and that meant it was shower time. Once a week, "whether we needed it or not," we had to take a shower.

Everything, even taking showers, was done alphabetically, so I took my usual place near the end of the line. There were a couple of W's behind me, but I always felt the guys at the beginning of the alphabet had some prestige. At least they didn't have to worry about the hot water running out.

There was no talking as we headed down the stairwell, just the sound of 30 pairs of stockinged feet thudding off the walls.

When we got to the bottom, I could see Jones at the end of the hallway, handing us off to Ol' Lady Howard. She was plopped in a chair just outside the shower room, beside a large wooden bin.

"Okay, take 'em off!" she yelled down the line, and we all stripped, holding our clothes in front of us. I could hear the water splashing off the tiled floor as the line began to move slowly. When each boy reached Ol' Lady Howard, he tossed his clothes into the bin and turned to face her for inspection. I knew what was coming. At thirteen, I always dreaded this part of the routine, especially weeks when the shower attendant was a woman.

When I reached her chair, I dropped my clothes into the bin, turned toward Ol' Lady Howard, and stared at the wall behind her. She stood up and poked through my hair with a short stick like a tongue depressor. She was searching for lice.

"Well, nothing up here," she said. "Now, spread 'em."

I stepped my feet apart. She sat down again and leaned forward to examine my crotch. With the same stick, she pushed my pecker first to one side, then the other, still looking for bugs. When the stick touched my balls, I could feel myself begin to harden, and she looked up at my face.

Sometimes in bed at night I got an erection for no reason at all. As each of us reached puberty, we developed irresistible urges, and had to find ways to satisfy them. I never thought of masturbating as "right" or "wrong," but the attendants called it "retarded behavior." Father Dudley would call it a sin. The attendants were always threatening to cut your pecker off if they caught you playing with yourself, so I was confused about what was "normal," and had tremendous guilt about beating off. But I couldn't resist because it felt so damn good.

The trick was not to get caught. You had to be discreet. Never in the shower because you were always watched in there. Maybe in the bathroom, but that was risky, too. Sometimes it was a competitive event—I jerk off, he jerks off—a friendly race to see who comes first or gets the most distance. Sometimes we did it to each other in bed under the covers. There was no emotion or "love" involved, just mechanics. No one at the institution ever hugged us, touched us, or held us close. Except for the beatings, masturbation was the only human touch we had.

Ol' Lady Howard paused in her inspection.

"Maybe you like this a little too much, Mr. Vitkus, do you?"

"No, Miss Howard," I said, still staring at the wall. "I just want to take my shower."

"Okay, but I'll be watching you in there with that soap."

"Yes, ma'am." I turned, and walked into the shower room.

Two much younger kids, whose names were also at the end of the alphabet, were waiting for me. Another attendant, this one a male, stood near the wall, out of range of the shower.

The older boys had to wash the little ones, so I grabbed the soap from the shelf—the same clunky strong-smelling stuff used in the infirmary—and took them both under the shower. When the cakes were new, they had hard, sharp edges. This piece had already been used by about 25 other kids before us, so it was rounded but still harsh.

I did each kid in steps—first one's hair, then the other—not because it was more efficient, but just so one of them wouldn't have to wait till the other was all finished. When I got down to their privates, I hesitated. I didn't want the attendant to holler at me for not washing this part, but didn't want to touch their genitals or the crack in their butts. I didn't want anyone calling me queer. So I waited till I saw the attendant glance toward the next boys coming in, and skipped to their legs and feet. Even so, the attendant must've thought I was taking too long, because while I was stooping down he whipped me across the back with a wet towel and I dropped the soap. I knew the sharp sting would leave a welt.

"Don't play with 'em, just get 'em done!"

The two kids ran out the door. I picked up the soap, washed myself quickly, then passed it along to the boy behind me. Out in the cold hallway, one of the little kids handed me his towel.

He was already starting to shiver. They had both used the same towel, which was probably passed from another boy before them. I tried to wring it out, but it was still so wet that all I could do was push some of the water off me, then got in line again, while another boy handed out the gray nightshirts that would last us till the next Saturday night.

The next day we were in for another fun afternoon of sitting in the day hall. Ol' Lady Howard was on duty, occupied as usual with her radio. It had been snowing since early morning, and she probably wanted to catch the weather. She ordered us to shut up, and we sat on the benches in silence. With plenty of practice, we all knew the drill.

I tried passing the time with my mind game of directing cockroaches on the floor, but without success. Only one of them made it anywhere near the crack I had designated as the finish line. The others scattered randomly across the floor, like they didn't know where they were going. Sometimes you just can't depend on cockroaches.

The radio newsman droned on, closing with the forecast... *more of the same, cold and snow through tomorrow. It's 19 degrees at WHYN.* Then they played one of those cheery station ID jingles, and the deejay started counting down the Top Ten. I wondered what it would be like to be able to buy one of those records myself.

While I was gazing through the bars at the snow, a sudden movement on another bench caught my attention. Harry gestured with his head toward the right corner of the room. One of the younger kids had discovered something better than cockroaches to pass the time. He had unzipped his pants and his hand was inside. This open display was really asking for it, but the look on his face said he didn't care where he was. Soon his other hand was assisting the operation, and in a minute his penis was saluting us all.

The resulting snickers got Ol' Lady Howard's immediate attention. "Mr. Jones, get in here right away!" she barked. "We have a 'small problem' to take care of."

Always eager to take care of any disciplining, Jones and another attendant arrived before the kid had a chance to put it back in his pants. They each grabbed an arm, jerked the kid up, and hauled him out the door, leaving the rest of us frozen on our benches.

"Into that bathroom!" Jones's voice echoed in the hallway, loud enough to be sure we heard. "And take off those pants—they're already unzipped anyway. In fact, take off all your clothes!"

I thought maybe they were gonna give the kid a cold shower, and that would be it. Or maybe even a scalding one to teach him a lesson—I had seen kids with burned backs. While I waited to hear the water turn on, the boy yelled, "Stop! Don't!" He was pleading frantically. "No! I won't ever do it again!"

"You're damn right, you won't. We'll see to that."

A piercing scream made us all jump—then loud, sustained, uncontrolled howling. When the cries finally dwindled to gasping sobs, the door opened and Jones led the boy back into the day hall.

He was wearing a diaper. The front was red with blood.

Sawdust

```
Showed much interest and made good progress in
printing class. Does fairly well using hand tools
in manual training class.
```
-1960 Yearly School Report

Of all my teachers, George Poole was my favorite. He taught Phys Ed, printing, and a woodshop class called Manual Training. An older man, with gray hair, a pot belly, and the same kind manner as Pete the baseball-playing attendant, Mr. Poole took me under his wing. He recognized that I had a brain.

In the print shop he showed me how to set type, selecting individual letters from a tray. "See how the *m*'s and *w*'s are wider, Donald?" He lined them up in a metal frame. "They take up more space. You can add spacers to other lines to make the margins even." And he taught me how to operate the press. When a page was set, I locked it in place and hit a foot pedal to slide it into the press, one sheet at a time. A roller spread ink across the type—I still like that smell—and the press squeezed shut. When it opened, out came a printed page, a finished product that made me proud.

In the woodshop, Mr. Poole was a constant source of encouragement. Each year, he helped us make stuff to display at the annual Belchertown Fair. He cut the raw lumber on a table saw, which we were forbidden to touch, then we used the wood for our projects. Usually we all made the same thing, simple stuff like bird houses or stepstools. But when I got a little older, around 14, I wanted something more challenging.

"I'd like to build a bookcase this year," I told Mr. Poole.

"Well, that is ambitious. You know, that won't be easy, Donald."

"Yeah, but that's what I want to make."

I could certainly never keep a bookcase on the ward. I didn't own any books. And I knew it would end up at the fair in the exhibit hall, and I'd never see it again. But none of that mattered. I liked the way the one in our classroom looked, with books lined up on those shiny, varnished shelves, and I wanted to make one.

Mr. Poole took a pencil from the pocket of the long gray coat he wore over his regular clothes, and drew a sketch on a piece of wood.

"Maybe something like this?"

"Yes, with three or four shelves."

"Okay, then, I guess you can try." He put the pencil behind his ear. "I'll find some plans for you."

Manual training was just one period a week, and we could only use hand tools like hammers, planes, and drills that you cranked like an eggbeater. A project like a bookcase would take a while. I wanted it to look good, with level shelves and square corners. One week, as I was having trouble making straight cuts with a handsaw, Mr. Poole stopped at my workbench.

"I'll tell you what, Donald. I'm not supposed to do this, but I like how you work. To finish in time for the fair, I'm going to let you use the table saw. Stay after today when the other boys leave. Don't tell anyone, or I'll get fired."

When the bell rang and everyone else had gone, Mr. Poole took me over to his saw. I stared at the exposed blade. Could a moron like me really run this thing?

"Whenever you use any power tool, Donald, pay attention because the machine is the boss. Never take your eyes off what you're doing. Never! Keep your fingers away from the guard, and press down on the wood so it doesn't kick back. This little rail here is called a 'fence.' You hold your piece against it, and pass the wood through, slow and steady. Watch."

He picked up a piece of scrap from the wood box, drew a line across it with his pencil, then pressed a red button beneath the saw. The blade screamed as he pushed the wood through. Then he hit another button, a black one, and the saw coasted to a stop.

He reached into the box and marked another piece. "Here, now you do it." I stepped behind the saw and looked at the blade.

"It won't cut if you don't turn it on. Go ahead, don't be scared." I pressed the red button. The motor roared and the teeth on the blade became a blur. "Okay, line up the mark behind the blade," Mr. Poole shouted. Seeing me hesitate, he added, "You can do this, Donald. Just be careful."

I placed the wood against the fence thing, and pushed it toward the blur. As the edge of the blade disappeared into the wood, I could feel the vibrating power. The blade spit sawdust onto my fingers and I smelled fresh pine.

"That's it," he yelled above the noise. "Don't push too hard, or it'll kick back on you. Let the machine do the work."

When I had cut all the way through, he pointed to the black button, and I turned off the saw. I had made my first-ever cut with a power tool. I had a grin on my face, and so did Mr. Poole.

That afternoon I made all the cuts I needed to build my bookcase. Mr. Poole had given me more than just permission and the thrill of using a power tool. He had given me his trust.

The Belchertown Fair arrived in October. A carnival of games, ox pulling contests, cotton candy and fried dough, a midway with a fun house and rides—it was all squeezed onto the town common, a narrow strip of green about a half mile up Route 202.

We always attended the day before Columbus Day, when the fair actually opened. That way the townies' kids wouldn't have to walk through the funhouse with some retard in there. At least that was my thinking. Besides, we were a source of free labor. On a weekday morning, while the real schools were still in session, a gray bus would drop us off so we could unload equipment and help set up the tents and booths. When we were done, we could go on the rides for free—I thought they were using us to test them for safety—a merry-go-round, Ferris wheel, and long swings that whipped you around in circles.

That year, before I went on any rides, I headed straight to the exhibit hall, a big white building that looked like a church on the edge of the common. The bookcase I had made would be on display there, and I wanted to see it.

Inside were pumpkins, baskets of shiny apples, and shelves of glass jars filled with carrots, corn, and colorful jams, many with blue, red, or white ribbons on them. Off to one side was a display of hand-sewn dresses, shirts, knitted hats, and all the stuff we had made in manual training—a public relations exhibit to show what wonderful things were happening at that place down the road. Against the wall, there it was—my bookcase, with a red ribbon on it! I knew it would be sold, and I'd never see the money, but maybe some *Leave It to Beaver* father would buy it for his sons' room, and I could feel good about that. Satisfied, I ran back outside and joined the others.

"Hey, Vitkus," Harry yelled, "let's go on the Scrambler!"

"Yeah, then the Tilt-a-Whirl a couple of times, and see if we puke!" Tim said.

We had the whole place to ourselves. That afternoon we zipped down the giant slide, screamed through the fun house, and from the top of the Ferris wheel took in the whole common, the midway, the booths, the oxen pull area, and the exhibit hall with my bookcase in it.

The morning after we had helped set up the booths at the fair, the gray bus brought some of us back uptown. This time, I was wearing a uniform. In addition to being a great teacher, Mr. Poole had organized a troop of Boy Scouts at the state school. When I heard about cool things like sleeping in tents, building campfires, and earning merit badges, I wanted in. Troop 509 met after dismissal every other week in the school auditorium. I don't know who provided the uniforms, but I wouldn't be surprised if it was Mr. Poole himself. When he handed me that shirt and red neckerchief, I was more than a Belchertown boy. I was a member of the Boy Scouts of America.

The Columbus Day parade kicked off the fair, and Boy Scout Troop 509 was one of the marching units. Harry led us, holding the staff of the American flag in one of those leather pocket things strapped around his waist, while Mr. Poole marched alongside us. Far ahead, I could hear the drums of the high school band and the sirens of the town's fire trucks. We were always at the tail end of the parade, but that didn't matter. I felt proud in that uniform, marching in step while people watched.

When we reached the end of the route, the crowd headed toward the common, and we were immediately shuttled back to the state school. A day later we got hauled back, not as scouts, but once again unpaid workers. It was cleanup time. Most of the rides had already been dismantled, and empty popcorn boxes, soda bottles, and candy wrappers littered the common.

I was assigned to pick up around one of the tents, so I started tossing things into a barrel. There was a lot of sawdust on the ground, and while I was kicking it around I noticed something shiny. I bent down and uncovered a couple of dimes. Sifting through the sawdust, I discovered three more, then another bunch. One of the coin-toss games must've been set up here. I had heard the expression "finders keepers," but we weren't allowed to have money. And I knew we'd all be searched when we got back to make sure we didn't have any cigarettes, matches, or maybe even weapons on us. It was standard procedure. I looked around. No one was watching, so I stuffed the coins into my underwear and finished cleaning up my area.

When the bus returned to F Building, Jones was waiting for us. "Line up!" he barked, and took us into the day hall. One by one, each kid in front of me passed inspection.

"All right, Vitkus, you're next." I stepped forward, and Jones ran his hands over my body. When he patted my back pocket, it clinked. I could feel a few dimes drop through my pants leg. Five of them rolled to the floor in a sprinkling of sawdust.

"Oh, what have we here, Mr. Vitkus? Did they pay you for your hard work and honesty over there, Mr. Boy Scout? Half a buck? Maybe more? Let's see exactly how much. Strip!"

I kicked off my shoes. Jones glanced inside and gave them each a shake. Nothing. But when I loosened my dungarees, several more dimes bounced to the floor, and now everyone could see the lumps in my underpants.

"Drop 'em!" Jones snapped. I did, and my shorts hit the floor with a soft thud. "Well, well, well." Jones glanced toward the others. "Will you look at that. A kid who shits money!"

He paused for dramatic effect. "Where did you get all this?"

"I don't know. I found it."

"Scout's honor, I found it!" Jones said, raising his eyebrows in mock innocence, and holding up two fingers in the scout salute. He liked an audience. "That's a pretty lucky find, ain't it, boys?" He was back in my face. "Whereabouts? Up your ass?"

I was determined not to cave in, not to allow him the pleasure. "I already told you. I just found it, that's all."

"Where, I said!"

"Somewhere. I'm not gonna say where."

"You damn well better, if you know what's good for you." He paused. "Tell me, were you in church yesterday?"

"What's church got to do with it?"

"Did you serve at Mass yesterday?"

"Yeah. So what?"

"Father Dudley tells me that some money was missing from the basket after he counted the collection. Could that be where you 'found' all these dimes, Mr. Trustworthy and Loyal?"

We never had money to donate, but the attendants and other workers did.

"What are you talkin' about? I never took no money from church. I'm an altar boy."

"Hmm ... a lying, thieving, Boy Scout altar boy. I think you need to do some penance."

Jones dragged me, still naked from the waist down, to the side of the room where there was a heating grate in the floor. "Kneel," he ordered.

As I lowered myself onto the grate, the steel squares pressed into my bare knees.

"Gimme fifty Our Father's and fifty Hail Mary's. No, make it a hundred. I'll be back in an hour. I wanna play checkers on those knees."

Camp Chesterfield

About 5:40 P.M. Donald thrust his left hand through a pane of glass and received two severe lacerations. Examination revealed the 5th extensor tendon to be completely severed...nearly complete severing of the 4th extensor tendon.

–August 4, 1957

It was June of 1957. School was out for the summer, and late one afternoon Mr. Poole and a couple of attendants loaded Troop 509—each of us lugging a sleeping bag that he somehow provided—onto the gray bus. My first campout! I had been thinking about this trip since Mr. Poole had first mentioned it months earlier and couldn't wait to find out what sleeping in a tent and building a campfire would be like. We were headed for Camp Chesterfield, a Boy Scout camp in a hill town about 30 miles away. My red neckerchief reflected in the glass beside me as the bus passed through the main entrance and onto Route 202. At age 14, this would be my first stay beyond the boundaries of Belchertown State School.

It wasn't much more than an hour's ride, but because of our late start, we arrived not long before sunset with little time for anything except to unpack our gear and get ready for bed. Camp Chesterfield was used by several troops throughout the summer, so our site was already set up with three dark green tents when we got off the bus.

Mr. Poole called out tent assignments. "Harry, Tim, Donald, and Roger, you guys bunk here." We tossed our sleeping bags through the open flap and climbed inside. The ground was covered by a wooden platform, but I could smell the dampness of the canvas. "I claim this one!" Harry blurted, flopping himself onto one of the four cots. Two on each side, they were all the same, but the rest of us scrambled for the others. I unrolled my sleeping bag, took off my shoes, shirt and pants, and crawled in. "Hey," Tim said, "somebody lock the door," causing laughter. Roger, the last one ready, tied the flap strings, and what little light there was disappeared. In the darkness, we imagined the week ahead. "I hope we go swimming a lot," Roger said. "Yeah, and hiking, too," Harry added. "I hear there are neat trails all over the place." "I wanna go fishing," Tim said. "Yeah, all of that stuff," I chimed in.

An hour or so later, when we were finally talked out, one by one, the others fell asleep. Except for the occasional creaking of a cot, it was quiet, much quieter than the ward ever was. Outside I could hear the steady chirping of crickets. With only a canvas door, and no overhead lights in my eyes, I drew the top of my sleeping bag over my head and nodded off.

"What the hell is that?!" I sat straight up, not remembering where I was. It was getting light. "That's Reveille," Harry said. He had been to Camp Chesterfield before. "Some kid in another troop is playing his bugle. Prob'ly goin' for a merit badge."

"Jesus!"

"Relax. It's better than Jones bangin' on your bedframe, ain't it?"

"Right."

Roger and Tim were stirring. "Boy, something smells good!" Roger said. We all dressed and went outside, where one of the attendants was manning a portable gas stove. "Okay, boys, line up." He said it not in a mean way, but like he was inviting us. Two trays on the table had scrambled eggs in one, and bacon in another. Separated! A third held pancakes.

I had never encountered this before. At Belchertown, all our food—whether it was oatmeal, carrots, or Jell-O—was smooshed together. They plopped it in a bowl and we ate it all with a heavy spoon stamped "Property of BSS."

Was this some kind of trick? Were we supposed to choose one or the other? I watched Roger hesitate, then take both bacon *and* eggs. Nobody hollered at him. I made a snap decision, dumped some eggs, bacon and even a pancake into the bowl of my mess kit, stirred them all into a sensible mush, sat down on a log and gulped it down in a hurry so no one else would steal it.

Ahead of us was a whole week in the woods—hiking, swimming, fishing, canoeing, crafts, campfires, songs and games, even just running around. We couldn't participate in archery or wood carving—no sharp implements for the boys from Belchertown—but with all the other fun stuff, that was no sacrifice.

As the days passed, swimming turned out to be my favorite activity. Mr. Poole gave us lessons in different strokes and showed us how to dive. I practiced as much as I could, doing laps along the line of floats, back and forth, then out to a buoy marker and back. I couldn't believe I was really doing this! I loved the freedom of movement, the feel of the water. Near the end of the week, Mr. Poole tested me, and I did well.

The night before we left, all the troops gathered around a bonfire to roast marshmallows on sticks before the closing ceremony. "Whoa, you really fried that one!" Tim shouted as my marshmallow burst into a dripping ball of fire. "That's just the way I like 'em," I lied, blowing out the flames on a marshmallow that now looked like a piece of charcoal. Faces flickered as another scout tossed a chunk of wood onto the fire, generating a flurry of sparks like a bunch of lightning bugs. I loved campfires, the jokes and stories, the warmth on my face, the smell of the smoke.

"Time for the awards," a scoutmaster from another troop announced. Mr. Poole and others gathered for the presentations, and when his turn came, Mr. Poole gave out a half-dozen merit badges to members of our troop. Harry got one for leadership, which was no surprise. I figured Mr. Poole was finished, but then he said, "Donald Vitkus, for excellence in swimming." I rose and he handed me a colored patch with a picture of a swimmer on it. "Thank you," I said, running my hands over the material. In our tent that night, as the bugler played taps, I fell asleep with the patch in my hand.

Before we left the next morning, Mr. Poole stitched the badge onto my uniform. I stared down at my chest. Merit! Me, Donald Vitkus, not patient #3394.

We packed up and piled onto the gray bus. The week had flown by. I had thoroughly enjoyed freedom in the outdoors with no attendants telling me where to walk, how long to sit, when to shower, when to pee, or to take these pills, line up, or shut up. All in a place where the only bars were trees in the woods. The bus pulled out, and I watched those trees pass by, every one a step closer to Belchertown.

Back in the stale air of the ward, I resumed the daily routine—get up, eat, sit in the day hall, then do it all over again the next day. I looked forward to our next troop meeting. When the day arrived, I collected my scout shirt from the boy at the clothes cubby. It still smelled of campfire. As I buttoned it up, I glanced down to check my merit badge. A ragged circle of pinholes marked the spot. When I returned from the meeting, Jones stopped me on my way to bed. "You think you look pretty special in that uniform, don't you, Vitkus?" He poked me in the chest where my merit badge had been. "Forget it. We have no favorites here."

I turned in my shirt and red neckerchief, and the kid in the clothes room handed me a gray nightshirt. Stenciled in black across the shoulders was `Property of BSS`. I climbed into bed and listened to Jones taking his headcount. "Twenty-one, twenty-two, twenty-three ..." I heard his key turn in the lock, and the steel door clanged shut on my summer.

A prolonged heat wave brought the dog days of August. Even with the windows open, the buildings became ovens of heat and humidity. Late one afternoon as we sweltered on the day hall benches, Jones sat with his nose stuck in a newspaper, occasionally swatting at a fly. His shirt, like ours, was soaked. "Line up!" he ordered abruptly, dropping his paper. "We're going for a walk."

We marched out in single file with me, as usual, towards the rear. It wasn't any cooler outside, and the air wasn't moving, but at least it was air. The line ahead turned down a sidewalk behind G Building, the home of older, more retarded patients. "Low grades."

At the back of the building was a cement patio, maybe four feet off the ground, surrounded by a black steel railing. The space was filled with thirty or more men, milling around in the sun. By the door, in a sliver of shade, an attendant leaned against the wall. A half-dozen patients paced back and forth along the railing, naked. A few shouted obscenities, babbled or moaned. Others, partially clothed but shoeless, wandered in endless circles. Some squatted and rocked, back and forth, back and forth. A couple lay directly on the blistering cement.

As we approached, a commotion erupted in one corner. Men began yelling, jumping, and flailing their arms. At first, I couldn't figure out what was happening, but then I saw the attendant spray them with a garden hose. Was he cooling them down? Bathing them? Had he been rinsing shit off the patio and absent-mindedly let the hose wander? No. I watched as he aimed the sharp stream directly at one man's groin. The patient screamed, covered his crotch with both hands, turned his back and crouched against the force of the cold water. The attendant burst out laughing.

"Hey, Jones," I yelled ahead. "What's going on over there?"

"None of your goddam business, that's what," he shouted, without even turning around. "Same goes for the rest of you! Just keep movin'."

While the men on the patio hollered and danced, we continued in silence. We rounded the building, but the screaming followed. Far in the distance, I could see the farm, where Buckie would be gently washing down the horses.

Back inside, it would be another night crammed in with 29 other guys. I thought about Camp Chesterfield. I thought about the men on the patio. Still awake after an hour or more, the walls closed in on me. I pulled the blanket over my head and drew back the corner of the sheet, uncovering the rubber mat that was supposed to protect the mattress if I peed in my sleep. Even 14-year-olds sometimes let go during nightmares. In winter months, I'd draw my finger up and down that rubber pad, creating static electricity under the wool blanket, tiny lightning displays that eventually lulled me to sleep. But that wouldn't work in the summer humidity, so I resorted to Plan B—rhythmically, quietly but persistently, banging my forehead against the steel rail behind my pillow.

I gripped the head rail with each hand and rocked. Bang. Back and forth again, in the darkness. Bang, bang. There were days when I left bite marks on my own arm, or peeled my toenails till they bled. In my twisted logic, if an attendant happened to be watching, there was a chance he'd go easier on me because I had already punished myself. It hurt, of course it hurt. Even a retard feels pain. But I was the one in control of the hurt, and I could stop any time I wanted. I slammed my head against the rail till I could feel blood on the steel. I banged myself to sleep.

A few days later I was brought downstairs to a meeting room. A bunch of people I didn't know were seated around a big dark table with papers in front of them. The women wore necklaces over their dresses, the men neckties and jackets. An attendant pointed me to an empty chair while the necklaces and neckties continued their discussion.

They talked to their papers, like I hadn't even entered the room. They used a lot of words I didn't understand, but "moron" and "retarded" were clear. Then phrases like "Number 3394," "his current I.Q.," and "possible transfer." Were they talking about moving me out of Belchertown State School? No, it couldn't be, no one had said anything to me. Besides, those times when I had escaped they called the cops, dragged me back, whipped me, and humiliated me. Now they want me out? Were they testing me after my week at camp?

Eventually one of the women turned to me. "Donald, how do you feel about this?"

"About what?" I kept my eyes down.

"How would you feel about moving someplace else?"

"A different building again? What'd I do this time?"

I could feel them staring at me.

"No, Donald. What would you think about moving somewhere away from here, some place on the outside, away from the state school?"

I hadn't anticipated this. I had enjoyed Camp Chesterfield, yes, literally on the outside. Not being locked up was fun, and I hated to come back. But these people were up to something. I was never allowed to make any kind of decision, let alone one like this. I didn't trust them. I had heard stories from boys who were sent out to farms, but had come back. *Yeah, they worked our asses off out there. It was hotter than hell. They made us pick from sunrise to sunset, and beat us if we didn't work fast enough. No breaks, no drinks. And after work you gotta go out and buy your own clothes and food and stuff. People stare at you.*

Were these people setting me up to be someone's slave?

"Donald? What do you think?" the woman asked again.

They expect an answer, just like that? I knew life could be better some place where there were no bars or heavy screens on the windows, a place where I could walk to the movies or a store on my own. I had run away twice to find a place like that, where attendants wouldn't whip me or slam me in solitary.

I had seen stuff about freedom on TV, Martin Luther King, colored people demonstrating and marching in the streets. Maybe they were trouble-makers, but so what? I saw Jackie Robinson, the first Negro to play major league baseball with those Brooklyn Bums. A lot of people didn't like that, but I admired him. I watched shows like *Leave It to Beaver*, where people lived in normal houses with their normal families. Beaver got into scrapes, yeah, but they never whipped him or locked him up.

And there were those few people who had actually encouraged me about getting out. Pete, teaching me about baseball and how to pitch. *Donald, you're not retarded. I know you. You can do better than this place.* Mr. Poole, risking his job, trusting me to use power tools. *You can do this, Donald. Just be careful.*

But Jones's voice echoed in my head. *You'll never make it on the outside. Face it, Vitkus, you're nothin' but a retard, a fuckin' moron. That's it. You just ain't smart enough to be on your own.*

When it came down to it, where would I go? I had no family, no nice house. Where would I eat or sleep? What about a job? It seemed like my whole future was being decided on the spot.

"Donald?"

The neckties and necklaces wanted an answer. Eight years of being locked up, always being told what to do and when to do it, had their effect. I couldn't think straight. Maybe Jones was right.

"I don't know," was all that came out.

Decades later, I would find this entry in my record:

> This case was considered at Staff today regarding an Institutional Survey to determine the suitability of patients for community placement. It was decided that this patient is unsuitable for such a placement.

The following morning, when Jones poked his head through the door and bellowed, "Rise and shine, you retards!" I was seething. I had been pissed off at having to come back from camp, and now I was furious at myself for not having the guts to get the hell out of this place when I had the chance.

I went through the motions of getting ready for breakfast. But as everyone else headed downstairs, I returned to my bed. I reached under my mattress, retrieved a cigarette butt and discarded matchbook I had found outside the attendants' canteen, and lit up. The result was Solitary.

> "This "M" Building patient was caught smoking in bed. He refused to answer any questions regarding where he got the match or cigarette. Placed in strong room. Posted for one month. Later threatened suicide and was banging his head against the wall. To prevent self-injury, he was given Thorazine, 50 mgm."

Those meds made me feel like a zombie, numb and listless.

When I was released, I was more angry and depressed than ever. In the breakfast line one morning, I watched a glob of oatmeal get plopped into my BSS bowl at the steam table, and headed toward a bench. On my way, a kid I wasn't friends with bumped into me and my oatmeal splattered to the floor. "You stupid shit!" I yelled in his face, knocked him down, and started punching. A circle formed around us. "Fight! Fight!" they chanted. I punched even harder and got in some good licks. I jumped onto a table and leaped across the rows, sending bowls of oatmeal flying before I got tackled.

"Goddammit, Vitkus! What the hell's your problem?" Higgins shouted as he dragged me up. He grabbed me by the shoulders, and spun me around. "Look at this mess!" The floor was strewn with oatmeal and overturned bowls. The other kid's lip was bleeding. "Stay out here till you cool the hell off!" Higgins pushed me into the hallway, and went back inside.

Left alone, I stared through the bars of a window that hadn't yet been re-fitted with a steel screen. Somewhere out there was Camp Chesterfield. Somewhere was freedom. I drove my fist through the window, grabbed onto the bars, and dragged my left wrist across the V of shattered glass. Blood dripped down the window and soaked through my sleeve. But in that moment I was in control of the life I wanted to end.

When Higgins heard the noise, he burst back into the hallway and saw my hand. "Jesus!" He grabbed a dish towel, knotted it tight around my wrist, and wrapped another around my hand. "I'm getting you to the hospital." The hospital was within walking distance, but Higgins drove me there, lecturing me about how stupid I was to pull a stunt like that.

The guy on duty was one of the ones we called "horse doctors." They didn't have medical degrees because they never passed the exams. So with no license to practice on the outside, they practiced on us. He took one look at my hand, and said, "Kid, you want me to cut that hand off for you? Is that what you want? You'll never get out of here with just one hand. You'll be a lifer for sure."

He called the Assistant Superintendent, who called in a real surgeon to sew me up. I had severed the tendons of the middle and ring fingers on my left hand, one of them completely, and spent four weeks in the hospital.

Superintendent Henry Tadgell later sent a letter about the incident to a person named Mr. Tito Lombardi:

> ```
> Your name is listed in the case record
> of our patient Donald E. Vitkus [#3394]
> as the only outside person interested
> in this boy. Therefore, we are writing
> to let you know of an injury received
> ```

by him. During a temper tantrum Donald thrust his left hand through a pane of glass and received two severe cuts which required major surgery. Donald is being cared for in our Hospital and should make a satisfactory recovery unless serious complications develop.

We should appreciate your letting us know of your connection with Donald and if you wish to be informed of illnesses or other special incidents in his case in the future.

He Gave Me the Finger

It produced what some call a chemical lobotomy, characterized by a trance-like walk known as the "Thorazine Shuffle"

I was no stranger to the hospital. Common childhood diseases spread with ease on the congested wards, and I had many of them—chicken pox and measles a month apart, and mumps a few years later. They all required isolation.

A captive population, we were also easy targets for medical experimentation. In addition to the high fluoride content in our water, we were exposed to frequent radiation. We were periodically herded into a truck loaded with x-ray equipment, with little concern about the cumulative effects.

I also seemed to be accident prone, getting my finger slammed in a door, stepping in front of a kid on a swing, hitting my head on a pole, splitting open a finger playing baseball, smacking into a water pipe, and falling off a sled. My record is sprinkled with reports about getting stitched up:

```
August 4, 1957. Surgeon: Dr. Adolf
Franz. Operation: Hemostasis, suture
of 4th and 5th extensor tendons. Wounds
closed. Sterile dressing and fore-
arm splint.
```

A more serious incident occurred when I was fifteen. In December each year, they flooded the baseball field to create a skating rink, an incentive for good behavior, and a way to let us blow off steam from being cooped up during the winter months. Hockey was out of the question because sticks could become weapons, but I enjoyed chasing other guys racing around the rink. One afternoon, as I tried to make a sharp turn, I lost my edge and came down hard, slamming my left knee onto the ice. Pain shot through my leg. The extreme level of fluoride in our water was likely a contributing factor, making my bones brittle.

Attendants had often accused me of hurting myself to gain attention. I didn't want to risk losing my privilege, so I got up, rubbed my knee, and skated some more till we were called in for the night. By the next morning, my knee had stiffened and swollen so much that it was easily noticed when I limped to the shower, and I was sent to the hospital. I had shattered my kneecap. Four days before Christmas, a "doctor" jabbed a pencil-sized needle into my bulging knee:

> Four ounces of thick, creamy pus were aspirated. The knee condition is still causing spiking temperatures. The entire left knee has been immobilized by a long splint. Elastic bandages have been carefully applied, ice packs to knee.

I developed a rash, and my temperature shot to 103. Nearly three weeks later, showing no improvement, I was transferred to Mercy Hospital in Springfield for surgery. The rash was attributed to merthiolate, an antiseptic which had been applied to my incision. Following surgery, I spent a week in recovery where the nurses eyed me like a strange animal.

It was mid-January before I was well enough to be transferred back to the state school hospital for convalescence, still with an open incision across my knee, on antibiotics, multi-vitamins, and a high protein diet. Upon my return, this note was appended to my medical report:

> This patient has not had visits from his relatives (foster parents) for the past nine years and the Social Worker (Miss Meyer) has been consulted. Another evaluation of his mental and intelligence status has been requested.

Two weeks later, another note followed:

> January 29, 1959. Patient this day statistically transferred to "D" Building in order to screen low grades from relatively bright patients.

Apparently the "relatively bright" referred to me, but it wasn't until the end of March that my knee had healed enough to discharge me from the state school hospital for the actual move to D Building. I had moved up a notch, but things didn't change much. The layout of my new building was identical to the old. For sake of economy, they were all the same.

So was the routine. One morning after breakfast, I waited in line near the door of the ward. It was 8 o'clock, time for meds. With a hundred boys in a building and only two staff on duty, sedating us had become a preferred method to maintain control, a way to make us sit in the day hall for hours on end without talking, spaced out on a bench or slumped in a corner. Lithium and Thorazine were chemical restraints used to supplement leather straps. Thorazine at the time was promoted by drug companies as a treatment "for mental defectives—head bangers, screamers, biters, and other disruptive types." It produced what some call a chemical lobotomy, characterized by a trance-like walk known as the "Thorazine Shuffle."

Maybe Jones was right, that I wasn't ready for life on the outside, but I certainly wouldn't miss this shit. I hated being forced to take pills. I didn't know what they were, but I knew how I'd feel in less than an hour. I would feel nothing. I wouldn't care what anyone did or said. I would be aware of my surroundings, but I wouldn't give a damn. No anger, no excitement, no fear, no happiness.

I was no longer considered a low grade, but the neckties and necklaces had decided I wasn't fit for community placement, so I was still here, now a 16-year-old retard waiting to enter la-la land. The attendant doling out the meds was a skinny guy with hairy arms. He didn't know me, not that it mattered much. I watched each boy ahead of me accept a tiny paper cup, head out to the water fountain, and come back in. I knew they'd all soon be in a fog, and I'd be one of them. By the time I reached the front of the line, I had made my decision.

"I'm not gonna take those," I said to hairy arms.

He looked at me like I had turned down a candy bar. "What?"

"I said, I'm not gonna take the pills."

"What do you mean, you're not gonna take them?" He probably never had anyone refuse before. "They're medicine. They're good for you."

"I don't care."

"They make you feel better." His voice was louder now, and he glanced toward the door behind me.

"No, they don't! I feel okay right now. I hate how they make me feel!" Somebody like this hairy bastard was always telling me what to do. If they're so good, why didn't he take them?

"Just take them, and go get your water." He lifted the cup toward me. "Here."

When I didn't put out my hand, he grabbed my wrist and I pulled away. He reached for my chin and tried to force my mouth open, but I clenched my teeth and shoved him backwards. Dozens of pills shot off his tray. Suddenly, my arms were wrenched backwards. Another attendant had grabbed me from behind and forced my wrists toward my shoulder blades till I thought my arms might break. When I screamed, the hairy guy jammed the pills into my mouth and shoved them toward the back of my throat with his middle finger. I struggled and gagged. Then, without thinking, I clamped down as hard as I could.

"Son of a bitch!" He yanked his hand back and stared at it. "Fuck!"

I tasted blood and felt something hard and sharp against my tongue. I had bitten his finger off at the first knuckle. In a rage, I tried to chew and swallow, but the thing was too hard. I felt a sharp punch in my back, and the bloody piece flew out of my mouth onto the floor. The hairy-armed attendant stooped to pick it up and grabbed a cloth to wrap around his pulsating stub.

The other guy pinned me to the floor, face down, kneeling on my back. I struggled, but he rolled me over and began forcing me into a strait jacket. He pushed my arms into the sleeves and pulled them across my chest like I was hugging myself. Panting in my face, he cinched the laces tight. When he finished, he dragged me by my feet into the hall, shoved me to the floor of another room, and slammed the door. The lock clicked.

Soaked with sweat, my heart pounding against the restraints, I laid on the floor and thought about what had just happened. I had bitten a fucking attendant's finger off! *Well, he deserved it, the bastard! Jamming his goddam finger down my throat!* The metallic taste of blood lingered in my mouth. I would pay a price. They'd probably yank a couple of my teeth, that's what they did to biters.

My arms ached and the canvas of the straitjacket stunk like a wet tent. I had worn these contraptions before and was sometimes able to do a Houdini by hooking my back on a table corner, but here there was no table. I squirmed futilely against the ties, exhausted myself, and fell asleep.

When I awoke several hours later, I recognized where I was. I was confined to solitary, the Dog House. I knew what to expect here. What I didn't expect was the duration.

Eventually, the straitjacket was removed, but I remained in solitary. Three times a day the door was unlocked and a boy pushed in my meals—two slices of bread and a tin cup of water. The rest of the time I did a lot of sitting and thinking. When I had to pee or crap, I hollered and banged on the door for an attendant to take me to the bathroom. Sometimes they didn't come in time. When I went on the floor or in my pants, they tacked on more days. When I mouthed off, they took out the mattress.

I was in solitary for 34 days.

I later regarded that as an achievement, a badge of honor—I had gotten to them, and they didn't know what else to do with me. When I finally did get out, I never saw that hairy-armed attendant again. He was probably transferred to another building, or he quit. In any case, no one ever tried to make me take pills again. And I still had my teeth.

Fourth Grade Grad

Likes to sing and did well in music class. Made satisfactory progress in beginner's piano lessons... His conduct in school has been very good. He has an agreeable disposition. He is in the graduation class of 1960.

–1960 Yearly School Report

On a humid late June afternoon, I stood in the hallway outside the school auditorium, tugging at my shirt collar, not used to wearing a necktie. Graduation day had arrived. I had just turned 17, a normal age for graduation, but this was from fourth grade.

I had done well in school for two reasons. First, I enjoyed the challenge of using my mind. It was my salvation. Secondly, school was a haven from physical and verbal abuse. Unlike most ward attendants, the teachers were encouraging. I wouldn't see them until years later, but positive remarks were common in my school file:

Donald did very well in Group IV this year. Has shown much interest in his school work and his academic work is at a fifth and sixth grade level. Has good general knowledge and is alert to the current news. Comprehends new work easily and shows reasoning ability. Does well in music class. Follows directions well and displays good sportsmanship in "Gym" class. He is in his glory in cooking

```
class. Neat and clean about his work
and follows directions well. Recently
joined the printing class and shows much
interest in the work. Conduct is very
good. Has an agreeable disposition.
```

An hour before the graduation ceremony, the teachers had lined us up on the stairs outside for pictures, girls in front, boys in the back. From behind his tripod on the sidewalk a photographer snapped shots of the BSS Class of 1960. Our black-and-white glossy—thirty of us in suits and dresses, squinting into the sun—would be added to the collection in the lobby display case. I don't know where the dressy clothes came from, but we looked pretty good for a bunch of retards.

After the class photograph, we lined up to enter the school auditorium and were instructed to wait for the music. That cue would be Mrs. Marshall, our music teacher at the piano, kicking off the ceremony.

Mrs. Marshall was a very proper woman who wore glasses decorated with shiny stuff like diamonds, and rings that sparkled. I enjoyed singing in her class. She taught me how to read sheet music, and over the last year I had begun taking piano lessons from her in the visitors' room. "You can't slouch at the piano, Donald," she said beside me on the bench. Mrs. Marshall sat like she had Jones's broom handle stuck up her backside.

She showed me where to place my fingers on the keys. I was surprised at how smooth they felt, and how easy they were to press. I plunked out a few notes, amazed that my own hands were making that sound. I looked forward to my lessons and pretty soon I was cranking out hits like "Twinkle, Twinkle, Little Star" and "Mary Had a Little Lamb." By the end of the year, Mrs. Marshall told me I was good enough to play at graduation. "What do you think, Donald? I'll be right there if you need help. You'll do fine."

I had my doubts.

Now graduation day had arrived. When we heard the music begin, the teacher at the door nodded. Inside the auditorium, it was even hotter. None of the buildings had air conditioning, except maybe the superintendent's house. A pair of fans at the back of the hall produced nothing but noise. Even with the windows open, there was no air.

I hadn't expected so many people. Except for the first two rows, left empty for us, most of the seats were filled, along with the balconies on each side of the hall. Mr. Poole was making his way down the center aisle, distributing the programs we had churned out a week earlier in his printing class. Several in the audience were already using them as fans.

As we approached the stage at the front of the auditorium, the girls turned left to their seats, and the boys to the right, where Mrs. Marshall was playing. She smiled as I walked by, but passing that close to the piano made my heart pound.

When we were seated, Mr. Poole handed each of us a program. Father Dudley would deliver an opening prayer, and everyone would recite The Pledge of Allegiance. The superintendent and head of the Board of Trustees would speak first, followed by our principal. Next was *Musical Interlude: America*. I didn't understand what an "interlude" was, but seeing the title made both my necktie and stomach tighter.

Each speaker delivered his remarks, but I didn't hear a thing they said. When the program reached the interlude, the two teachers who had led us into the auditorium marched the class onto the stage. I headed to the piano, sat down on the bench and pulled myself closer. As I opened the sheet music, the pages rattled in my hand. Mrs. Marshall took her place by the stage, and when it looked like I was ready, she started waving her arms, counting aloud, "One, two, three, one, two, three" and pointed in my direction.

"My Country, 'Tis of Thee" wasn't a very complicated song, and I had gotten it down pretty well in practice. But this was show-time. I felt a trickle of sweat drop down my back. I started off okay, and the class came in on cue. But by the time we reached the third line, my left hand wasn't cooperating with my right, and I was hitting the wrong notes. I froze. I just stopped playing. The class kept going, but they had lost me at the "land of the pilgrims' pride."

Mrs. Marshall immediately joined the singing in a loud voice, and not missing a beat, sat down beside me and finished the song.

She made it look like we had planned to share the part. At the end, everyone clapped, but I was so embarrassed I wanted to disappear.

When the ceremony was over, I returned to D Building to get out of my sweaty clothes. But before I could change, Miss Meyer, a social worker, stopped me. "Donald, you have visitors," she said, and took me to the waiting room.

Visitors? For the kid who 'receives no mail or visitors and does not go on vacations?' Who would want to see me? Could it actually be my mother? After all these years, had she finally come for me?

Downstairs, a man and woman were sitting in the visitors' room. They were both dressed up, too, like for some special occasion.

"Donald, this is Mr. and Mrs. Lombardi," Miss Meyer said. I didn't recognize their faces, but I knew the name, the last foster parents I lived with before I was brought here. I hadn't seen or heard from them in eleven years.

"Hello, Donald," the woman said stiffly. "Congratulations." The man just looked at me. He didn't try to shake my hand, and I didn't offer.

"They saw you graduate," Miss Meyer told me. "They were watching from the balcony. They want to take you out."

I was stunned. Take me out? Where? What did that mean? "Oh," was all I could say.

They were both wrinkled and gray. These were the people who had dumped me at Belchertown all those years ago. The ones who had walked me up the steps of the administration building after that long ride when I was six years old, and then turned their backs. The people who had tied me to a chair in their kitchen because they had trouble managing me.

They walked me to the parking lot—the same lot I had watched all those Christmases for a car that might be my mother's—and the man opened the back door of their vehicle for me to get in. Mrs. Lombardi got behind the wheel, and in a few minutes we were uptown at the restaurant with the two cows heads. They chose a booth and sat opposite me. Mrs. Lombardi told the waitress, "Just coffee for us," then pointed at me. "He'll have a hotdog and Coke."

Beyond that, neither of them spoke. When our order came, they stirred their coffee and watched me eat. Where the hell had they been all these years? How come they never answered letters about me? What did they want from me now? I was aching to ask, but had been trained not to question, not to look people in the eye. So I stared at my plate and chewed. When they finished their coffee, they brought me back to the state school. I didn't even get a sundae.

A few days later, they were back. The Lombardi's wanted to take me out again, this time to their house for two weeks. I still couldn't figure these people out. Maybe now that I had graduated, I was important enough for them to care about? I was acceptable now, smarter, fixed? What would I do there for two whole weeks? How was I supposed to act? For eleven years I had never been in a house, anyone's house. Except for Camp Chesterfield, I had never been away from the state school.

They put me in the back seat of their car again with a paper bag of shirts and pants from the clothes room. This would be a much longer drive than the trip to the restaurant. I stared out the window as we passed through places I had never seen, town after town, lots of buildings, lots of farms and woods. Sometimes we went really fast on a long, straight road, but the trip still took a couple of hours.

We finally arrived in front of a big white house, the kind that *Leave It to Beaver* lived in. I didn't know where we were, but it was a two-family in a residential section of Somerville in eastern Massachusetts, almost a hundred miles from Belchertown—another planet.

They took me inside to two other people seated on a couch in the living room. One was a cop. What did I do? Did I screw up already? The other was a woman with stiff hair like the social worker at Belchertown. Mrs. Lombardi said they were her son and daughter.

"Come with me, and I'll show you the room," the daughter said, and I followed her upstairs with my bag. "This is where you'll sleep, you can leave your things in here." There was only one bed! "The bathroom is across the hall." It had a single toilet with some kind of cover. On the sink was a bar of white soap in a dish, and a really small brush in a cup beside a bright-colored tube. Yellow towels hung from a rack on the wall. A mirror above the sink showed me a kid that looked out of place. My clothes didn't seem right for here.

The woman took me back downstairs to the living room. I'm not sure they knew what to do with me. "You can sit there." She pointed toward the couch, turned on the TV across the room, and left.

The Lombardi's had raised their kids in this house, and now the policeman lived with his own kids next door. They were a family and I felt like an intruder, an alien. I didn't know how families acted, or how I should act. What should I do when they were in the room? Could I speak? What would I say, anyway? I half expected that they were going to put me to work, cleaning the toilet, mopping the kitchen floor, washing the dishes.

At mealtimes the table was set with napkins, real glasses, dishes and silverware, laid out on a flowered tablecloth. Meat, vegetables, and potatoes were served separately, not smooshed together. Besides a spoon, each setting, even mine, included a knife and fork. Weren't they afraid I might use them as weapons? Is that why they had made it a point to show me the cop in his uniform? I stuck to the spoon. I didn't know how to use a knife and fork, anyway.

Nobody tried to talk to me much, either at meals or any other time. Course, I didn't make any attempt to interact with them, either. I was used to eating in silence and sitting in silence in the day hall. I spoke only to ask permission. Where should I sit? Can I go to the bathroom now? Do you want me to take a shower today? Is it time to go to bed? And I was sure not to look anyone in the eye when I asked.

Mostly I just watched TV. A guy named Cassius Clay, only a year older than me, was training for the summer Olympics in Rome. He liked to talk tough. Martin Luther King was speaking about civil rights, and white cops were battling crowds of Negroes in the streets with tear gas, dogs, and night sticks. It made me mad to watch. I saw news reports about Negroes who had the nerve to sit at a counter at a five-and-ten-cent store in North Carolina and expected to be served lunch. Why were they so upset? They were out on the street walking around, weren't they? Slowly, I began to realize they were fighting for their rights as human beings.

One day when I was tired of watching TV, I asked Mrs. Lombardi for permission to take a walk, something I never could do unsupervised at Belchertown. She said yes.

I wasn't running away because I didn't understand cities or where I was going. I just walked. Aside from my brief escape attempts, this was the first time I walked anywhere beyond the state school. I wasn't scared, but amazed, both by the freedom to be on my own, and by what I saw. The streets were filled with traffic—cars, buses, and taxi cabs—and the sidewalks were busy with people. I got lost, but kept walking. When I came to stop lights, I waited till I saw others cross. Were they watching me? Was I acting okay? I passed stores with brand new clothes and shoes in the windows, and restaurants with inviting smells. It never occurred to me to step inside any of these places. I didn't have any money, and I didn't know how to handle it, anyway. I came to a sign that said Harvard Square where the sidewalk was jammed with people, many not much older than me, carrying books. I asked for directions and eventually found my way back to the Lombardi house.

Walking and watching TV. That's how I spent my time there. When the two weeks were up, with no explanation they drove me back to Belchertown. I guess the experiment was over. The Lombardi's apparently didn't want to have anything more to do with me. The feeling was mutual.

Parole

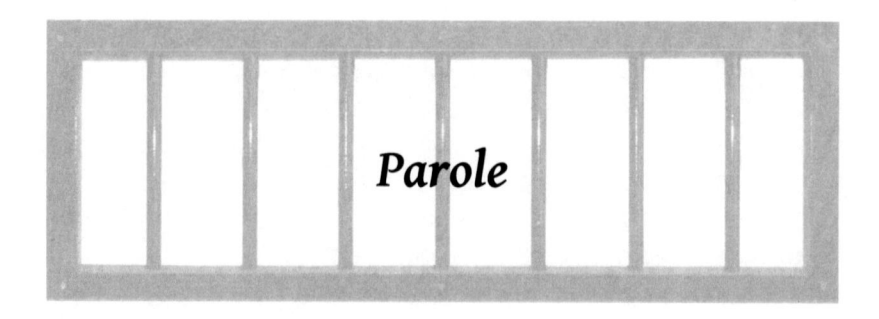

Patient was placed on parole today with Sister Superior, Our Lady of Providence Home for Children, Riverdale Road, West Springfield, Mass.

–June 28, 1960

I had completed my education at Belchertown State School. My I.Q. test results had roughly doubled since my admission. I couldn't wait to get out and prove that I really could make it on the outside. But I wasn't yet old enough for regular employment, and what to do with this smart moron presented a challenge to the authorities:

> June 15, 1960. Dormitory physician brought up problem that this boy, recently graduated from school, has an I.Q. of 80. He is, however, only 17. Social Service have been considering problem; they can hardly place him before he is 18.

In late June, Jones approached me one morning after breakfast. "There's a car waiting for you, Vitkus." He handed me a bag of clothes. A car? Now what? Where was I going? Why? Jones saw the questions on my face. "Don't worry. You'll be back."

In the parking lot, a lady social worker directed me to the back seat of a state vehicle, climbed in the front, and the driver took us out the main entrance. An hour or so later, we turned up a long driveway to the top of a grassy hill, and stopped in front of a brick building. A sign on the lawn read "Brightside." I had arrived at Our Lady of Providence Home for Children in West

Springfield, Massachusetts, also known as Brightside, operated by the Catholic Church. I didn't realize it, but I had spent my last day at Belchertown State School.

We entered an office where a lady in white stood by a desk. I figured she was a nurse, but she had this creepy hat with a band down to her eyebrows, and a dish towel thing on the back. On her chest was a huge bib, spotless bright white and stiff like cardboard. A wooden cross hung from a chain around her neck, and a string of beads dangled from her waist. Except for her face, she was draped in folds of white cloth. The weirdest thing was that she didn't have any hands. She looked like a ghost.

"Hello, Miss Miller," she said, with a slight bow to the social worker lady. Suddenly, her hands appeared from behind that bib. "Please, have a seat." She turned to me. "Donald, I'm Mother Superior." She did look pretty high class in that outfit, but she wasn't my idea of a mother. She reached out to shake my hand. "Welcome to Brightside, you can be seated, too. Place your bag by the chair."

Her voice was soft, but firm. The cross on her neck dangled in mid-air, then bumped the desk as she sat down. She opened a folder and signed a couple of papers.

"Donald, you are now officially on parole."

Parole. Like I was a convict on release. Another lady in white walked in, dressed almost the same. "Sister Mary Agatha will take you to your room." Already I had met a mother and her sister.

The second ghost led me back outdoors and up the hill to another building. Without unlocking it, she opened the front door and we climbed a set of stairs to a room with four beds. "This is where you will stay, Donald," she said. I looked around. Beside each bed was a dresser, and the room had a window with no bars or heavy screen. "This bed will be yours." She pointed to one in the corner.

"Do I put my clothes here, Ma'am?" I figured it wouldn't hurt to be polite on my first day.

"Yes. And call me 'Sister,' Donald. I'm a nun."

"None what, Ma'am?"

"I'm a nun of the Sisters of Our Lady of Providence."

"Oh. If you're none of them, why do I call you Sister?"

She smiled. "Our Lady of Providence is the name of our order. We're all called 'sisters.' Well, except for Mother Superior."

"Does she order you around?"

"She's what you might call my boss, yes. You'll figure it all out. Leave your bag by the dresser, you can deal with that later. It's almost lunch time and we need to get to the dining hall."

'Sister' led me down a stairwell heavy with the smell of something cooking, and I suddenly realized how hungry I was. We entered a small room where the food scent was overpowered by bleach and detergent.

"George, this is Donald," she said to a boy at a huge stainless steel sink. She had to speak loudly above the clatter of dishes, but even then she didn't sound gruff like Jones or most of the attendants at Belchertown. "Donald, this is George, one of the boys you'll be rooming with."

"Hi," he said. He was a husky kid, a little older than me, with an apron tied around his waist.

"Hi."

"Donald will be working here with you from now on. I need to go out and supervise lunch. I want you to show him what to do."

"Yes, Sister." He looked too young to be her brother. As she left, George leaned over the counter and lifted up a metal shade that opened to the dining hall. The place was full of kids, some my age, others younger, eating at long tables.

"They're all orphans," George said. "There's over a hundred of 'em here, even some babies."

Orphans, I could identify with that. The aroma of the food made my stomach churn. "Do we get to eat now?"

"Not till they're done, that's the rule. And don't talk to any of them. That's another rule," George continued. "The nuns will get on your ass if you do. For that matter, you're not supposed to talk to the nuns, either, 'cept about work." One of the kids brought his tray to the counter. George grabbed the plate and sponged leftover carrots down a hole in the counter.

"How come?"

"You're from Belchertown, ain't ya?"

"Yeah."

"You know how you can't look an attendant in the eye? It's sorta like that. There's a lady supervisor you'll see roamin' around. It's okay to talk to her. She's not a nun, but she's Catholic. They don't hire anybody who ain't. Just do your job and you'll be okay. When they bring up their trays, scrape the dishes and put them in the rack. The glasses go on the side, the plates in the middle. Put the silverware in this basket."

He pushed the rack through strips of rubber hanging from the opening of the dish washer. The setup was a lot like I had seen in the infirmary and our dining hall at the state school, but I let him show me anyway.

"When they come out, let 'em dry for a couple of minutes, cuz they'll be damn hot. Then stack 'em on these shelves. When everybody's gone, you go out and wipe down the tables and mop the floor. I'll show you that later. Then you're done and you can eat. We get two hours off after lunch, then do it all again at supper. And breakfast."

There were about a dozen boys like George in my building at Brightside. I thought I recognized a couple of faces, and eventually learned they were all from Belchertown. That's not something you just blurt out to a new kid.

We got up at 5 each morning, time enough to shower and be at work by 6. Here I could shower with no attendant watching, and I didn't have to wash down any younger kids first or share a bar of soap. I even had a towel all to myself.

When I was dressed, I walked down the hill with the other boys to the orphans' building, again, without an attendant. It was weird not being supervised all the time, but I could get used to that.

The cafeteria was on the first floor of the orphanage. The nuns and orphans lived on separate wings of the second floor, which also included a nursery for babies.

Our first duty was to set the tables—a plate, plastic glass, spoon, knife and fork, even a cloth napkin at each setting. The nuns prepared the food in the kitchen, and carried it to the tables in large bowls and platters. When the orphans finished eating, we cleaned up and then it was our turn, but in a separate smaller room. We served ourselves while a nun watched to make sure we didn't take too much. I felt like we were getting the leftovers, but at least it was real food, not ground-up mash. I was amazed to find that we were allowed to use knives and forks. Weren't they concerned I might use one as a weapon? After all, I was on parole. Not to draw attention, I took just a spoon. I didn't know how to use a knife or fork anyway.

At lunch a few days after I arrived, Sister Mary Agatha placed a knife and fork by my plate and sat down beside me. "Donald, use these. Watch me. She picked up the fork in one hand, the knife in the other, then stuck the fork into the slice of ham on my plate. While she held the meat in place, she cut off a piece with the knife.

"Now you do it."

By now, the rest of the boys were watching. I didn't know which hand to use for which. With the fork in one fist, I stabbed at the piece of meat, and sawed at it with the knife in my other. Seventeen years old, and I was learning how to use a knife and fork.

In our dormitory, we were free to watch TV in the basement. It was right out in the open, not locked in a cage! I never turned it on myself, and always let one of the other guys change the channel. Often I went upstairs and sat on my bed, discovering what it was like to spend time alone, unsupervised. I could be alone here, not under constant supervision. There was nobody here to force meds down my throat. I was free to walk the grounds, where there were no screaming naked patients getting hosed down. There was no smell of pee or shit, no solitary. The world looked different with no bars or axe-proof screens obstructing the view. I resolved never to go back to Belchertown.

At the same time, these new freedoms confused me. I didn't know if I was doing right or wrong. I wasn't used to making decisions. In a strange way, being told what to do and when to do it had been comforting. What were the boundaries here? Was it okay to walk downtown on my own? Others did, but would I get picked up by a cop and hauled back, maybe back to the state school? *You'll never make it on the outside, Vitkus. You're a moron.* Was Jones right?

On the other hand, I was a teenager, conflicted and growing more rebellious. True, I wasn't locked up any more, but who were these nuns to boss me around? Do this, do that. Don't talk to the orphans. Don't look at the student nurses. I felt like a servant following orders.

In September the orphans headed back to the classroom. They attended Catholic schools in the area. Boys came to the dining room in white shirts and ties, the girls with white blouses and plaid skirts, like they belonged to some kind of club. They talked about homework, tests, and dances. I heard older kids mention things like equations, Latin, something called "home eck," and a whole class of fresh men.

With graduation behind me, school was one thing I didn't have to worry about. I had enough stuff to learn myself. One of the Belchertown boys showed me how to use the washing machine in the basement, and where to hang my clothes on the line outside. I had my own bureau drawer to keep neat.

The toilets here, inside stalls with doors on them, had seats and a roll of paper on the side. Toilet paper! I learned how to use it, but figured the seats must be for girls, so I put them up and sat on the porcelain. It never occurred to me to shut the door, and the other boys were okay with that. I didn't want to be screamed at by an attendant for hiding behind a door. Besides, the stalls were confining. Even though the latch was on the inside, they reminded me of solitary.

Sunday mornings were a challenge. The church, a regular parish of the Springfield Diocese with its own congregation, was a short walk from our building. Mass was before breakfast at 6:30, and if you didn't go to church, you were going to hell. Sometimes I said to hell with it and stayed in bed. No one checked on us, so the only risk was that one of the other kids might rat if you didn't show up at Mass. But I could depend on George. He always went, and when he came back, I asked him what the sermon was about so I could report to Sister if she pumped me about it later.

I also learned my birth date. I knew I was turning 18 because that's when you got placed on parole, but at Belchertown actual birthdays were never revealed. Why would a retard need to know information like that, a party?

"Donald, this is your date of birth," Sister Mary Agatha told me, handing me a card. "May 12, 1943," it read. I wasn't sure what to make of it. "You'll need to learn it for filling out forms like job applications," she added. "Below that is your Social Security number. You need to memorize that, too, for work."

Since I would actually get paid for working here, another challenge was handling money. Except for the time I picked up dimes at the Belchertown Fair, I had never had cash in my pocket. At Brightside I earned ten bucks a week, for six-and-a-half days, with Sunday afternoons off. Payday was Thursday, and at the end of my first week I was looking forward to a pocketful of quarters. That afternoon in the dish room Mother Superior handed me another piece of paper with my name on it.

"What's this? Where's my money, Sister?"

"That *is* your money, Donald. It's called a check. One of the other boys will show you where to cash it. Take this with you." She handed me a little blue book with my name stamped inside, along with that long Social Security number. "You must deposit five dollars every week. The rest is yours to spend in a proper manner."

They had set up a savings account for me at a bank on High Street in the center of Holyoke, about three miles away. After work I walked downtown with George. "On the way back, we'll stop over there." He pointed at a corner grocery. "That's where we get cigarettes, soda, and comics."

He taught me how to wait for the light to cross Riverdale Street, and at the bank he showed me the ropes. "Just sign your name here on the back of the check. Ya gotta use ink." He signed his check with a pen hooked to a chain on the counter. They must've thought we'd steal it, which I probably would have.

"Now get in line over here with me." He pointed to a woman sitting behind bars, fancier than the ones at Belchertown. They were painted gold, with curls at the top. "That's the teller," he said.

"Oh. What do I tell her?"

"Just give her your check and bank book, you idiot. Tell her you want to deposit half of it."

I followed his directions. The lady stamped the book and counted out my money—four dollar bills, a half dollar, two quarters, two dimes, and a nickel—the real thing, not play money like they gave us at Belchertown to learn coins and denominations. I stuffed it in my pocket.

On our walk back to Brightside, George and I stopped at the grocery. I couldn't wait to spend my own money on my own cigarettes, but I hesitated at the door. Was it okay? Even with George's lead, I felt like I was sneaking in. At the cash register, I watched him buy a pack of Luckies. "And you, sir?" the cashier asked. She called me 'sir.' I scanned the rack behind her. A shiny pack with a red crown and fancy lettering caught my eye—Chesterfield, like our Boy Scout camp. That became my brand. I paid the lady, and she even gave me a free book of matches. Outside, George showed me how to tap the pack on my palm to get the first cigarette out, and we both lit up. I thought I looked pretty cool smoking a whole cigarette, not a butt from the sidewalk.

The next payday I walked downtown on my own. There was a bus stop near Brightside, but I still wasn't sure if "retards" were supposed to be using it. Besides, it was only a 45-minute walk, so why waste my money? At the bank, I cashed my check, but this time I didn't hand over my bank book. I had better uses for my money than giving it to the teller lady.

With ten bucks to blow, I headed to a movie theater that George had shown me. On the big overhead sign, with flashing yellow lights that looked like they were moving around it in a circle, was: "Double Feature—The Lone Ranger and Hopalong Cassidy." Two of my favorites. In front of the entrance was a tiny building with a window in it, and a lady sitting inside. I watched another kid slide his money through a hole at the bottom of the glass. The lady pushed a button, a ticket popped up, and she pushed it through the hole. I checked around to see if anyone was watching. Was it okay for a retard to enter a movie theater unattended? The aroma of hot popcorn convinced me.

Inside was a counter of brightly lit shelves crammed with candy bars, a soda machine, and a shiny silver pot erupting popcorn in a glass case. I bought a box of popcorn and a Three Musketeers, dropped a dime in the slot of the soda machine and pressed the root beer button. A paper cup came down behind a little window and filled up, all by itself. I carried my loot into the theatre, walked down the carpeted aisle, picked out my own seat, and watched, with no one watching me.

That weekend, while I was mopping the cafeteria floor, Sister Mary Agatha told me I had visitors. "There are some people at Mother Superior's office who want to see you when you finish up here."

"People to see me? Who?"

"It's Mr. and Mrs. Lombardi."

Those two again? Why were they hounding me now, just when things were getting better? They probably wanted me to go back to their house and work for them, be the boy to do all their chores, for free.

"I don't want to see them."

"Donald, they were your foster parents."

"Big deal. I don't care."

"Apparently, they came a long way to see you."

"They had no need for me all those years I was at Belchertown. I wasn't good enough. Now that I've graduated and I'm on parole, they think I'm better?"

"Maybe they had their reasons."

"I been to their house, and I hated it. They ignored me!" I was getting cranked up. "No! I don't have to talk to those two, and I'm not gonna. I don't want nothin' to do with them."

"I see." Sister Mary Agatha turned and left.

The following week I got hauled into Mother Superior's office. She thumbed through some papers at her desk, making me stand and wait. "It looks like you've been enjoying yourself, Donald," she said, eventually.

That was a curve. I thought I was there to get reamed out about the Lombardi's. "Well, it is a little better here than Belchertown," I said. Then added, "Sister." I still wasn't sure whether to call her 'Sister' or 'Mother.'

She reached into a drawer and held up my bank book. "You haven't been saving your money, as you were told. You disobeyed, and that's a sin."

"I, uh, guess I forgot how to get to the bank, Sister." I put my hands behind my back.

"You know better than to tell me that, Donald. Now you're lying. That's a sin, too." Sin was big with the nuns. "If you can't save money, how are you going to manage on your own? Do you want to go back to Belchertown?"

That was still a real threat. "No, Sister."

"Then see to it that you get to the bank next week. And this time, you're to deposit the entire ten dollars. Is that understood?"

"Yes, Sister."

"Good. Now, on your knees."

Like the movie theater, her office was carpeted. I didn't have to kneel on a heating grate.

"What do you have to say for yourself?"

"I was wrong, Sister. I'm very sorry. I disobeyed, and that was a sin. It won't happen again, Sister."

My records show that when my mother gave me up to the state, she had requested that I be brought up Catholic. I was getting my dose of it now. I hadn't forgotten Father Dudley's dismissal of what happened to Ronnie at Belchertown—*That's a state issue, not a church issue.* But religion was the thing at Brightside, and I had to go through the motions. Even so, I didn't care for the priest here, either. Monsignor Powers was the big boss. Mother Superior supervised the nuns, the orphans, and us state boys, but Monsignor Powers ran the whole place. I felt uneasy around him, the way he strolled in that black suit and shiny shoes. The nuns catered to him, and he loved it. They served his meals in a separate room off the orphans' cafeteria. I could see him in there at his private table, a napkin under his chin, reading his paper. He was well taken care of.

One morning after we had finished serving, I was eating my own breakfast when Sister Mary Agatha came by. "Donald, Monsignor wants some topping for his toast. Take this to him." She handed me a bowl of strawberry jam with a dinky little spoon stuck in it.

I put it down on the table. "I don't want to."

"I didn't ask if you want to. You have to. He's your priest."

"I don't have to do nothin' for him. He's not my priest, and I don't believe in God anyway."

"Donald! Bring Monsignor his jam!"

"No. And you can't make me."

With my newfound freedom and no restraints or physical threats, I pushed the limits, questioning, challenging. Why do I have to go to Mass? Why do us Belchertown boys have to eat by ourselves? How come we can't talk to the orphans? Are they better than us?

That afternoon I was back in Mother Superior's office. "Donald, this incident is going in your record," she said, scribbling something down. "It will be reported to the social worker at Belchertown. You are here on parole, don't forget that. What do you have to say for yourself?"

I was terrified about being sent back. "I'm sorry, Sister." I looked at the floor. "I shouldn't have done that. I was wrong, Sister. I should respect Monsignor Powers. Yes, Sister, I really do believe in God."

All this apologizing aggravated the hell out of me, but I swallowed my pride. After all, I was still supervised here, but not so strictly, and the environment was certainly a world better than Belchertown. I had money in my pocket, the freedom to spend it, and a growing sense of independence. I knew the state was responsible for my welfare until I turned 21, so I made up my mind to settle in for the duration of my parole.

4-F

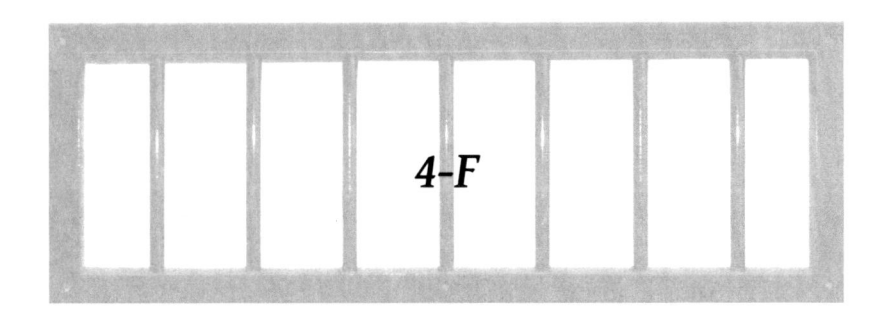

Donald was today discharged from Placement.
                           –June 13, 1963

"I've seen you here before," the girl beside me shouted. I pretended not to hear her above the loud music and the whir of the skates circling the hard wood floor. On a warm summer afternoon, I had walked downtown to the Top Hat, a roller skating rink that was one of my favorite Holyoke destinations.

"What's your name?" she said, a little louder.

"Donald." I kept my eyes on the floor in front of me.

"Hi, Donald, I'm Susan."

I didn't know how to react.

"Afraid you might fall? Is that why you don't look at me?"

I began to feel dizzy, and it wasn't from circling the rink. Socializing with the opposite sex, at no matter what age, wasn't part of the curriculum at Belchertown State School. Except for those Valentine's Day dances when we could hold a girl at arm's length, they were completely off limits. Girls were aliens. As little boys, we watched them like dogs watch cats. But now I was no longer a little boy.

When I didn't answer, she said, "Let's stop," and rolled to a bench by the rail as I followed. "Sit, it's okay," she said, patting the bench beside her. Now I couldn't ignore her. I sat down, and stole a sideways glance while other skaters zipped by. She had blue eyes, and blondish-brown hair like me. She was short, maybe a little chubby, but I thought she was pretty.

"Do you like this music?" she asked, edging closer.

"Yeah, it's okay."

At the state school, the message was clear. Don't talk to girls, and don't touch them. No one wanted retards making more retards. The story that they'd cut your balls off if you got a girl pregnant—a pretty strong deterrent—was still fresh in my mind. A few guys talked about making out with girls under the bleachers in the gym, or getting laid in the network of steam tunnels that carried heat to all the buildings. Most of that was brag, but pregnancies did happen. Every now and then a girl would go away for a while and then come back, thinner.

"You're not bad on skates. I haven't seen you fall once. Will you be here again next week?" she asked.

"I don't know. Maybe. I mean, I guess so." I felt like I was getting away with something, just talking to her.

In 1961, the United States had a military draft, and since I had turned 18, I had to be registered with Selective Service. My social worker, a woman named Ethel Johnson, gave me my registration card and told me to carry it at all times. It said, "Donald Vitkus, Class 4-F," which meant nothing to me. I stuffed it in my wallet and forgot about it.

Later that summer, I was loading the dishwasher at Brightside when Miss Johnson came by. "This is your last shift, Donald," she said. "When you're finished here today, pack up your clothes. You'll be leaving Brightside tomorrow."

I had made it more than a year without being sent back to Belchertown, despite all the threats. "What did I do, Miss Johnson? I got here on time. I haven't talked back to the nuns, and I put some money in my bank book. You can even check it."

"It's nothing like that, Donald. You haven't done anything wrong, you're just moving."

"Moving? Where am I going?" I had adjusted to the routine at Brightside, and was seeing more of Susan at the rink, even going to movies with her.

"I've found a nice place for you. You'll like it."

That's what they told me when I was six, on my way to Belchertown.

The following day, when I got into the back seat of Miss Johnson's car—I always sat in back—I was expecting a long ride, but in just a few miles she pulled over. Across the street was the Yankee Peddlar Inn, a high class Holyoke restaurant with a fake white horse and carriage out front. We weren't far from Brightside. I had walked this area before.

"This is where you'll be living, Donald."

She pointed to a gray house next to us, a regular house, not an institutional building. It had a small porch in front. She took me up the sidewalk, rang the bell, and stepped right in without waiting for anyone to answer. I followed her into the hallway. It smelled like cabbage cooking. A woman came from what I guess was the kitchen, gray-haired and wrinkly, wiping her hands on her apron. "Donald, this is Mrs. Skibinski, your landlady. That means you'll be paying rent to her."

"Nice to meet you, Donald," she said softly, extending her hand. A little stooped over, she had to turn her head up toward my face.

"Hello," I said, and shook her hand.

"Come on up, and I'll show you your room. Miss Johnson can wait here." She gripped the railing as I followed her up a carpeted staircase. She wore the same old lady shoes as the nuns, black with fat heels. At the top, she paused. "This is the bathroom. Keep it clean." Through the open door I could see the toilet—it had a seat on it—beside a small white sink with a mirror above it. On the opposite side was a matching bathtub, on raised feet that looked like animal claws. We continued up another flight of stairs, bare and more narrow. There was less light here, and it was warmer. "And this is your room," she said, opening the only door.

Inside was a single bed and dresser, nothing more. A light with a pull chain hung from the sloped ceiling. There was a closed window at the back, a closet on the side, and wallpaper with bunches of maroon flowers and swirly leaves everywhere. The floor was dark brown, wood, not tile or cement. The place smelled a little musty, but it was clean. There'd be no cockroaches to watch here.

I would live in the attic, and there would be no socializing with the family. Fine, I didn't know how to socialize anyway. Mrs. Skibinski would keep an eye on me, check my room—sometimes when I was in it—and report back to Miss Johnson.

"Leave your towels and bed linens by the door at the end of each week. I'll take care of them." She put her hands on her hips. "No hot plates and no visitors. Especially girls. Those are the rules," she said, then headed back downstairs.

I looked around again. No rows of beds! For the first time in my life, I would be sleeping alone.

As for rent money, Miss Johnson had that covered, too. She had found me a job within walking distance at the Soldiers Home, a hospital for aging and disabled veterans, a half mile up the hill on Cherry Street. Washing dishes, what else? That was my vocational path at Brightside, so I was qualified. I would also get my meals there. All my career training was paying off.

I alternated morning and afternoon shifts with staggered days off, never two in a row. Weekends were the best because the kitchen manager wasn't around. She often threatened to report me if I didn't mop the floor or follow other orders, but that was never a problem. I always did what I was told.

I had to buy tickets for meals and ate in the kitchen. It never occurred to me to bring my own lunch because I didn't know how to shop for groceries, and I had no place to store food, anyway. I was earning enough money to buy a single meal on days off at a local diner, and still have a little left over to continue to see Susan. I had moved only about four miles from Brightside, so we could still get to the Top Hat or movies downtown.

One afternoon Mrs. Skibinski called me downstairs. A door-to-door salesman had stopped by, and asked if she had any tenants. I guess he didn't know I was from the state school. He picked up what looked like a heavy suitcase, placed it on the bench in the hallway, and opened it up. Inside were several books with shiny covers that looked like leather. Each one was labeled with letters of the alphabet. The guy was selling *Encyclopedia Britannica*. He gave me his spiel, and before I knew it, I had signed up to get smart. Weekly payments would eventually get me a whole set, A to Z. Over the coming months, as each volume arrived, I lined them up on the floor against the wall of my room. I didn't have a TV or radio, so I spent my time reading, especially anything I could find under science. This retard had his very own set of encyclopedias.

I had overheard those conversations among the orphans about school after fourth grade, homework assignments and tests. I knew I was missing something, and I wanted to learn stuff. I also began hearing guys in the dish room at the Soldiers Home talk about something called "the draft," and a "lottery." They asked each other what their classification was, and their chances of getting called up. I thought about my 4-F card, but didn't want to sound stupid, so I never talked about it or asked what it meant. I tried looking in my *Britannica*, but that didn't help. From watching TV, I knew another way to find stuff out, and I headed to the Holyoke Library.

It was quiet inside and everyone looked like they knew what they were doing. A few people had newspapers spread out on big tables, while others were thumbing through cards in tiny file cabinet drawers. Shelves of books were everywhere. I had no idea where to look, so I asked a lady sitting behind a desk.

"Excuse me, how do I find out what 4-F means?"

"4-F? Do you mean about Selective Service?"

I didn't know the term, but she was wearing glasses, so I figured she was smart.

"Yes, the service."

She handed me a folded paper from a stack on the counter. "This brochure explains all the Selective Service Classifications."

"How much is it?"

"They're free, you can take one."

"Thank you."

Inside was a chart with a column of numbers and letters, almost like a report card. At the top was "1-A: Available for unrestricted military service." Near the bottom, I found "4-F: Not Acceptable for Military Service, physically, morally, or mentally." It didn't take much to figure out which word applied to me. The state had done it to me again—they had registered me as a retard. They had controlled my past and now they were controlling my future.

I took the card out of my wallet and stared at it. There it was in black and white—"4-F." Another goddamned label. Since I didn't have a driver's license, this was my only form of identification. Who would ever want to hire me when I showed them that?

I had seen ads on TV about good jobs, training and education in the Army, but now that was out of the question. I thought about getting an attorney, somebody like Perry Mason who would fight for my rights. Who was I fooling? I didn't know where to go or who to call, and I couldn't afford one anyway. I just knew I had to get rid of that freakin' label.

The next day after work I went downtown again, this time to City Hall, and found an office marked Draft Board. A woman inside who was pounding away at a typewriter paused and looked up. "Can I help you?"

I took the card out of my wallet and put it on the counter. "Yes, this needs to be changed," I said. She came to the counter and examined my card. "What do you mean? Is something wrong, is your name spelled wrong?"

"It says I'm 4-F. I want it changed."

She looked at me like I had a screw loose. "This is your classification, sir. I don't have any authority to change that."

"Who does, then?"

"This is how you were registered with Selective Service."

"Well, I want to be selected. Who can change this to 1-A?"

"The Draft Board decides these things. I'm just their clerk, but I'll see what I can do, sir." She still had that look. "We'll let you know."

"Okay, thank you." I felt like she was just putting me off, but what else could I do?

A couple of weeks later Mrs. Skibinski handed me an envelope. "Miss Johnson was here. She said I should give this to you."

"Thank you," I said and took it upstairs. Inside was a new Selective Service card labeled, "Donald Vitkus, 1-A." I could hardly believe it. I had no idea how the designation changed. Apparently, all it had taken was a trip to the draft board. I took my old card out, ripped it up, and replaced it with my new identity.

In the coming months, I continued working at the Soldiers Home, seeing Susan as often as I could when I had time off. She had introduced me to her parents, and we occasionally had dinner at her family's home in South Hadley. They had to encourage me to sit at the table with them.

One afternoon when I returned from work, Mrs. Skibinski stopped me at the door again. "I guess you're getting important," she said, and handed me a letter from the post office. It had my name on it. I had never received mail before in my life. Who would be writing to me?

On my bed upstairs, I read:*"Mr. Donald Vitkus, you are hereby required to report to the Springfield Induction Center for service in the United States Army."* This must be a mistake. I was 1-A in my wallet, but still a retard in my head. I never thought the Army would really want me, a guy with a fourth grade education. I read it again and again to make sure. If it was a mistake, I wasn't going to ask questions. In another month, I'd be wearing a uniform. I'd be somebody.

First thing the next morning I showed the letter to the kitchen manager at the Soldiers Home. I had to give her notice that I'd be leaving in a few weeks, but more than that, I wanted to see the look on her face.

Finally, someone wanted me, and it was Uncle Sam. I couldn't wait to tell Susan.

The Basics

"You tryin' to convince me you're a retard to get out of the Army?"

I soon found myself stripped to my underwear, standing in a line of recruits at Fort Dix in New Jersey. It was July of 1964. Hours earlier I had said goodbye to Susan, boarded a train, and left Massachusetts for the first time in my life, with no idea what to expect.

I moved past examiners who listened to my heart, told me to cough while they held my balls, pushed sticks down my throat, and shot needles into each arm, then on to another line for my fatigues. One guy gave me pants, the next shirts, another underwear and socks—three pairs of everything. This was no wad of clothes from the cubbies at Belchertown. This stuff matched, and it was all my size! Next I got a brand new pair of boots, and a kit with a toothbrush, razor, shaving cream, deodorant, and my own bar of soap. All this, plus a duffel bag! I jammed everything in and wrestled the bag to the rear of a crowded bus, shoulder to shoulder with guys from all over the country.

Crouching to look through the open windows, I watched building after building pass by. Formations of men were marching or running everywhere, chanting in rhythm, their T-shirts dark with sweat. When the bus rolled to a stop, a guy on the curb hollered, "This is it, gentlemen, your home sweet home, for the next eight weeks." He wore a Smokey Bear hat and had three stripes on his sleeve. "Welcome to the United States Army! Step off and line up. You are my property now, gentlemen! Line up along the curb, facing that building. Right over there. Move it, move it!"

Following the guys in front of me, I lugged my duffel down the aisle. When I reached the door, my bag shifted, I lost my balance, stumbled down the steps, and fell right at the man's feet. "Shit! I mean, I'm sorry. Sir."

He stared down at me while everyone else froze. When I got to my feet, he was in my face. He was actually a couple of inches shorter than me, but seemed taller. "What's your name, clutzo?" He wasn't hollering, but he sounded like he was.

"Donald."

"You got a last name, *Donald*?"

"Vitkus." Then I added, "Sir."

Any minute, they'd all see me for the retard that I was. I tried to look at the ground like Jones always forced me to do, but this guy was too close. He pushed his chest into mine, forcing me back a step.

"Don't you walk away when I'm talkin' to you, Vitkus!" He jabbed me repeatedly, targeting my breastbone, his finger like a gun barrel. "And don't call me *Sir*. Call me *Sergeant*!"

"Yes, sir. Sergeant."

"Look at me when I'm talkin' to you!" he snapped.

I forced my eyes upward, but not all the way. A name tag on his chest said *Sgt. Nittoli*. His shirt didn't have a wrinkle on it.

"Vitkus. I'm gonna remember that name. I'm gonna be on your sorry pimpled ass, Donald Vitkus, until the very fuckin' end." He paused, to let that sink in.

"Vitkus, do you know what you just did?"

"I tripped and fell. I didn't mean to drop my bag on your feet. It's heavy. Sorry."

"Sorry, *Sergeant*!"

"Yes, sorry, Sergeant."

He looked me up and down while the others watched.

"You know what else happened here, Vitkus?" Suddenly, his voice dropped, confidential but intense. "Your goddamn heavy bag dirtied my shoes." He looked at his feet, then repeated the message, emphasizing each word. "Your fucking heavy bag dirtied my shoes." His eyes returned to my face. "I suppose you're sorry for that, too," he said calmly. Then, through his teeth, he added, "Get down there and brush them off!"

I squatted. They were the blackest, shiniest shoes I had ever seen. They looked pretty clean to me, but I wiped them off with my hand anyway.

"Now pick up that fucking heavy bag and get your sorry ass in line with the rest of these losers."

With that introduction, I became Sergeant Nittoli's project.

Days later, with the temperature and humidity both around 90, he led us on a five-mile run. Nittoli was about 30, hard-nosed and muscled, all Army. In full gear like the rest of us, he was in his element. After a mile or so, he turned, back-pedaled easily, and saw me lagging at the end of the pack. He began running beside me, step for step. "What are you, a pussy or something, Vitkus? That pack too heavy? Or maybe it's the boots? You need a pair of high heels?" He wasn't even breathing hard. "Afraid you're gonna break a nail or somethin'? You wanna go back to the ladies' barracks to fix your hair?"

My shirt was drenched and I was gasping for breath, but Nittoli was hardly breaking a sweat.

"Maybe your tits are bouncing too much, that it? Take that shirt off and lemme see if you need a fuckin' bra." I tried to pick up my pace. "You wanna be a soldier? This is the United States Army! A quitter never wins, and a winner never quits. Move your ass, turdface!" And he jogged back to the front.

It didn't get better. At parade drill, when Nittoli barked *Left, march!* I turned right. When he ordered *Halt!* I took an extra step. I was trying hard to get it right, but the harder I tried the more I screwed up. Maybe I really was a retard. There seemed to be no doubt in Nittoli's mind.

"Goddammit, Vitkus! You understand the word *Halt*?" He stood beside me, flailing his arms and yelling into my ear like it was a megaphone. "You got a brain in there, asshole? They teach you your right from your left in that retard school? Yeah, I seen your record. Fourth grade education! You tryin' to convince me you're a retard to get out of the Army? I got news for you. I'm gonna *make* you learn!" He thought for a second. "Which hand do you jerk off with?"

Masturbation was so common at Belchertown that the question didn't surprise me. "This one, sergeant." I raised my left hand.

"Right. You're left-handed."

Now I was really confused.

"Vitkus, when I say *left*, pretend you're reachin' for your pecker, then head in that direction!"

A couple of guys behind me snickered.

"You assholes get a yuck outta that? *Forward, march!*" he barked. For the rest of the afternoon, we marched everywhere. "*Left! Right! About face! Double time!*" We marched to the mess hall, we marched to the firing range, we marched to the obstacle course.

Being a leftie continued to be a challenge. On the firing range, I had to lie facing the targets the same way as the others, which meant I had to learn to shoot an M-14 right-handed. On the march, I wanted to carry my gun over my right shoulder because it felt awkward on the left. "Goddammit, Vitkus, switch sides!"

True to his word, Nittoli rode my ass for the entire eight weeks, from hand-to-hand combat, to scrambling over barriers, under barbed wire, crawling through sand and mud under live ammo. And running, running, running. His tactics were a lot like Jones's, but their motives were worlds apart. The Army had a purpose. He was pissing me off to motivate me, and he was succeeding. I had fought not to be labeled 4-F, fought to get into the army, and now would fight to stay in.

Nittoli cited me repeatedly for uniform violations—my boots weren't shined, they were untied, my uniform wasn't pressed, my hat was crooked. "Vitkus, where the hell is your goddamned belt?" I never wore a belt at Belchertown after Ol' Lady Howard hung me on that hook. "When the enemy's chasing your sorry butt and your pants are around your boots, what are you gonna do? You don't belong in this man's Army, you freakin' retard!" *You freakin' retard!* is how Sergeant Nittoli came to address me. I was determined to prove otherwise, both to him and to myself.

On one miserably hot July morning, we were up for inspection. At 0900 hours, Sergeant Nittoli came through the barracks, accompanied by a Major decked out in ribbons and brass. We stood at attention as the pair worked their way down the aisle, examining each man's wall locker, uniform, and "rack," the army's term for bunk. When they reached me, the Major looked me up and down. "Your name tag is crooked, soldier," he said. "Yes, sir," I said and reached to fix it. "Not now!" Next he looked at my rack. I had trouble forming the taut hospital corners and wrinkle-free blanket that were the Army's idea of what a bed should look like. "This man's rack is a mess, Sergeant."

"Yes, sir," Nittoli said. I knew what he was thinking. Without another word, he stepped around me, picked up my mattress, and heaved it out the window. We were on the second floor, and I would have to retrieve it.

One August afternoon, with a mean thunderstorm brewing, I sat on my footlocker shining my boots. The barracks was sweltering. Others were also getting set for inspection the next day, checking their uniforms, the layout of items in their lockers, and cleaning their guns. I had learned that, among other qualities, the Army valued two things—shiny shoes and a shiny belt buckle. Sweat trickled off my nose as I daubed a rag into the can of polish at my feet, spit on the toe of my boot, and snapped the rag back and forth. The buckle would be next.

"Private Vitkus, stand at attention!" I was startled by Sergeant Nittoli's voice, firing from just above my head. I leaped to attention, realized I still held my boot in one hand, the rag in the other, and let them both drop.

Even in this humidity, Nittoli's uniform was crisp, immaculate—his sharply creased trousers perfectly bloused into his boot tops. He was like that all the time. I knew I could never reach that level of military precision. I just knew it. He had already reamed me out earlier in the day for missing a station on the obstacle course, and now I figured I was in for more of the same.

"I'm talking to you, Private Vitkus. I've told you before, pick your head up and face me when I'm addressing you. My voice comes from up here, not down there."

"Yes, Sergeant." I forced myself to stare straight ahead. I could feel his breath on my face, but he was yelling like I was somewhere down the hall. Outside, thunder rumbled closer, and rain began to drum the metal roof of the barracks.

"Vitkus, are you trying to get out of the military on a Section 8?"

I felt like I was back at Belchertown, being made an example of in front of everyone else.

"No, Sergeant."

"Do you know what a Section 8 is?"

"Yes, Sergeant."

"What is it?"

"That's when something is wrong with a person mentally, and you kick them out of the Army."

I also knew a Section 8 often involved a dishonorable discharge for sexual perversion, but I didn't say that. All the Belchertown guilt and confusion about masturbating, touching other boys, and what is "normal" behavior was in my head in an instant.

"That's right, Vitkus. Come with me."

I followed him down the row of bunks, and he turned into the lavatory at the rear of the barracks. We stood there, in front of one of the stalls and he pointed to the toilet.

"You see that horseshoe-shaped thing, soldier?"

"Yes, Sergeant."

"Here in this man's Army, we call that a toilet seat. You a man, Vitkus?"

"Yes, Sergeant."

"And that seat has got to be down when you're sitting on the fuckin' toilet." His voice was echoing off the tile walls. I knew the others could hear. "Get in there right now, Vitkus, drop 'em, and sit down!"

I followed the order. I pushed down my underpants, and sat on the toilet seat. A flash of lightning sent the image of the crying boy with the bloody diaper through my mind. I was sweating even harder.

"So how does that feel, Vitkus? Is your ass happy?"

My throat tightened.

"I asked you a question, soldier!"

It just didn't feel right not to be on the cold rim of the bowl, but I knew what I needed to say. "Yes, sergeant, my ass is happy."

"Goddammit, soldier! Look at me!"

When I glanced up, his face was strained and his eyes narrowed, the same look Jones used to get.

"On your feet!"

I reached for my skivvies.

"Did I tell you to pull those up?"

I rose and looked straight ahead.

"Now turn around."

I shuffled my feet.

"You see that seat in the down position?"

"Yes, Sergeant."

"Well, good. In fact, fucking wonderful. Now flush." I pressed the handle and the sudden rush of water matched what was happening outside.

"Face me."

I turned.

"Vitkus, it's come to my attention that you've been seen sitting on the toilet with the seat up. Right on the goddamned porcelain! What the hell is wrong with you? If you're pissing, I don't give a flying fuck. But when you shit, that seat is down, do you understand? I don't ever want to hear about this situation again, because if I do, there's gonna be a problem. Do I make myself clear?"

"Yes, Sergeant." I wondered who the rat was. What was the big deal, anyway?

"You know, Vitkus, sometimes, when sergeants don't see eye-to-eye with privates, we go out back and we work out our differences. And the guy who ends up with the most bruises keeps his mouth shut. Have you seen guys around here with black and blue marks?" He didn't wait for an answer. "That's because they've been behind the barracks with me to learn my point of view. Do we understand each other, Private Vitkus?"

"Yes, Sergeant, I understand."

"Great. Now pull up your shorts. You look like an idiot talkin' to me with your dong hangin' out."

In Country

I was no longer "Patient #3394 who receives no mail." I was a soldier with a girl back home.

When I completed basic, I was shipped to Camp Wolters, a small Army base just outside Mineral Wells, Texas. I was attached to the 864th Engineering Battalion, a unit of mechanical engineers, heavy equipment operators, and construction personnel trained to build roads, bridges, structures, and landing fields. My job was in support, specifically food services. I worked in the kitchen serving food, washing dishes, and sweeping up—the career path that had been paved for me at Belchertown. But in Army lingo, I was an "Executive Cook."

In April of 1965, we were ordered to pack our gear and get on a train to an unknown destination. We were "on maneuvers." In a few days, I was looking at the Golden Gate Bridge. I had joined the Army and was seeing the world. Outside of San Francisco, we boarded the *USNS Eltinge* and left port on May 13.

A World War II liberty ship just out of mothballs, *The Eltinge* was a gray rust bucket with constant mechanical problems. Between breakdowns we limped across the Pacific, and just beyond the International Date Line the ship lost all power. No engines, no electricity. It was stifling below deck, and the bobbing ship sent waves of guys puking over the railing. Dead in the water for days, we drifted back across the date line until we were rescued by another ship and towed 500 miles to Midway where we got a break from seasickness while our cargo was transferred to *The Barrett*, a Navy vessel diverted to pick us up.

A month after disembarking from San Francisco, we dropped anchor in a quiet bay. I climbed into a landing craft crammed with a hundred other guys in full combat gear. It was mid-day and the air of tension made me realize this was more than a training mission. As we approached the beach, the front ramp of the craft dropped down, and we waded ashore. It was hot, humid, and quiet. The sun bounced off bright white sand, magnifying the heat. It felt like we had actually gotten closer to the sun, and my helmet and fatigues didn't help. For the first and only time in my life I was standing on foreign soil—the wide, sandy beach of Cam Ranh Bay. We had been deployed to the Republic of South Vietnam.

Like most of us, before I got to Vietnam I didn't know a thing about it. I might have heard it mentioned on TV, but U.S. involvement wasn't big yet, and I had never paid much attention. The 864th was among the first U.S. Army engineers to arrive. I remember only one building on the beach, a house that reminded me of the superintendent's residence at Belchertown. The rest was nothing but sand. Our mission was to construct an airfield long enough to accommodate large aircraft, even B-52s, to bring in more troops and supplies for the war that was ramping up farther north.

While other guys pushed sand with dozers and poured cement, my main tool was a P-38, a can opener. I handed out C-Rations. There was nothing to cook. Everything came in a can—ham and eggs, macaroni and cheese, baked beans—often the same stuff for days on end. When supplies came in, we got what we got.

When I wasn't prying tin, I patrolled the perimeter of the construction site. With the intense heat, most of the work was done at night, under minimum lighting. The heavy equipment operators couldn't hear small arms fire and they needed protection.

Besides my M-14, sometimes I lugged an M-60 machine gun with heavy cartridge belts. I had never touched one in basic, but in Nam my commander said, "Here, this is your job. Take it out to practice, it's yours." I quickly learned to brace myself when I pulled that trigger, by lying down or getting on one knee. Otherwise, I ended up on my ass.

I had stayed in touch with Susan throughout basic and our relationship had grown more serious. We expected to continue seeing each other when I finished my military commitment. Vietnam didn't alter that plan. I wrote often, and couldn't wait for her return letters. I was no longer "Patient #3394 who receives no mail." I was a soldier with a girl back home.

I adjusted to conditions in Nam more easily than many others. That's not to say I didn't screw up, but Sergeant Nittoli had trained me well, and enforcement of regulations was more relaxed "in country." I didn't have to worry about uniform infractions here. Nobody cared if my shirt wasn't pressed, my boots were unlaced, my belt buckle wasn't on center, or even if my zipper was down. I could wear the same clothes for days, go without showering or shaving, and not be ordered to do pushups, or strip and remake my bunk.

Another plus was that no one wore stripes in combat because identifiable leaders made primary targets. With no visible signs of authority, there was nothing for me to rebel against—no one lording his superiority over me with a set of keys dangling from his belt, or wielding a baseball bat to modify my behavior.

In Nam I didn't have to sneak butts off the sidewalk or even buy them in a store. They were free. Every C-ration came with four no-name cigarettes. They were a bitch to light because humidity dampened the matches, but I didn't have to resort to heating a wire in a boys room light socket. You just had to be damned sure the flame or glowing butt wouldn't be seen by the enemy. I also got introduced to pot, which was readily available, and enjoyed more than my share. We lit up freely in front of superiors. Unless you were scheduled for duty, no one cared.

There were no holds barred when it came to language, even when talking to officers. "Fuck" and all its fucking variations, along with all other four-letter words were as accepted as any other descriptive terms, as long as you obeyed orders and didn't show disrespect.

The lack of privacy was no problem. We showered under 55-gallon drums of water, painted black and heated by the sun. Clean water was in short supply, so you had to be quick, but I was used to that. Toilets were wooden boxes with holes cut in the top, like outhouses with no sides. Buried in the sand beneath the box was another drum with the top cut off to catch the deposits.

They attracted clouds of flies and stunk like hell, so you didn't linger to read *The Stars and Stripes*, but we had toilet paper. When the honey pot filled up, some poor bastard had the job of removing the box, tossing in contaminated fuel, wrapping a rag around a long piece of wood and lighting it. Believe it or not, shit burns.

On the negative side, the climate was a nightmare. It could be 115 degrees in the shade. In the dry months, wind-driven beach sand was everywhere. Sand got into your tent, into your eyes, and into your teeth. It also got into the machinery. We were constantly devising metal or canvas guards to keep fine grit from clogging air filters, and at night I slept with my M-14 inside my sleeping bag to protect it from jamming.

In monsoon season, July and August, the sky unplugged and released torrents of rain. Wind gusts blew the rain sideways, into our equipment and under our ponchos. I picked leeches out of my boots, which were a breeding ground for mold and jungle rot.

The humidity spawned swarms of mosquitoes. I kept my shirt tucked in and tied the ends of my sleeves and pants with twine in a losing battle to fend them off. A single mosquito buzzing in your ear is a pain in the ass anywhere, but here they meant malaria. Medics distributed pills to combat diseases like malaria and hepatitis on a regular basis. Waiting in line for meds before lunch one day, I was seized by a sensation of gagging on a finger shoved down my throat. I panicked and refused the pills, even the salt tablets the medic was handing out for dehydration.

"You're holdin' up the fuckin' chow line!" someone yelled. Two guys grabbed me, dragged me to the shower, and threw me in. When I returned later soaking wet, they watched as I swallowed my anxiety, and the pills. But from then on, one of them, a guy named Phil, was assigned to be my meds buddy, to make sure I took them, wherever we were.

On another occasion, I was assigned guard duty. It was well after midnight when I finished, and I headed straight for the rack. Even after sunset the tents baked us like bread rolls, but I pulled a blanket over my head anyway, a habit that followed me from Belchertown. With the heavy equipment cranking away, I was soon asleep.

Some time before dawn, I was jolted awake by a punch in my face. I was attacked by someone hammering away in the blackness. Bam, bam! I was getting pummeled in my chest, arms, and face by what felt like two or three assailants. We must've been ambushed. I struggled to defend myself, but snarled in the blanket, I couldn't fight back. Disoriented, my heart pounding, I shrank into a fetal position for protection.

Then, as suddenly as it had started, the beating stopped. I could hear heavy breathing. "Vitkus, you fuckin' idiot! What the hell are you doin'?" I recognized the voice. The blanket was yanked from my face, not by the enemy, but a guy from my own tent.

I touched my face. My lips and nose were bleeding. Was this some kind of weird training exercise? "What the fuck?" was all I could say.

"You were bangin' your goddam head on the bed! That's what the fuck! And loud! Whomp, whomp, whomp! You pull that shit with VC around, you'll get us all killed! We'd be dead. Jesus fuckin' Christ!"

"Hope you enjoyed your blanket party, you FNG!" another said, still panting. "Do that again, we'll throw you another one, even better." He flung the blanket over me, and everything went quiet.

An FNG was a "Fucking New Guy," who hadn't experienced combat. Lying awake the rest of the night, I thought about what I had done. In my sleep, my head banging compulsion, a strange comfort at Belchertown, had returned. It didn't work here.

In the morning, our commander officer noted my blood-dried face. "Jesus, Vitkus, you look like a cock that lost the fight!"

I glanced at the guys around me. "Yes, sir. I fell down, sir."

"Really? You fell?"

"Yes, sir. I was trying to find the latrine in the middle of the night, and I tripped on something."

"Looks more like you hit someone's fist with your face. You sure that's what happened?"

"Yes, sir. That's what happened. I'm sure."

He looked at the others, studying their non-reaction. "Well, accidents do happen. But I suspect this one won't happen again, will it?"

"No, sir. It won't happen again."

Despite such setbacks, I actually made rank, and was promoted to E-4. Briefly. The Army preaches that "To command, one must first learn to obey," and my mouth still had trouble with authority. When an officer from the Tan Son Nhut Air Base outside Saigon paid an inspection visit and told us that we looked like slobs, I said, "You'd look this way, too, if you weren't sitting behind a desk." Then I added, "Sir." He didn't respond, but I got written up under an Article 15, the Army's non-judicial system of discipline. They docked my pay, and I was busted back to plain old Private. I had been an E-4 for three months.

It was just as well. Always having been told what to do, I bristled at giving orders myself, and didn't expect anyone to listen to me. I couldn't discipline or say no. *You want to take off from your post to go get laid? Okay by me.*

Most of our pay was sent home, but we still had military scrip allotted to us each month. Local entrepreneurs saw a ready market of American consumers, and there was no shortage of places to drink, see a show, and get laid. Everybody was happy. Prostitution was a thriving business, girls in tight dresses outside every bar, drumming up customers. "Hey, GI, you wanna buy me tea?" She flashes a tit. "C'mon, don't be shy." They were probably on commission. The military was always warning us about VD, so in addition to free cigarettes, they also passed out condoms. The Army thought of everything.

And the ladies looked great. As a horny 22-year-old who grew up segregated from the opposite sex, these were high class women. Most of them were young, but after a few drinks or hits, the old ones looked pretty good, too. My sales resistance was low.

The back rooms had plenty of beds available, complete with mosquito netting. My pecker itched for a different reason. The first time, I was nervous. I wasn't sure what I was doing. I figure the hookers got a pretty good deal because I didn't hug or kiss, just got right down to business. They didn't seem to mind. And they didn't have to hand out coupons for me to come back. Badly hung over one morning, I woke up beneath the netting, a woman's back toward me. She rolled over to face me and smiled. She had no teeth.

Although I had acclimated to military life, being in a war zone under the constant threat of combat was still scary. What frightened me as much as the potential of enemy fire was the prospect of accidental hits from our own air support. Low-flying F-4's screamed out of nowhere. Hueys—the helicopter gunships that became the signature of the Vietnam War—and B-52's heavy with bombs and napalm flew overhead. What if somebody screwed up, and the payload fell short?

I was also terrified of failing as a soldier. I needed to prove that I wasn't 4-F material, that I could hold up under combat, that I wasn't a moron.

Early one morning on patrol with three other guys, I stepped through the vegetation as silently as possible, watching for hidden booby traps that might blow my leg off or worse. With little more noise than the leaves scraping our uniforms, we were guided by hand signals from our point man. It would take a couple of hours to complete the loop mapped out for us, a circuit on the perimeter of a construction area where the 864th was laying concrete pads for tents to accommodate a buildup of troops. Our job was to flush out anyone who might not like the idea. I prayed my jungle fatigues made me a less visible target.

It was slow going. The sun had already cooked the area into a steamy mass of tangled vines and rotting undergrowth. The smell of napalm, a sweet combination of fuel, laundry detergent, and nutmeg, hung in the air. Attracted by the rivulets of sweat running down my face, a squadron of mosquitoes was enjoying an early lunch at my expense.

As I reached for my canteen, sharp popping erupted to our left. I dropped to the ground. A series of single shots repeated—sniper fire from an enemy invisible in the dense foliage. Our leader pointed to a thicket about 50 meters away. We opened fire, sending a barrage of rounds into the jungle. I was shooting at bushes and trees. A few more pops came from behind the wall of vegetation. Then nothing.

The exchange had lasted less than a minute, but that was more than enough time to match my heartbeat to the rate of gunfire. My ears were still ringing some time later when we came across a body in a growth of giant ferns. My first up-close look at a black pajama. My gut churned. Had I just killed a human being? Sprawled face up, he looked younger than me, and not very big. Blood glistened through his shirt. His eyes were still open.

The immediate question was who would get credit for the kill. Three confirmed kills earned you a pass into town. I let the others decide. I was trying not to puke. I had been trained for combat, trained to kill, but nothing prepared me for what I was feeling. I knew I had been changed.

After three months in Cam Ranh Bay, the 864th relocated to Na Trang, about thirty miles north, to an air base under development by the U.S. Air Force for the remainder of my tour. Late one day, I retreated to my tent to write to Susan. Glad to be off duty, I stretched out on my bunk with my sleeping partner, my M-16, beside me. Phil, my meds buddy, came in, but his mission was to smoke some pot. Our commanders never cared if we got high. As long as we weren't slated for guard duty or assigned to patrol, they looked the other way. Marijuana was a way to deal with both stress and boredom, or even the stress of boredom.

When I saw what Phil was up to, I took out a Thai stick of my own that I had purchased from one of the friendly Coke girls, traveling sales ladies who peddled cases of ice-cold Coca-Cola with a little pot on the side. We both lit up. The drone of heavy construction equipment outside become white noise, mellowed by marijuana.

"Ya know, these fuckers are the best meds," I said lying on my back, watching the smoke curl up toward the canvas.

"Right, and I don't even have to force you to take 'em." Phil laughed from his bunk. He toked long and deep. "What're you gonna do when you get back to the states, Vitkus?"

"I don't know, go back to my old job, I guess. Washin' dishes till I can find somethin' better. You?"

"First thing, I wanna get laid—priorities, you know—and not by some dick-sucking slope, either. An all-American broad—you know, a blonde maybe—hair down to her shoulders, nice lips, long legs, big tits." I leaned over and watched Phil take another drag. He drew the joint down to his fingertips, touched a fresh one to the glow, and dropped the stub into a doobie cup.

"I got a girl named Susan waiting for me," I said, building a pretty good buzz myself.

"You *hope* she's waitin'," he said.

"Yeah, I was just gonna write to her. We started seeing each other before basic. We met while …" My sentence was cut short by bursts of gunfire. We grabbed our rifles, ran outside and dove into a bunker, one of many dug and sandbagged around the perimeter exactly for this purpose. The shooting was sporadic, in short rapid bursts. Whenever you're under fire, it seems like a lot, even if it's intermittent and random. Neither of us spoke. I could hear the occasional quick "zhing" of rounds passing overhead. Adrenaline battled the pot in my body, a weird sensation that made me feel more in control while I was scared shitless, focused intently on saving my ass. I didn't return immediate fire because my tracers would give us away. The shooting continued for several minutes, then paused. During the lull, I peaked over the rim to scan the jungle, watching for a flash. It was dark now and the jungle was pitch black. I ducked down and waited, hoping I wouldn't soon be filling a body bag. Eventually, after a few more rounds, more distant, the shooting stopped altogether.

Minutes passed, an hour, maybe more. In the darkness, I stretched my legs a bit. "Hey," I said, barely above a whisper, "must be clear by now, don'tcha think? Haven't heard nothin' for a while." Phil didn't answer. I remembered the blanket party lesson, how important it was to keep quiet. Suddenly tired, and with the danger apparently passed, I nodded off. I didn't wake up till just before dawn, with birds yammering above the usual creepy sounds of jungle nighttime. In the faint light, I could see my buddy a yard away, still asleep.

"Hey, sun's comin' up," I said quietly. "It's clear. Let's get outta here." No response. Taking a big chance by startling him out of his sleep, I leaned over and nudged his shoulder. It was sticky. His head rolled back, and a trickle dripped down his cheek. Just below his helmet, in the middle of his forehead, was a shiny dark hole.

I served ten months in Vietnam. In the process, I failed my meds buddy, the guy assigned to keep me healthy. It's a memory that haunts me with permanent guilt. Experiences like that, magnified by my years of institutional abuse, would manifest themselves in post traumatic stress reactions decades later. In the middle of the night, I would wake up screaming, holding my hands together above my head because I was handcuffed, being led to court martial, for not keeping my buddy alive.

On May 23, 1966, I received an honorable discharge from the United States Army. I had served my country overseas and returned a combat veteran.

Don't Touch Me

I couldn't stand having someone's arms around me, and that included my own wife.

I was out of Belchertown, out of Brightside, and out of the Army. What now?

Even with my military experience, I felt too damn retarded to do anything but wash dishes. I went back to the same room on Northampton Street in Holyoke, and until I could figure out something else, back to the Soldiers' Home where they were required to hold my job open for me.

I was seeing Susan again, and I enjoyed being with her. For the first time in my life, another person wanted me. We had discussed marriage before I completed basic. I felt like I was in love, but didn't know if it was the real thing. How was I supposed to feel? Love wasn't something I encountered at the state school. I sure liked sex—the toothless prostitute in Vietnam had shown me that. I knew that wasn't love, but wanted more of it, and I'm embarrassed to say that I got married for sex. That's the way it was.

We were married in a small Catholic church in South Hadley. Since I had no family, during the ceremony Susan's grandmother sat on my side of the aisle. She also helped us get an apartment in a block she managed on Lyman Street in Holyoke, a walk-up on the fourth floor—two rooms, a gas stove, and an icebox. I still didn't have a driver's license, so we walked a lot and did our shopping on High Street, which was lined with stores back then. We had very little money, no credit and no car, but we had each other. Maybe, at last, I could look to the future.

Susan found office work at Scott Graphics across the bridge in South Hadley. I realized I couldn't be a dishwasher the rest of my life, so I looked for something better, maybe factory work. With more than twenty mills, Holyoke was known as The Paper City. Factories built along a system of canals and dams off the Connecticut River ran through downtown, providing jobs for waves of immigrants in the early 1900's. Now they provided one for me. I was hired at Eastern Specialties, a plant that made rolls of paper for teletype and adding machines, within walking distance on Appleton Street. It was unskilled labor with a lot of heavy lifting, and didn't require more than a grade school education, but it was the first job I ever got on my own.

Although Susan wanted children, the idea of fatherhood terrified me. I barely knew how to take care of myself—what would I ever do with a baby? How would I raise kids? More importantly, would my genes screw up their lives? Would our children be morons?

Another not so minor problem was that I didn't like being touched. Susan enjoyed snuggling, but I recoiled at anything that approached being held. I didn't know how to accept or provide intimacy. I didn't even like handshakes or pats on the back because physical contact at Belchertown meant only beatings or restraint. I got smacked with a fist, broom handle, or baseball bat—whatever was handy—tackled by an attendant, laced into a straitjacket, or thrown in solitary. I couldn't stand having someone's arms around me, and that included my own wife. But Susan wanted kids and I wanted sex, so I would have to overcome the challenge.

If I had been born a couple of years earlier, having children would never have been possible. As the "retarded" offspring of an "immoral mother" whose own grandfather was "an excessive drinker and below par mentally," I probably would've been sterilized. Eugenics was common practice in state schools because folks in the Commonwealth didn't want retards begetting more retards, a further burden on society. That was part of the argument for isolating people like me from the rest of the population. The Nazis had nothing on us. Threats of sterilization still existed at Belchertown if you got caught masturbating or having sex. Luckily for me, the Supreme Court ended that policy, and my parts still worked.

Being Catholic, Susan and I didn't practice birth control, and before long she was pregnant. My fears proved unwarranted. In

1968, Susan gave birth to David, a healthy, normal baby boy. I was proud and thankful. Susan quit her job to be a fulltime mother, and I became the breadwinner, happy with that arrangement. My job was to support my family. That's what a father was supposed to do.

To make up for some of our lost income, Susan got part-time work she could do at home, sewing clothes for a textile company. But like any young mother, she needed to get out of the house. "I'm going to my class," she called from our bedroom one night after supper. Her mother was teaching ceramics in South Hadley, and Susan decided to give it a try. "David should sleep, but if he starts to cry, check his diaper."

Dave was almost two years old. "Okay, I can handle that," I said from the kitchen. I was used to changing diapers at Belchertown. The smell and mess never bothered me.

"If he's dry, you might have to give him a bottle," Susan added, and was out the door.

"I can do that, too," I said to myself. "Nothing to warming up a bottle." I sat down to thumb through some magazines and enjoy the quiet.

An hour or so later, I heard Dave begin to fuss, then cry. When I went in to check, the sky beyond the window was lit up. Flames leaped from the roof of the paper mill directly across the street, and thick smoke poured through shattered glass. As I bent over his crib, Dave reached up. He needed to grab his little arms around my neck and hold on to his daddy. The "pick me up" in his eyes tore at me. Sirens blared and down in the street police were evacuating the area. The fire was growing and we had to get out. I turned my son away from me, lifted him at arms' length and carried him, his legs dangling, down the stairs and out the door. I was some father.

That same year, Susan became pregnant again. I was still leery about having kids, and now we'd have two. This time it was a girl. While I wasn't comfortable taking care of Dave, I was petrified with handling Annemarie. I had never been allowed to associate with girls at Belchertown, and now I had a little girl of my own. I would have to lean on Susan to raise her.

For a while, things went according to plan. While the kids were growing, Susan handed out the hugs and discipline on the home front, and I brought home the bacon. Eventually, though, assuming all the parenting began to take a toll on Susan. It wasn't easy cleaning, cooking, doing laundry, and shopping with two little kids around her ankles.

"Here, they're yours!" was the greeting I got one day after work. "They're driving me nuts."

"Jesus, Susan, I just walked in the door. I put in sixteen hours today. I just want to go to bed."

"What, and this isn't work? These are your kids, too, you know!" She nudged them in my direction. "David, Annemarie, this is your father. Donald, these are your kids."

With tension growing at home, I began to have problems at work. My job at Eastern Specialties was mostly grunt work, which I didn't mind. But they started to treat me like a retard, and that got under my skin. I began screwing up on my job, deliberately. The more they called me a retard, the more I acted like one, and I got fired. I had failed myself and failed my family.

Resolving to do better, I went looking for work. U.S. Envelope, a print and packaging factory in West Springfield, needed someone to fill in while one of their men was on grand jury duty, and I applied. They hired me as a temp, apparently they liked my work, and when the other guy returned, I was taken on permanently.

I poured myself into my new job, taking overtime, even double shifts when they were available. I remembered the trust Mr. Poole had shown in me at Belchertown in building that bookcase, and his message that I could take pride in my work. Whether it was showering patients, printing forms, or shoveling shit, work made me a productive human being. More than a moron.

The new position paid better, and I was able to set aside money for a car and driver's license. I bought a junk Toyota and spent hours in the driveway doing brake jobs, replacing the water pump, anything to save money. Susan's father offered to help, but I refused, sometimes not too gracefully. "I can do this myself. Just leave me alone!" I would holler from under the hood. It didn't matter how many skinned knuckles I earned, how many "fucks"

I uttered, or how many wrenches I winged across the yard. I wanted to show that I could handle it.

The kids were smart. When they were outside, they learned to stand clear.

"Don't go near Daddy," Annemarie would tell Dave.

"Why, is he mad at us?"

"No, but he's working on the car. I think he's mad at himself."

When Dave turned five, we enrolled him in school. Susan went back to work, and we alternated shifts so someone would be home with Annemarie. That seemed to ease the burden on Susan, and we all fell into the new routine, until Dave's behavior raised some red flags. In first grade, he came home early one day, and before long he started showing up even earlier. Apparently he made up some excuse to leave the classroom and then made his way home. He said school was boring. In second grade his attitude worsened. Despite being placed with a strict teacher whose classroom was next to the principal's office, Dave grew more obstinate. It upset me that my son wasn't doing well, but I didn't know how to handle the situation, or care to, and let Susan deal with it. She started taking Dave to a child psychologist, and my concerns, those worries about my genetic background, resurfaced.

On the other hand, Annemarie enjoyed school. Two years behind Dave, she was a better student, creative, with a strong interest in art. She didn't get into mischief like Dave, and pretty much stayed under the radar. I thought she was doing well.

When it was time for Dave's transition to middle school, Susan and I were called to a meeting with a special education teacher. We were to bring Dave. We met in her classroom after dismissal, some distance down the hall from the others. Colorful posters filled a bulletin board, and a couple of beanbag chairs were pushed into a corner near a TV stand. Mrs. Spencer, a woman with gray hair in her 40s, spoke about our son.

"All Dave's teachers say that he would do much better, Mr. and Mrs. Vitkus, if he paid attention and applied himself." We sat at student desks, facing each other. "When he gets bored, that's when he starts getting into trouble. Does that sound accurate to you, David?"

"I guess so," Dave said, his eyes down.

"And you get angry and start acting out. Is that right?"

"I don't like school." Dave's knee bounced up and down against the desktop. "The stuff the teachers make us do is stupid. They..."

"It's not stupid, and neither are you!" Susan interrupted. "You can do better. We know that," she added, giving Dave the eye. "I agree," Mrs. Spencer said. "The reason for Dave's outbursts might be that he's frustrated by trying to understand."

"The psychologist says he understands fine, he's just stubborn," Susan countered. "Dave likes to read. He always has his nose in a book at home. He's just not interested in school books."

Mrs. Spencer raised her eyebrows. "Oh, what does he read?"

"Well, right now he's reading a textbook about logic." Dave had a fascination with the Mr. Spock character of Star Trek, and Susan had recently picked up the book at a yard sale.

"I see," Mrs. Spencer said. She didn't sound convinced.

I had heard enough. "I have to tell you something, Mrs. Spencer. Maybe some of this is my fault. I grew up at Belchertown State School. It was a place for retards."

The woman's face changed. "I'm aware of Belchertown, Mr. Vitkus." She shifted in her chair and folded her hands. "It's possible that David has a learning disability. He might be a candidate for Chapter 766, you know, the new Special Education program here in Massachusetts."

"I've heard about that. I don't want our son labeled a 'Sped!'"

"We're not talking about labels here. David hasn't been doing well in a regular academic classroom. He's acting out and leaving the building. We could design a program geared to his special needs."

"He doesn't have 'special needs.' He just needs to focus," Susan insisted. "We know he can do the work. David is not dumb."

"No. That would be another label, wouldn't it?" Mrs. Spencer turned to Dave. "What do you think, David? Why not give it try for a year?"

"Whatever," he shrugged. "School is school. I won't like it anyway."

In the end we consented, and that September Dave was placed in a Special Ed class. Our son spent fifth grade segregated from the "regular" student population, a year in which he was suspended six times, and had 52 disciplinary letters sent home about his behavior. What had I done?

Luckily, Susan persisted on Dave's behalf. She took him to American International College in Springfield for testing, where he was determined to be of above average intelligence with age-appropriate math skills, and the reading comprehension of a high school senior. In sixth grade he was returned to regular classes, was placed with a great teacher, and began to find success.

While the kids were going through school, I began thinking about returning to the classroom myself. Until I had heard about it from the orphans at Brightside, I didn't even know that school existed beyond the fourth grade. How could I convince my son about the value of an education if I hadn't completed my own? My military service qualified me for the G.I. Bill and free schooling, but when I had returned from Vietnam, I never gave it much thought. My priorities were marriage and a job.

One day I read in the paper that the local high school was offering evening courses for adults. Since I was on the third shift, I could attend classes before work. Best of all, Uncle Sam would actually pay me to go to school, and the idea of a few extra bucks was appealing. The time was right. Getting my high school education—not a GED, but a legitimate diploma—became my second job.

I studied English, math, and history, two classes a night, four nights a week, which meant even less time with the kids. And if I got called in for overtime, I spent the weekend on homework. I still didn't consider myself smart enough for high school, but I got decent grades, mostly C's. I thought maybe the teachers were just passing me. In a few years I had earned enough credits to fulfill all my requirements, and in April of 1976, I was a 33-year-old graduate of Chicopee Comprehensive High School. I framed my diploma.

Juggling work and school wasn't easy, but the added paycheck every month was good motivation and my success in school rubbed off on my performance at the plant. I worked my way up to operator, running a multi-color press, turning out a continuous stream of Oreo cookie bags, Three Musketeers and Almond Joy wrappers. Packaging sold product. It had to be perfect, and producing a smooth run carried a fair amount of responsibility. Maintaining even ink coverage and aligning the colors on six different rollers required constant attention and adjustments. The challenge gave me a sense of accomplishment. I was a long way from the print shop at Belchertown.

When the kids got old enough to stay on their own, Susan and I were able to go out every now and then. She introduced me to Jeff, one of her shift supervisors at Scott Graphics, and his wife Nancy. We enjoyed each others' company and became friends, going out for movies, bowling, pizza and beer.

Things were looking good, but despite the value I placed on work and the self-esteem it provided, every now and then I just screwed up on the job. Even though I knew better, I took risks like climbing the ladder on the side of the press while it was running, or letting my shirt tail hang out so it might get caught in the machinery, or not wearing my safety glasses. Negative behavior had been a way of getting attention from ward attendants at Belchertown. It said, *I exist. Look at me. I'm not faceless, I'm not a number. I'm a human being.* I realize now that somehow that behavior carried over into my work at the plant. On one level I knew that what I was doing was wrong, but what the hell? There was a union and I was paying my dues. Let them protect me. What else am I getting out of them?

It wasn't a smart choice. I'd get reprimanded, written up, the union rep would speak up for me, and I'd go back to my job and produce good work for a while. It was a cycle I couldn't seem to break. I probably should have been fired. Years later, I would discover why I wasn't. I learned that Charlie Hill, the president of U.S. Envelope, had a son who had grown up with me at Belchertown. He understood. And each time a supervisor wanted to fire me, Charlie intervened on my behalf.

I had just punched in one night when Jenkins, a machinist, stopped by my workstation. He often updated me at the beginning of a shift about how a run had been going.

"Before you start, Donald, you need to come with me." He beckoned with his finger. Jenkins was also president of our local, United Paper Workers 579. I respected him for standing up for our rights, and I figured this must be union related. I followed him to his station, where he didn't waste words.

"Vitkus, what the fuck are you doin'?"

I had been half expecting something like this, but played dumb. "What do you mean?"

"You know goddamn well what I mean. You're screwin' up your jobs."

I knew Quality Control had had their eyes on me. Jenkins grabbed a sample off his bench. It had been rejected by inspectors. The printing was blurred, a double image. "You see that? What is this shit?" He had warned me about this twice the week before. "I calibrated your press yesterday. This ain't the machine's fault."

"I don't know. Maybe I haven't been paying enough attention."

"I'll say you're not. You're acting like a fuckin' retard!" There it was again, that label. Jenkins knew about my background. I had never lied about it on job applications. Without warning, he threw me against the tool crib and poked me in the chest, like Sergeant Nittoli at Fort Dix. I didn't resist.

"Listen, Vitkus, I have to represent you because you pay your dues. I know the work you're capable of turning out, and this ain't it. If you don't shape up, you're gonna be fired, and I won't be able to help you." He held his thumb and forefinger to my face. "You're this close to losing your job."

"Okay, okay, I get the picture," I said. I hated him at that moment. I hated him for his threat, and I hated him for his authority, but most of all because he was right. I did know what he was talking about—my mind wasn't on my work. I had learned that Susan was developing more than an interest in double-dating with our friends. She was seeing Jeff after her shift.

Jenkins grabbed me by the collar. "You goddamn well better get the picture. Now pull your head out of your ass and get back to work."

The next week, I was suspended.

"So this is what you do behind my back?" I hollered at Susan across the kitchen table. "It's not enough to see him at the bowling alley, I guess. Are you scoring with that bastard in other ways, too?"

Susan sat with one elbow on the table, the tips of her fingers touching her forehead. She stared at the tablecloth. "It's not like that."

"Oh. Then what *is* it like?" I leaned forward. "Look at you. You can't even face me."

Susan pressed her hands to her face, covering her eyes. "Jeff is just nice to me."

"He's nice to you. Well, I guess so! And what, I'm not?" I knocked over my chair and yelled down at her. "Nancy told me all about you two. I'm an idiot for not seeing it myself."

"Please, Donald! He knows how to treat me, is all I'm saying."

"Sure he knows how to treat you," I yelled. "He's a goddamn high-and-mighty shift supervisor, and I'm a piss-ant press operator! I hear he's had plenty of practice treating women, by the way. Yeah, Nancy told me that, too. You're not the first, you know. You think you're special? As soon as he feels like it, he'll dump you and there'll be another broad to take your place."

Susan looked at me, tearing up. "Is that what I am, Donald? Your broad? When do you hold me? When, since we got married? When was the last time you said you love me?"

"What are you talkin' about? I gave you a ring. We've been together fifteen years." My fist hit the table. "We've got two kids, don't we?"

"And when did you ever play with them, show them any attention?"

"What do you mean? Dave's in junior high, he doesn't want me to play with him. The same with Annemarie. She's with her friends all the time."

"Because you never spent any time with either one of them before! Where were you when Annemarie needed a hug from her father? Why couldn't you take Dave fishing or play catch with him once in a while? Didn't you say you liked baseball when you were growing up? Where were you at our kids' birthday parties?"

Each year Susan bought birthday presents and made cakes for Dave and Annemarie. Never having had a birthday party, I was actually jealous of seeing my own kids unwrap presents, so I stayed in another room till they were finished. I should have felt guilty, but I couldn't share in their happiness.

"Don't try to make this about the kids, Susan."

"It's about all of us, Donald. It's called family. What the hell, why should Dave and Annemarie expect any different now? They've given up on you, Donald, and I can't blame them." Susan was sobbing hard now.

"I earn good money at work. I support them. Them *and* you."

"Jesus, Donald, I'm not talking about money!"

"No. And you're not sleeping around, either!"

"When have you hugged me, Donald? When was the last time? *I love you, Susan.* Why can't you say those words?" Susan took a gasping breath, like a little kid after a cry. "*Love?* Jesus, when have you even touched me, if it wasn't to get laid?"

The questions stung like a strap across my back.

I thought I loved Susan, but I couldn't bring myself to demonstrate that I did. Like a self-conscious eight-year-old, I was embarrassed to hold hands in public, and I didn't know how to tell her I loved her, even in private. It wasn't that my mind formed the words and the phrase got stuck in my throat. The words just weren't there. I didn't have the vocabulary of affection. I knew in my heart that I had married for sex. And now I didn't know how to answer.

"So Jeff loves you?" I said. "Jeff is all touchy-feely, and you think I'm a moron, is that it?"

Susan shook her head and sighed. "No, Donald. I don't think you're a moron."

Back at the plant, the human resources manager told me if I wanted to keep my job, I'd have to see a psychiatrist. It was obvious, he said, that I needed some kind of counseling. "Here's her number. Make an appointment."

A goddamn shrink. There it was again, the shadow of Belchertown. I had already been through years of psychotherapy to deal with my past. Now I was lapsing into those insecurities. I wasn't good enough. I was a retard who didn't know how to give my wife the intimacy she craved, or how to relate to my kids. I was a good provider, but a lousy husband and father.

I knew what a psychiatrist would tell me. *That was then, this is now...you need to put all that behind you...try to live in the present...keep your mind on your work.* Blah, blah, blah. I didn't want to hear any more of that crap, but what choice did I have?

In her office the following week, Dr. Know-Everything directed me to a chair by her desk. There would be none of that lying-on-a-couch stuff. She pulled up a stool, reached for a pad, and the grilling began. "Why do you think you reacted that way? What do you think is causing your discomfort? How can you focus better on your work?"

She stared down at me from her stool. I was a patient again. Who the hell does she think she is, a fucking attendant? I refused to look up, and resisted telling her about my marriage problems. At the end of the session, I told her I wasn't coming back. But I did. Week after week, as each consultation approached, my stomach tensed, and after each one I felt even worse.

It was during those sessions that Susan asked me for a divorce. We had been married 15 years. I didn't fight it. I knew she couldn't be happy with me. Eventually, the appointments ended and I was able to keep my job, but I lost my marriage and lost contact with my kids.

I didn't realize it until years later, but Susan suffered from chronic depression that eventually resulted in a nervous breakdown. Combined with my institutionalization and inability to show affection, our marriage was a Molotov cocktail waiting to be lit.

The divorce knocked me for a loop. Dave now says I went off the deep end, and I suppose he's right. When I returned to work, I was no longer a press operator. I was still on the payroll, but had been demoted to machine adjustor. Over time I came to realize that Jenkins had been trying to save my ass. For months I went through the motions, getting up in the dingy apartment I had moved to in Southwick, going to work, coming back to eat and sleep, then doing it all over again the next day. I would have to work my way through the bitterness.

It would take years.

Return

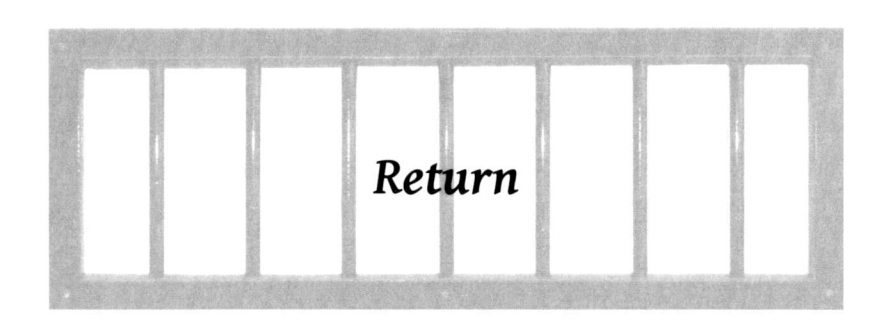

```
D. M. D. Form A-5
                                                                    Admitted to
            ......BELCHERTOWN STATE SCHOOL......  Nurs. II
                         Name of Institution

                    PATIENT'S WARD CARD

    N. B.—THIS card must always accompany every patient in all changes from ward to ward and
attendants on ward are responsible for the same. The card must be returned to the office when the
patient leaves the institution. When necessary, a new one can be obtained from the medical department.

Name  Vitkus  Donald Everett                    No. 3394
Admitted 2:00 PM     July  13   1949   Age  6   Height 3' 11"
          Hour         Date              Date of Birth  May 12 1943
Weight  46½ pounds   Eyes  Hazel          Hair  Blonde
       Personal peculiarities and habits. Cautions as to escape, Self-injury, Violence, etc.
Religion  R. Catholic  Baptized  yes       Confirmed  no
First Communion  yes 1-1-55  How Supported  State  Clothing  State
Remarks
                                        R. A. Kinmouth  , M.D.
                                                  Admitting Physician.
```

Purple lights flashed through smoky haze as the stripper gyrated to a pulsing heavy metal beat, making love to her pole. Each bump and grind brought cheers from the guys below, as they played tuck-a-buck and soaked up more Bud. Anthony's, a strip joint in South Hadley, wasn't the kind of place you'd bring your son, but Dave had actually brought me. He and his buddy Nate had just finished fourteen weeks of training at the Western Mass. Police Academy in Agawam. It was 1989, seven years after the divorce, and Dave had called me to celebrate his graduation.

Dave had been in junior high when Susan and I split. I made attempts to stay in touch with my kids, but Susan put obstacles in the way, and when I had visitation opportunities, I often didn't take advantage of them. We were both to blame. Susan would agree on a time when I could visit and then change plans, or I would "forget" to show up. It was a control game we played, and the kids suffered for it. Except for birthdays and occasional phone calls, I had very little contact with Dave during his high school years, and almost none with AnneMarie. Caught in the middle, children of divorces sometimes side with one parent. AnneMarie chose Susan, and I didn't hold it against her.

"You know, I've never been in a place like this," I yelled across the table to Nate.

"The hell you haven't," shouted Dave. "Look at that shit-eating grin! You don't have to play Mr. Innocent, Nate knows you were in the army."

Dave looked like he could be my younger brother, same build, a little over six feet tall, but broader. We shared the same hazel eyes, prominent nose and ears, even the same walking posture. But fresh out of the academy, he was in shape. You knew from his upper arms that this would be a cop not to mess with.

It was by chance that I had discovered he was going to police school. I was working a second job at a human service agency in Agawam when I saw a group of cadets through a fence on the other side of the street running in formation. One of them looked a lot like my son. When I later mentioned it, Dave admitted, "Yeah, that was me, Dad." He hadn't told me because he knew what my reaction would be. I hated authority figures, people in uniform, and my own son was becoming a cop.

"Yes, I did basic at Fort Dix and served a year in Nam," I told Nate.

"Wow, that must've been tough."

"Yeah, it was a real bitch, all right," Dave interrupted. "Tell him about all the weed, Dad. Tell Nate about that broad in Saigon, the one with no teeth."

He was busting my balls and I was enjoying it. I didn't want to miss another milestone in Dave's life. Even though I resented his becoming a cop, it was easier to talk to him now that he was grown. As a young teen, he had been hurt by the divorce, but now with a reason to celebrate and the beer flowing, we rediscovered what we had in common. That night at Anthony's, we laughed and exchanged war stories—his academy training and my time in boot camp, all those drills, all those orders to obey—father and son re-connecting after so much lost time.

Following his graduation, Dave was hired onto the Northampton Police Department. It was nice to have a son again and we stayed in touch. He introduced me to a young woman named Laura who, two years later, became my daughter-in-law. One afternoon they invited me to dinner at their house in Whately, and over coffee the conversation turned to family.

"I want to congratulate you, Dave, you've done all right. You have a great wife, nice place, an important job, a good future. Not bad for the son of a moron."

"Thanks, Dad, but stop that moron crap. You've got a high school diploma, and you've got a good job, too. You served your country in a war that shouldn't have happened. You're not a moron."

"Yeah, well I was raised like one. I never even knew my birthday. I know my mother's name was Veronica, but that's all that I know."

Laura had heard this complaint many times before. "Donald, your records are available to you now. Why don't you just go ahead and get them?" Her tone was encouraging, not critical. "What are you waiting for? Just do it."

"She's right, Dad."

Laura was right. When I was discharged from the state system in 1963, my records were sealed. None of us former Belchertown patients were allowed to access our own files. Our pasts were locked up, just like we had been. But that ban was finally lifted sometime after Ben Ricci and the Friends of Belchertown brought a class action lawsuit against the Department of Mental Retardation in 1972. I had always wondered about my family background, but had never returned to ask for my file. I didn't want to go anywhere near that place. Besides, I was scared of what I might find out.

On a sticky summer afternoon in the early 1990's, I returned to Belchertown State School for the first time in more than three decades. Dave had picked me up after work. Although he had an idea how I felt about this trip, I'd never told him much about what the place was really like. And after all this time, I wasn't sure what to expect myself. But as we drove through the entrance, the sight of those buildings triggered a flood of memories—Jones and his ring of keys, solitary, the stench of shit smeared on the walls. I was thirteen years old, being returned by another cop, not Dave, after a thwarted escape attempt. The bars on the windows were long gone, but I was looking through them. I wanted to run away all over again.

We passed only one car on the way in. The grounds were deserted. Dave parked in the lot by the administration building and I was six years old, being hauled up the ten granite steps to be admitted as a "moron."

Inside, the building trapped the humidity. I felt closed in, half expecting someone to ask if I would like to wear a monkey suit. Maybe this was a mistake, but it was the only way to find out who I was.

The place was full of movement. Perspiring workers were emptying the drawers of filing cabinets, and loading stacks of cardboard boxes onto hand trucks.

We had an appointment with the records clerk. "I know this looks a mess," she said in her office, a bit out of breath, "but actually your timing is good." A lazy ceiling fan wasn't helping much, and she slid her hand across her forehead. She looked old enough to be retired. "In a few days, all this stuff will be in Boston. Please have a seat. I'll get your file, Donald." She was nicer than I anticipated.

She stepped into a back room and returned with a brown accordion-type folder. Seven or eight inches thick, it looked heavy. It was so floppy she balanced it in both hands and set it on her desk, making sure the worn label faced Dave and me. In typewritten letters, it read: `Vitkus, Donald Everett, No. 23-3394`.

Inside this scuffed cardboard was the institution's version of my childhood, the only existing record of my first eighteen years of life.

"I'm sorry I haven't been able to go through this yet. It's going to take some time, but we can do that together right now, if that's all right with you, Donald."

"Sure," Dave said for me when I didn't answer. I was glad he was there. I needed his moral support. Besides, with his police background, Dave knew a lot about legal documents.

"There might be a few things that I can't let you have, especially if a report mentions another patient by name. But if it's not subject to confidentiality and something we don't need to keep on file, you can take the original. Otherwise, I'll give you copies."

"Okay," Dave said. He took out a pad for notes. This would be a process of discovery for him, too. Neither one of us trusted the state, and even though this woman seemed cooperative, she might suddenly decide not to let us take anything with us. "Does this include all of my dad's files, everything?"

"Yes, everything we have—school records, maybe even report cards, medical data, discipline forms—everything from the time he was admitted till the day he was discharged. As you probably know, there are no patients here anymore, and we have to be out of here in a month. All these cartons are heading to the state archive building. We're getting ready to lock up for good."

Lock up. I winced at her phrasing. As far as I was concerned, the whole place should've been bolted shut half a century ago.

"You ready for this, Dad?" Dave sensed my anxiety.

"That's why we came, isn't it? Let's have a look."

One by one, the records lady placed each paper on the desk in front of us. Most were state forms with typewritten information filled in, others with handwritten responses. A few items immediately caught our attention.

First was a form addressed to the Division of Child Guardianship, Department of Public Welfare in Boston. The top line read:

```
I hereby request that you receive and
provide for my child, Donald Everett
Vitkus, who is dependent upon public
charity in accordance with the provi-
```

sions of chapter 119, section 38, of the General Laws.

It is signed, Veronica Vitkus.

"Look, that's your mom's signature, Dad!"

I gazed at the line he pointed to. My mother. The mother I watched for through that window to the parking lot all those years, all those Christmases. Both her name and mine were neatly signed, a careful penmanship with fancy capital letters. In the same handwriting was the date: June 8, 1943. I stopped to figure it out.

"I was 27 days old."

"Jesus," said Dave, his voice hushed. He was jotting notes as fast as he could.

Another paper had the heading: DESCRIPTIVE APPLICATION FOR ADMISSION TO BELCHERTOWN STATE SCHOOL. Line 1 read: Applicant's name VITKERS, DONALD. Beside the cross-out, in handwriting different from my mother's, was: Vitkus, illeg. Apparently somebody didn't know how to spell my name, but he or she knew I was born illegitimate. It was dated June 8, 1949, six years to the day after my mother had signed me over to the state foster care system. It also listed my date of birth, May 12, 1943, information I was never allowed to know while I was a patient. Birthdays give you a sense of identity, and might be cause for celebration.

Further down the page were these two lines:

Place of birth: Waltham Mass
Name of father: Don Williams alleg

"Look, Dad, he's got the same first name. You were named after your father!"

"What does 'alleg' mean?" I had forgotten about the heat, but sweat was dripping down my back.

"It means 'alleged,' the records lady explained. Dave scribbled some more. "It's okay," she said, "I'll give you copies of everything you need."

Don Williams...I was named after my father, a man I never knew? A man who never visited or wrote all those years when I was a patient? Where the hell was he then? Is he still alive? Do I look like him? Should I even care? Questions ricocheted through my mind. I didn't know what to make of any of this. There was too much to take in, too much to read. This was all about me, but it felt like someone else's story.

Next came a black-and-white photograph, a 5-by-7 picture of me. Typed in the space above my head was: `Vitkus, Donald Everett #23-3394`. At the bottom was the date, `August 7, 1953`. I stared at the photo. I was ten years old, seated in a wooden chair, dressed in a light T-shirt with flamingos on it and dark pants. Facing directly into the camera, my eyes were narrowed, in what looked like a "Go ahead, make my day!" Clint Eastwood squint. Like a post office mug shot.

"Hey, Dad, you looked like a wiseass, even way back then! Cool!" Dave was trying to lighten me up. He had stopped writing now.

These file photos were actually called "Run-away shots," taken each year so attendants would have pictures to give to the police in case someone escaped, someone like me. Each photograph was accompanied by a sheet of ten fingerprints, each one labeled, like I was some kind of criminal.

Another shot showed me at seventeen. My face was less round, my features sharpened. My hair was more grown out, neatly combed. I still wasn't smiling, but my eyes were open, a confident look. Wearing a T-shirt with narrow horizontal stripes, I was slim, athletic-looking. It was a pose that could pass for a fashion ad in today's newspaper flyers.

"Boy, get a load of that!" Dave jabbed me with his elbow. "The girls must've thought you were a hunk."

Page by page, the record lady placed the documents we could have in a separate pile, then took out a packet of about a dozen pages stapled together. The top sheet read: `28163 VITKUS, Veronica`.

"Oh my God, this is all about your mom," Dave said. "My grandmother! And it looks like you have a sister. Holy crap!"

The first entry was dated `12/20/38`:

```
(MAC) Ltr frm Loretta M. Baker, Visitor,
    Girls'    Parole    Branch,    referring:
```

> Patricia Ann, born 12/14/38, the [illeg.] child of Veronica Vitkus, born 12/12/22 in Cambridge; Catholic. Mat. grmo. Died in Sept., 1936. Mat. grfa. rptd to be a heavy drinker and a poor provider.

A sister. "Patricia Ann." Another name I'd never heard of. She would be four years older than me, and I never knew she even existed. Does she know about me? Do we look like we're related?

The rest of the paragraph was no less jarring. The word "parole" tightened my stomach. My mother had been on "parole," just like I was at Brightside. Her mother died when my mother was just 14, and her father was a drunk.

From another pocket of the file, the clerk removed a half dozen or so small black cards. They looked like photocopied negatives of index cards, white printing on black. One bore my mother's name. Under a heading of Children were: Patricia '38, Donald '43, Sandra '45, Michael '46, Charlene '48.

There was that name "Patricia" again. "Who are these other people?" I asked.

"They must all be your brothers and sisters," the clerk said.

"Jesus, Dad, you had family all these years and never knew it! Two of them are younger than you!"

Should this make me happy? It was like reading about strangers in a newspaper. By mid-afternoon my stack of papers had gotten pretty thick, and so had the questions piling up in my mind, each new name, each date and scrap of information raising more questions than it answered.

"Well, I think that's it," the woman said finally, wiping her eyes. She checked the bottom of the file to be sure. "Yes, we're done." I felt done in, exhausted, like we'd been at it all day. My shirt stuck to my back. "I'll run these off for you," she said, turning to the machine behind her desk. When she finished, she stuffed everything into a manila envelope with a red string at the top and tied it shut.

"Here you are, Donald. I hope this is helpful. You have a lot to look at."

"Thank you."

"Yes, thank you for your time and cooperation," Dave added.

Out in the fresh air, Dave put his hand on my shoulder. "You still okay, Dad?"

"Yeah, I'm all right."

I looked at the envelope in my hand, full of names I'd never heard, and information I never knew. This would take time to absorb, a long time. Do I really have family? Where are these people? Do they know that I exist? I walked back down those granite steps, thirty years after being discharged.

"But what do I do now?"

Roots

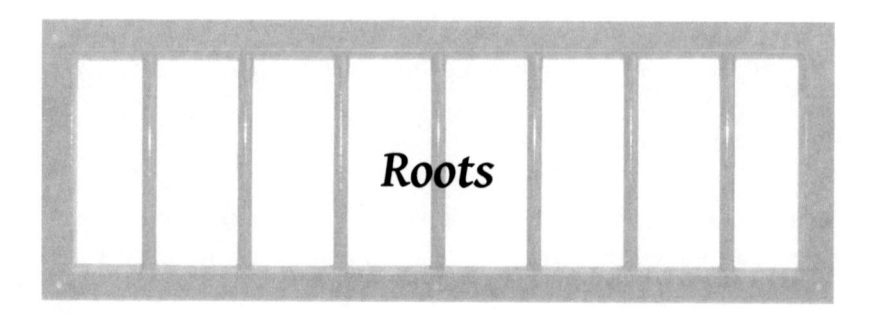

Mother returned from her work and gave birth in rooming house to a child; then walked down two flights of stairs and tel'd Mrs. Quinn, a former building mother in Waltham, who arranged for ambulance...and she and child were taken to the Waltham Hospital.

–May 12, 1943

When I left the state school that day, the last time I would be there before the place was forever locked shut, here's what I knew: I had a mother named Veronica, an aunt named Alice, and I was apparently named after a guy named Donald. I had sisters named Patricia Ann, Sandra, and Charlene, and a brother Michael. My grandfather was a drinker, my mother a delinquent, we were all involved with the state's social welfare system, and I was a moron. Names and labels on a piece of paper.

In the weeks and months following our visit, Dave and I pored through all the records we obtained, laying out bits of information from a puzzle of broken parts, and surmising how they might fit together.

Among the documents was a packet of entries from the Massachusetts Division of Child Guardianship, detailing the first years of my life. One section, Dictation on Family, focused on my mother, while another, Dictation on Child, chronicled my journey through a series of foster homes after my mother handed me over to the state. Most people can't remember a lot about what happened in their infancy and pre-school years, so it seems ironic that I have this look into my past. Four decades later, I was able to piece together some of the events that must have led to my being admitted to Belchertown State School.

In 1910, a Lithuanian immigrant named Stanley Vitkus, "alias Witcox, alias Vitcus, alias Victus," the man who would become my maternal grandfather, settled in Lawrence, Massachusetts. He was barely out of his teens when he arrived in America, probably looking forward to a bright future with plenty of work to be had in the textile mills of this place called Lawrence.

Four years later, another immigrant from Lithuania landed in the city, a young woman named Marcella Gatski. Stanley and Marcella apparently began seeing each other, and my future grandparents were married in a Catholic church on January 28, 1917. He was 27, she was 24. Most likely they spoke broken English, but were ready to raise a family in their new land. Just before Christmas in 1922, Marcella gave birth to twin girls, Alice and Veronica. One of them would become my mother.

For a time, the family was apparently getting by okay, until Stanley lost his job in the early years of The Great Depression. They moved to Cambridge, where the records show they received six dollars a week on public welfare. Stanley eventually got work with the WPA, President Roosevelt's Works Progress Administration, but things were sliding downhill. Social workers in their reports described Stanley as a heavy drinker, in poor health, a poor provider, and below par mentally.

As they aged, the years took a toll on my grandparents. In her early forties, Marcella died of erysipelas, a serious skin disease, at Haynes Memorial Hospital, leaving Veronica and Alice unsupervised at age 14, while their father was out drinking. By 1937, Veronica had come under supervision of a probation officer, and appeared before the Newton Court as a juvenile delinquent. Later that year, notations indicate she came down with the same illness that had killed her mother, but Stanley refused to let his daughter be taken to the hospital, where she might die as his wife had. He denied entry to a visiting district nurse, until the nurse returned to the house with a police escort, finding Veronica sick in bed. The Visiting Nurses Association made daily stops to the "Witcox" home, and the Society for the Prevention of Cruelty to Children took an interest in the case when Stanley's drinking put Veronica in fear for her safety.

In August of 1938, with the situation deteriorating further, Stanley sent his fifteen-year-old daughters to a school for delinquents in Lancaster, about 35 miles away. Veronica, five months pregnant, was committed as a stubborn child. Four months later, two days after she turned 16, that stubborn child gave birth to Patricia Ann, the first of what would be five illegitimate children, including me. Now Veronica was more than just stubborn. She was labeled immoral and, in grade 9, her schooling was over.

The records did not indicate what became of Alice. My grandfather would live another 30 years, apparently alone. He died of pneumonia in 1968 at Boston State Hospital, where he had probably been committed.

With a baby daughter to support, Veronica moved to Lowell to live with an aunt, possibly so her aunt could take care of Patricia Ann while Veronica looked for a job. Like many other women in the midst of World War II, Veronica found work at a defense plant, the Clifford Manufacturing Company, earning $24 a week. A social worker stated that Veronica considered putting Patricia Ann up for adoption, and—the record is unclear here—may have placed her in foster care. At some point, Veronica moved into a rooming house, and began seeing a Navy man, 26-year-old Don Williams of Dracut. She told the social worker he was assigned to convoy duty on "the *U.S.S. Pittsburgh*...one of the most heavily armed cruisers, and they were in the thick of the French invasion." Don Williams was a widower with no children. But one day, while he was somewhere across the Atlantic, that status changed:

> [5/12/43] Mother returned from her work and gave birth in rooming house to a child; then walked down two flights of stairs and tel'd [telephoned] Mrs. Quinn, a former building mother in Waltham, who arranged for ambulance...and she and child were taken to the Waltham Hospital.

The next entry stated:

```
Donald, born 5-12-43, is the second [ ]
child of Veronica Vitkus...Mother is to
return to her job and will contribute
towards the support of Donald. Donald
was baptized at St. Joseph's Church,
Boston, on 6-8-43.
```

The blank space apparently masked out the word "illegitimate," and the line on my birth certificate where my father's name should appear was blank. After what was probably a brief church ceremony, I wasn't brought home to a celebrating family. That same day my mother filed the following document, a standard form, with the Division of Child Guardianship, Department of Public Welfare, Boston:

```
I hereby request that you receive and
provide for my child, Donald Everett
Vitkus, who is dependent on public
charity in accordance with the provi-
sions of chapter 119, section 38, of the
General Laws.

I hereby agree to pay to the Department of
Public Welfare the sum of $3.00 per week
...in part reimbursement of the expense
of supporting the above named child.
```

My mother's signature and my name were in identical neat handwriting. At 27 days old, I had become both a member of the Catholic church and a ward of the state. My mother could go back to work.

Patricia Ann, who was four-and-a-half years old when I was born, was floating somewhere in the foster care system, and, at the age of six, was eventually adopted by a family in 1945.

My mother came to see me several times after she gave me up. I was five weeks old on the date of her first recorded visit, a Sunday in late June. She reported that, because she was working, she could come only on weekends. A social worker approved Sunday visits, "providing this does not lead to any misunderstanding or complications."

But things did get complicated a year later, when my mother arrived, accompanied by a man in a Navy uniform. My father was home on leave in July of 1944, and he and my mother came to see me:

> ...no permission of any kind had been given; mother and alleged father visited 7/14 at 5 P.M. - stayed 2 hours; alleged father a sailor, very quiet and courteous, has dark curly hair and brown eyes, tall and thin...

My quiet and courteous alleged father was later ordered "not to visit baby again." Don Williams and my mother had been hoping to get married while he was on leave, but there just wasn't enough time, and in three days he was headed for the South Pacific. I was fourteen months old, and that two-hour visit was apparently the only time the man I was named after ever saw me.

Two months later, my mother was alone:

> 9/13/44 - Mother to office for permission to visit child; Address - 85 West 6th St. Lowell; not working, staying with aunt at this address. Brought child a red knit suit.

And that's the last time I ever saw her.

Over the next five years, I would bounce from one placement to another, a total of six foster homes in Roxbury, Norwood, Framingham, Wellesley, and Billerica, all in the Greater Boston area. Statements from foster mothers and social workers show that there were concerns about my development. At various hospitals and infirmaries, I was treated for bronchitis, tonsillitis, skin rashes, and a broken leg when I tripped over a chair while at a medical appointment. As an infant, I rocked in my crib and banged my head at night during sleep. I was slow to walk, slow to talk, and slow to associate with other kids.

At age three, I was sent to the Wrentham State School for psychological testing and determined to have an I.Q. of 41, but was described as "surprisingly cooperative and well-behaved." In various reports, I was noted to have "very large hands and feet" for age, a peculiar walk, a nice sun tan, and was a tall scrawny little boy who looks undernourished. I was circumcised at age three. At age four, I was teased, hit, ordered around by other kids, and characterized as "timid, nervous, and fearful." But by age six, I had come into my own. My foster mother said that I was the hardest of all the children, very stubborn and very hard to manage at times, with a quick temper.

My Case Record Folder included D.M.D. [Department of Mental Diseases] Form A-81:

```
Descriptive Application for Admission
to Belchertown State School:

Applicant's name: Donald Vitkus illeg
Date of birth: May 12, 1943
Place of birth: Waltham, Mass.
Name of father: Don Williams alleg
Maiden name of mother: Veronica Vitkus
Physical Examination and Condition
Well developed and well nourished.
Height 47" Weight 46 lbs.
Head measurements 20 X 17.5 X 14.
```

I was a six-year-old bastard, my mother was committed to an institution, they weren't sure who my father was, but they had my hat size down to a T. The form was dated July 8, 1949, six years to the day since my mother had signed me over. Belchertown State School would be my residence for the next eleven years:

```
First Staff Note: July 20, 1949: This
patient was seen at Staff Meeting today
for the first time since admission to
the Institution. When interviewed he
was pleasant, cooperative and answered
all questions courteously. Is living
in Nursery II at the present time and
```

will be transferred to "F" building shortly. Diagnoses made today, Clinical: Mental Deficiency, Familial Type. Psychological: Moron

With that warm welcome, I was admitted to Belchertown State School and certified a "Moron"—an indelible label like a tattoo on my arm.

Courting My Family

Dear Sir: Would it be possible for you to get in touch with any member of the family of our patient, Donald Everett Vitkus, born 5-12-43 in Waltham, Mass. the son of Veronica or Marcella Vitkus, alleged father Donald Williams?...This boy has had no visitors or mail from any member of his family since his admission to Belchertown on 7-13-49.

–January 27, 1959
Letter to Board of Public Welfare
140 Cabot Street, Lowell, Mass.

Obtaining my Belchertown file triggered a three-year search to track down my family. I wanted to find out who I was, to find my mother—the woman who had thought enough of me to bring me a "red knit suit" on her final visit.

Dave and I were both on night shifts, and met after work in the parking lot at the Northampton Police Station. He'd be standing beside his cruiser, often still in uniform. He knew how I felt about authority, and I'm sure that was ball-busting. Besides, wearing his uniform on personal business wouldn't be ethical, and he always changed into civvies before we left.

With the Internet not yet developed, we had to go where the information was. We hit city halls and courthouses across New England, hoping to uncover any further ties to my origin. All those hours in the car allowed time to sift through issues that had accumulated in the years we had drifted apart. We didn't argue, but openly let each other know how we felt about the changes in our relationship as the result of the divorce. Seeking my past, together with my son, nurtured bonds that hadn't existed before.

We searched genealogical societies, birth records, death records, marriage records, microfiche and newspaper clippings in Connecticut, Rhode Island, and New Hampshire looking for clues about my family. Most of all I wanted to find my mother, but I was motivated more by revenge than by love. I wanted to ask why she gave me up to the state to be raised as a retard, and why she never visited or wrote. Where was she all those Christmases? I wanted to tell her in no uncertain terms how I felt about being abandoned. I had developed a backlog of pent-up anger, and wanted to hurt her, maybe even physically. Of course, I didn't say that to Dave.

We made countless phone calls—"long distance" and expensive back then—to town clerks and court officials throughout New England. We drove the Mass Pike east to Boston, a hundred miles and two hours each way, too many times to count, poring through files at the Office of Vital Records on Tremont Street. There are fourteen county courts in the Commonwealth of Massachusetts, and we hit every one, along with many of the probates.

Each stop was a shot in the dark. There was no standardization of records from one town hall or courthouse to the next, and filing systems were erratic. Every now and then we'd stumble across a reference in a court docket index containing a name and hearing date that might be relevant, but never much to go on. It was a tedious, frustrating process, and I wasn't always patient with the receptions we got.

At one courthouse Dave stopped to use the restroom while I went into the clerk's office. The woman behind the counter was stapling papers. "Can I help you, sir?" Her tone said she didn't want to be interrupted.

"Yes, my name is Donald Vitkus," I said. "I'm looking for records of my family—birth certificates, death certificates, adoption records, anything you might have."

"Were you adopted, sir?"

"No, I was a foster kid and raised in an institution. My mother wasn't married."

"Well, if your siblings were adopted, we might have records, but they're not available." She continued stapling.

"What do you mean, they're unavailable? You just said you might have them."

"Records of illegitimate births and adoptions are sealed. I can't show them to you without a court order."

I put my list of names on the counter. "These might be my brother and sisters! You don't understand! I've been looking for them for years."

"I have to follow the regulations, sir. I don't have the authority."

"I'm damned sick of authority." My fist came down beside her stapler. "Who the hell are you to deny me? This is *my* family, not yours!"

"I'm sorry, sir."

Out in the hall, Dave heard my shouting and ran in. "Dad, calm down. I'm sorry, ma'am" he told the clerk. She looked startled, but not intimidated. "My dad grew up in an institution and he's pretty emotional about this stuff." Dave spoke with the confidence of a cop. "I apologize. Sometimes he doesn't understand how these things operate."

"I understand enough!" I shot back.

"Dad!"

We left empty handed. Back in the car Dave said, "For Chrissake, Dad, you gotta behave in these places. We were in a courthouse!"

"I don't give a shit. That piss-ant clerk had information I want. Who the hell is she to tell me no?"

"She's not just a clerk, goddammit, she's an officer of the court! She has the power to arrest you."

Fuck it. For my entire life, someone—an attendant, a social worker, a court or military officer—had wielded power over me. I was 23 when I was discharged from the Army, but never registered to vote because I knew I'd be refused by some high-and-mighty office worker. It was the law. I had been institutionalized with an I.Q. of 41, and left with a fourth grade education. How could I be trusted to make an informed voting decision? In my thirties, I tried to secure a gun permit, and the local police chief denied me.

I had grown up with retards, I'd be a threat to society. It didn't matter that I had served my country and handled a machine gun in Vietnam. That was different.

Dave started the car and we passed the next ten miles in silence. He knew I had a thick skull and he let his message sink in. "Don't get discouraged, Dad," he said eventually. "I know this is tough. Look, you want to make one more stop? Just for the hell of it? We're not far from Cambridge."

I had cooled down by now. "Sure, what the hell, you're the driver. Why not?"

My record showed I had spent a year in foster care in nearby Somerville, so stopping in Cambridge made sense.

When we arrived at the courthouse, Dave said, "This time, let me do the talking." Inside we sat down at the desk of a probate court officer, a younger woman with dark eyes. She didn't smile, but appeared receptive.

"We know this is spur of the moment," Dave said, "but my father and I are looking for records dating back to the 1940s that contain any mention of who we believe to be members of his family." The woman turned from Dave to me, taking a moment to study my face. "I'll see what I can do," she said, and jotted the names we told her on a slip of paper—Patricia, Sandra, Michael, and Charlene Vitkus, my sisters and brother—who were all just that to me, names on a slip of paper.

"Let me take a look," she said, and stepped out. Dave turned to me. "Who knows?" he said, shrugging his shoulders. Several minutes later, the woman returned with a folder. "I found these about Michael and Sandra, but I can't release them to you without checking with the judge."

Holy shit, actual records, I thought.

"We understand," Dave said, "we've been at this for a while."

"I know how frustrating these searches can be," the woman said. She paused, then placed the folder on her desk and looked at us. "Is the copying machine running?" she asked, and turned her head toward the next room, where we could hear someone running off copies. "I'll be back," she said, and left us alone again.

I looked at Dave. "That was weird. What the hell was that all about?"

"Maybe she's giving us a chance," Dave said.

"No, I don't think so. She's setting us up. If we use that machine, we'll be screwed."

She returned in a short while and glanced at the folder, unmoved on her desk. "Judge Foley would like to see you," she said, and led us into an adjacent courtroom, empty except for a man in a white shirt and tie, seated behind the bench.

"The court is here to serve the public," he said after introductions. "I can't release this information directly to you today. What I can do, though, is send them to a third party who will do some checking for you. Are you willing to sign a court order to that effect?"

Dave nodded to me. "Sure, that would be okay," I said. At least this guy was cordial. I understood the court didn't want people showing up on someone's doorstep and saying, *Hi, you don't know me, but I'm your brother. What do you think?*

He forwarded the records to a private investigator named Ann Henry, who worked for an agency called T.R.Y. (Today Reunites Yesterday) in Northampton, back in Western Massachusetts. Her job was to reunite adoptees with their birth families, if that's what everybody wanted. She would make the overtures to my siblings.

But first she had to find them, and who knows how long that would take. We had spent three years just to get this far. Even though the court was trying to help, I couldn't get beyond my distrust of any state agency or authority. In my eyes, Ann Henry was part of the system with no real interest in me, and I didn't expect to hear from her again.

In the meantime, Dave and I continued our search for any available information about my parents. Except for what I had found at Belchertown, we had little to go on, just the names of my mother and alleged father, and their birth dates. It wasn't long before we realized that locating my father, with a name as common as Williams, would be very difficult. Within the given time period, there were so many "Donald Williams" entries scattered from Massachusetts to California that it would take forever to track them down. Finding the right one would be like hitting the lottery. The name "Vitkus," on the other hand, was a different story.

Among the stops we made was the Family History Center in Bloomfield, Connecticut, a microfilm service affiliated with the Mormons. It was there that I came across the name "Veronica Jordan." The surname didn't mean anything to me, but the birth date, December 12, 1922, matched my mother's. Also listed was an Alice Vitkus, the other name I had discovered in my file when I was supposed to be cleaning the matron's office at Belchertown some 40 years ago. Could this possibly be my mother and her twin sister?

I took the information home and began contacting Social Security. I called field offices in cities across Western Massachusetts—Holyoke, Northampton, and Pittsfield. I called the regional office in Boston and national headquarters in Baltimore. If I met a dead end, I called the same number again the next day, hoping to reach a different person, someone who might offer a sliver of new information. I spoke to one woman in Baltimore so many times that she began to recognize my voice.

"Mr. Vitkus, you keep calling us. I don't know how much more we can help you."

"Look, I know I'm being a pest but I was raised in an orphanage and I'm looking for my mother. I just want to find out more about my family. Is that so much to ask?" I was trying hard to keep the edge off my voice.

"No, of course not. Give me the names and dates one more time, and I'll get back to you."

Good to her word, the next day she told me she had located a record of payments to a Veronica Vitkus Jordan. "I need to caution you. I have no way of knowing whether this woman is actually your mother or not. She applied for disability assistance and was receiving benefits, but the payments stopped at some point in the late 1940's." She paused. "I'm sorry to tell you, Mr. Vitkus, that she probably has passed away."

That wasn't a shock, just information. I didn't say so but, in fact, I was happy to hear it. "I see. Can you tell me where she was?"

"The last payment was sent to an address in Andrews, South Carolina."

"Thank you."

My vengeful gut said my mother deserved to be dead for abandoning me. On the other hand, I still wanted to know more. I was a little surprised that the agent had released even that bit of information. Maybe it was because may mother was deceased so privacy was no longer a concern, or maybe the woman just wanted to get me off her back. It didn't matter. Later, in a library atlas, I located Andrews, a town of fewer than 3,000, midway between Myrtle Beach and Charleston. Back to the phone. I called funeral homes and area newspapers, hoping to locate an obituary, but without success. Eventually, I reached a librarian in Charleston who seemed willing to help. I gave her my information and she said she'd get back to me. When I didn't hear anything for a long while, I figured this was another dead end. But several weeks later, she returned my call.

"Mr. Vitkus, I apologize for taking so long, but I was finally able to locate an obituary for a Veronica Vitkus Jordan, who passed away in Andrews. Would you like me to send a copy to you?"

"Yes, please."

"Okay. You know, I have it right here in front of me. I can read it to you now if you'd like."

I learned that Veronica Vitkus Jordan had passed away more than twenty years previous in 1972, and was buried in Andrews Memorial Cemetery, about sixty miles north of Charleston. She had just turned 50. She was born on December 12, 1922, and had children named Patricia, Sandra, Charlene, and Michael, all a match with my records from Belchertown.

All Veronica's Children

Several months after meeting with the judge in Cambridge, I got a call from the agent he had appointed to contact my siblings. "Mr. Vitkus, this is Ann Henry from Today Reunites Yesterday in Northampton." By then, I had nearly forgotten about her. "I know it's taken a long time to get back to you, but I have some news. I've located your sister Patricia. She's living in Florida, and she's interested in meeting you. Would you like me to arrange that?"

It took a few seconds for the words to register. I had been waiting my whole life for an event like this. "Yes, of course," I said.

"Good. Her married name is Patricia Reed. She'll be giving you a call."

Ann had sent Patricia my photo and documents, explaining that she had a brother in Massachusetts who was searching for his family. Actually, a half-brother because we have different fathers. Born out of wedlock five years before me, Patricia was already in the foster care system by the time I came along. My mother had put her up for adoption, so my sister had no idea that I existed. She called a few days later.

"Hello, is this Donald?"

"Yes, this is Donald."
"Well, hello, brother. This is you sister Pat calling from Florida."
"Yes, I was told you'd be calling."
"How are you?"
"I'm okay. You?"

It was a friendly but awkward conversation. Neither one of us knew quite what to say to the stranger at the other end. As I listened to the voice with a southern accent, I tried to picture this sister I had never seen. She sounded nice, but it was hard to tell by one short phone call. We exchanged information and she agreed to fly north to meet me.

I was 51 years old, about to meet my sister for the first time. How would I react? What would I think of her? Would I see a resemblance? Would she know anything about our parents? What would she think of me? What more would we even have to say to each other?

Conflicting emotions welled up in me. I was excited about meeting family, but what I now recognize to be misdirected anger was also surfacing. Patricia had been lucky enough to be adopted, raised in a home, not an institution. I couldn't separate anticipation from anxiety, and actually felt jealous of this sister I hadn't even met. Experienced at her work, Ann Henry had cautioned me about this mixture of feelings. "Take it slow, Donald. You both have a lot of ground to cover and probably a lot of baggage. What happened five decades ago wasn't your fault, and it wasn't Patricia's, either. Try to remember that."

On the agreed upon day, a warm spring morning in May of 1994, Dave and Laura came to my apartment in Southwick to meet this aunt that Dave had never seen. The three of us waited at the top of my driveway. I had stopped smoking years ago, but reached into my shirt pocket for a pack of cigarettes that wasn't there. I checked my watch. "They're late. Maybe she changed her mind," I said, pacing.

"We know you're anxious, Dad. This is a big moment," Dave said. "For all of us," Laura added. "Don't worry, Donald, I'm sure she'll be here."

Eventually, a car pulled up. I stepped forward, but hesitated. "Go ahead, Dad," Dave urged. The driver's door opened, and

Patricia stepped out. For the first time in my life, I looked into the eyes of a blood relative. I wanted to hug, but couldn't make my arms do it. Instead, I shook my sister's hand. And cried.

We asked each other a lot of questions that day. It's hard to feel close to a sister when you meet as grown-ups, but Patricia was easy to talk to. And I didn't let my confused jealousy ruin the occasion. In fact, I didn't mention anything about Belchertown because I didn't want her to think her brother was a retard. I said I was raised in an orphanage, and let it go at that.

A few weeks later, Patricia, Dave, Laura and I met again, this time at a restaurant on Boston's North Shore, where my sister—by now we were calling her Pat—had been raised. We asked to be seated in a booth away from others and ordered coffee. When we had settled in, Pat began. "You know, I always had a suspicion that I was adopted. When I was growing up in Medford, there were no baby pictures of me anywhere in the house. The youngest photo I saw was taken when I was probably three or four years old. I also have a vague memory of being brought into a big building at some point, standing in front of a huge brown desk, and seeing this man in a black robe. I had no idea why I was there, but that must've been the day I was adopted."

"And adoption cases were sealed in court, so you couldn't find out," Dave said.

"Right." Pat stirred her coffee. "Another hint that I was adopted came when my father had a stroke. I was still little, but for some reason I was the only one who could really understand him when he tried to speak. That didn't set well with the rest of the family, and I couldn't figure out why. Actually, we were thicker than mud, dad and me. The more I think about it, I believe I came into that house because of him, the man who raised me. He's the one who really wanted to adopt me, not the woman I called Mother."

"At least you had someone to be raised by," I said. "You weren't abused, were you?"

"No, they were good to me, don't get me wrong." Pat lowered her voice and leaned forward across the table. "But when he passed away, I felt like the wrong parent had died." She paused to let that sink in.

"Wow, that's pretty strong," Laura said.

"I know. But she just never treated me the way I should've been treated. Years later, when I was married and living in Brockton, I'd invite my mother to spend winters with me. She was getting on in years, and I thought I could help her through the cold and snow. *No, that's okay,* she'd say. *I'm going to your sister's in Syracuse.*" Pat raised her palms in frustration. "Now I ask you, where's the weather worse? She also had a habit of calling my kids by the names of my sister's children. It wasn't senility, believe me. My kids came second in her heart. So all those years, I just had a feeling that I was adopted. Then I got that call from Ann Henry."

"She's good at her job," Dave said. "Before we got hooked up with her, Dad and I spent tons of time searching city hall and court records across the state, all over New England. We finally stumbled across your name, and Michael, Sandra, and Charlene's in Cambridge District Court. It's very possible you have records there, too."

"Could be, who knows?" Pat said.

Later on that visit Dave took Patricia to Cambridge, and she returned with a portfolio of her own past, including two different birth certificates. They each showed the same date and location, December 14, 1938, at the Good Samaritan Hospital, operated by the Salvation Army. And both listed her mother as Veronica Vitkus, and left the father's name blank. But one recorded the birth of "Patricia Vitkus," and the other "Patricia Spring," for her adoptive family.

Other papers interwove with the records Dave and I had obtained from Belchertown, and together Pat and I were able to reconstruct some of our past. Our mother had five children—Patricia, me, Sandra, Michael, and Charlene in that order—all of whom she gave up to be wards of the state. Except for Patricia, we all had the same father. Patricia's earlier research showed that when our mother learned that Sandra, Michael, and Charlene were being abused in the foster care system, she regained custody. She tried to get Patricia back, too, but Pat's adoption had already gone through. It's still a mystery if she made any effort to find me.

When I was critical of our mother, Patricia said, "What happened wasn't her fault, Donald. You know, she and Alice were only 13 when their mother died. They were left to be raised by our grandfather, a falling-down drunk who couldn't hold a job, and who beat them. So they were pretty much on their own, and what are you gonna do when you're thrown to the streets of Boston?

"I found out years ago that my real father was a taxi driver with 19 charges for sex offenses on his record. That's documented," she said. "For all we know, our mother might have been raped by this guy when she was just fifteen. When those Navy ships came into Charlestown during the war, sailors walked across the bridge straight into the combat zone, where there were no holds barred. They were looking for sex, and took all they could get. That's probably where our mother and her twin sister hung out." Patricia paused. "Your father was in the Navy, wasn't he, Donald?"

"Yes. Donald Williams. Most likely, I was named after him."

Several months later, more fragments fell into place. Ann Henry had located Michael, Sandra, and Charlene in South Carolina. By now, they had all married, so my sisters' names had changed yet again, making them even harder to trace.

I learned that my mother herself eventually married—another Navy man like my father. She apparently liked men in uniform. Her husband agreed to adopt her three kids, and he became their father of record.

Like Pat, none of these three siblings had any idea that I existed. Ann Henry first contacted Michael. I can imagine his reaction. He probably thought the whole thing was a scam when one day this woman from Massachusetts called and said, 'Hey, you know what? You have a brother.' I wouldn't blame him for being skeptical.

She arranged a meeting for all of us, including Pat, who also was a complete stranger to the others. We would gather just before Thanksgiving at a hotel in Savannah, Georgia. As nervous as when I had met Pat, I was about to face the rest of my family, siblings who until now were just names on file cards I had once stumbled across at Belchertown State School. The same questions ran through my mind. What would they look like? What would they think of me? What do you say to a brother and sisters you've never met? I hoped for the best, that we might establish a bond, that at last I'd have birth family.

When we stepped into the lobby, more than twenty years since our mother had died, the five middle-aged children of Veronica Vitkus were in the same room for the first time ever. As soon as I saw Michael, there was no doubt that we were brothers. We mirrored each other—the same facial features, the same build, even what my son Dave later called the same "mad scientist" hair. Michael walked like me, gestured like me, and he talked like me. We weren't twins, but the genetic tendency that had given my mother a double was still an influence. We later discovered from Sandra and Charlene that Pat looked a lot like our mother. They said she even shared the same hot temper when she was crossed.

Our reunion was cordial, but despite the resemblances, meeting my brother and sisters was like talking with strangers. Although we were family, we lacked even the ties that classmates would feel at a school reunion. I had expected it to be different, hoped to feel a closeness, but it didn't happen. Too much time had elapsed, and our lives had taken drastically different courses.

A year later, again around Thanksgiving, I headed south to see Charlene. Despite my disappointment at not feeling a bond with my siblings, I still had questions about my mother. Charlene seemed to be the best one to provide answers. The youngest among us, she was more able than the others to accept what had happened in our family, and was receptive to meeting again.

The weather was good and I was in no hurry, so I decided not to take the interstate. Travelling secondary roads would give me a chance to see more of the country. It was late Thanksgiving afternoon when I crossed into North Carolina, enjoying the scenery along U.S. Route 220. Outside Charlotte, I noticed a blue light flashing in my mirror. I moved onto the shoulder to let the cruiser pass, but it slowed and pulled in behind me. A beefy, unsmiling state trooper with a Smokey Bear hat like Sergeant Nittoli approached my car.

I rolled down my window. "I wasn't speeding, was I, officer?"

"No, sir, you weren't." He stared at me through mirror sunglasses. "In fact, you were going a little slow. License and registration, please."

I pulled my registration from the glove compartment, and slipped my license out of my wallet. The officer examined them, then leaned into my window.

"Have you been drinking, sir?"

"No, sir." I hadn't.

"Wait here," he said, and returned to his cruiser. Passing drivers slowed and turned their heads to get a look at me.

In a few minutes he was back. "Why are you on this road?"

"I'm on my way to see my sister in South Carolina. What's the problem, did I miss a toll or something?"

"You were swerving back and forth."

He was probably right. Dave had told me I drive like an old man, drifting from one side of the lane to the other.

"I'm gonna ask you again, sir. Why are you traveling on this highway?"

"I told you, I'm headed to visit my sister." I wished I could read his eyes behind those glasses. "Is this a special road or something? Is it just for certain people? It's public, ain't it?"

"I'll ask the questions, sir. Were you in a mental institution in Massachusetts, sir?" He pronounced it 'Massatoosetts.'

"Yes, when I was a kid."

"Did you escape?"

"No! Well, yeah. I mean, I tried to, a lot of us did. But that was a long time ago."

"Is that what you're doing now?"

"Look, officer, I don't what they told you on your radio. I was in a state school when I was growing up. I'm on my way now to my sister's house. If I haven't broken any laws, I'd like to continue. I'm an American. This is still a free country, ain't it? I served in Vietnam." It was on the tip of my tongue to add that my son was a cop in 'Massatoosetts,' but didn't.

"Out of the car."

He opened my door and half pulled me out. "Walk along that line."

I did, but shuffled a bit, a habit I retained from the state school. He took me to his cruiser and opened the back door. "Get in." He shut the door and I could hear it lock. There were bars in front of me.

He returned to my car, opened every door, and searched the entire vehicle. Everything he found—my extra clothes and shaving kit, a map, pencils, empty soda cans, gum wrappers and other trash—got tossed onto the road. He popped the hood, searched under it, then opened the trunk and pulled out everything that was in there—an oil spout, rags, jumper cables, the jack, even the spare. Everything. Then he got down on the road and looked under my car.

When he finished, he walked back to his cruiser and opened the door. "If it wasn't Thanksgiving, I'd be hauling you in. Be on your way, and don't stop."

I retrieved all my stuff from the pavement, and drove on, careful not to drift. I looked forward to seeing Charlene. She had a sense of open-mindedness and compassion, and recognized that I carried a lot of conflicted feelings about our mother. It was late by the time I arrived, so we met at a McDonald's where I got coffees for us.

"It's hard for you to realize Donald, but our mother was a good woman," Charlene told me as we sat by a window. "She really was. If she had known what it was like where you grew up, she would've gone there to get you. She would have. I'm sure of it."

Then why didn't she try to find out, I thought. How come three of us got to enjoy birthdays and holidays, a stable home, a mother's touch—while I was left in that hell-hole?

"I built up a lot of anger over those years."

"I'm not surprised, and I don't blame you. But our mother loved her children," Charlene continued. "She protected us. If anyone tried to bother us, they had her to contend with." A fry machine beeped behind us as Charlene's eyes dropped to the table. "Looking back, though, she wasn't a happy person. She never said anything to any of us about what happened, but she cried a lot. Especially around Mother's Day."

"You know I was born on May 12."

"When we were little, we'd ask, 'What's wrong? Why are you crying, Momma?' And she'd say, well, 'Today's the day my brother got shot down in the war,' or something like that. You could tell she was keeping things buried deep inside." Charlene had twisted a napkin in her hands. "She cried lots of times, Donald. And she drank. She always said she had her hell right here on Earth, so she wasn't worried about what came afterwards. She made her mistakes and had to pay for them." Charlene looked directly at me. "She loved you, Donald. She missed you. Back then, if a woman had a child out of wedlock, she was shamed, ruined. There was no help."

"I know."

Charlene stared through the glass at the passing traffic, then turned back. "Would you like to visit her grave? It isn't far from here...I can drive you."

It's an awful thing, but in my younger years I actually wanted to piss on my mother's grave. Her absence gnawed at me. I had longed for her, desperate to fill in the voids, and that loneliness transformed into anger. Her obituary had led me here, and I was honored that my sister now offered to share my mother's resting place with me.

"Okay," I said.

My mother was buried in the memorial cemetery of Andrews, South Carolina, now a town of about 3,000. "Here's her marker," Charlene said, leading me to the site. The flat bronze plaque, embossed with rose branches, read: *Veronica Marcella Vitkus Jordan, Dec. 12, 1922—Dec. 15, 1972, Wife, Mother and Friend.*

I didn't kneel or bless myself, or say any prayers. I didn't tear up. And I certainly didn't pee on her grave. Instead, a faint relief eased over me, as another piece of the puzzle shifted. This was the final resting place of the woman who had brought me a red knit suit on her final visit. The memories of no phone calls, "receives no mail, has no visitors," and staring out the ward window for a car that I wouldn't recognize lingered. But at last I was beginning to know my mother.

Southern Hospitality

"Donald, if it's okay with you, I'd like to be your stand-in daddy."

On one of my trips south to find my family, I found a new wife. I was introduced to a woman named Pat, and we were quickly attracted to each other. She was pretty, with short brown hair, blue eyes, a ready smile, and a southern accent. As soon as we met, I enjoyed talking with her because she seemed to understand me better than anyone ever had before. I invited her north to Massachusetts, where we went to movies and restaurants together. I liked taking her on road trips, showing her New England, sometimes to an attraction like the Bush estate in Kennebunkport, or Yankee Candle in Deerfield, where scented candles filled the air in a year-long Christmas village. But often I had no destination in mind, just the fun of driving my old Toyota with Pat beside me. She made me feel special, important. It was on one of those trips that I turned to her and said, "You know, Pat, we should get married." That was my proposal, and she said yes.

We had both been married before, and we weren't kids. Pat was 42 and I was 52, so our wedding, about a year after we met, would be a quiet affair with a few of Pat's friends in attendance.

June 16, 1996, was a steamy Sunday in Columbia, South Carolina. It had rained all morning, and the early afternoon brought heavy thunderstorms. Our ceremony was scheduled for three o'clock, and at 2:45 it was still pouring. But the rain stopped abruptly, like someone turned off the faucet, the sun came out, and we gathered in a small garden outside the Unitarian church. Pat was beautiful in a pink and white dress. I wore dark pants and a dress shirt, no jacket or tie. The trees were still dripping as the minister recited a ceremony by Marianne Williamson, a spiritualist whose writing Pat admired, explaining that each of us was a gift to the other.

"Donald, do you take this woman Patricia to be your lawful wedded wife, to love her and to honor her, nurture and sustain her, through times of darkness as well as light, henceforth and forevermore?"

"I do."

On the way to dinner afterwards, Pat pointed upward. "Look at that, Donald, it's beautiful!" An enormous rainbow, bigger and brighter than I'd ever seen, arched across the sky in front of us.

"That's a sign our marriage was meant to be."

"I think you're right," Pat said, taking my hand.

It sounds Hollywood, but that's really how it happened.

Pat grew up in Fieldale, Virginia, a town of less than a thousand in the southwest corner of the state with little more than a post office, grocery store, and a local restaurant. I visited her parents a couple of times before we got married. I didn't know what they'd think of their daughter seeing a Northerner. Having watched the civil rights marches as a kid on that Belchertown TV, I expected racism, rednecks and backward thinking, but that's not what I found. Her family accepted me as one of their own, and I was greeted in town with genuine southern hospitality. In the store, at the post office and on the street, people I didn't know stopped to talk. They were in no hurry.

"Y'all should get used to that," Pat's 'Daddy' Bill told me at the kitchen table.

"That's right," said Glenna, her mom, setting a bowl of homemade vegetable soup in front of me. "You Yankees are always rushing here, rushing there, workin' up your blood pressure."

"We pretty much all know each other in Fieldale," Bill added, "and we like to chat."

Both in their sixties, Pat's folks were comfortable in who they were. Glenna was a tiny dark-haired woman, about five feet tall, not much over 100 pounds. She kept an immaculate country kitchen and always had a pot of soup simmering for me. Bill had retired from Appalachian Power, where he had worked as a linesman for 42 years. Nearly bald with a gray beard, he had what Pat called 'absolutely gorgeous blue eyes.'

"Just don't go wanderin' around in the woods," he warned. "You might get shot by a moonshiner."

I laughed at what I thought was a joke.

"No, I'm serious. They see some stranger snoopin' around, they might think you're one of them revenuers."

Glenna's kitchen was the heart of their home where family and friends congregated. She was a caretaker, always thinking of others. Guests were drawn to her table by the aroma of roast pork, fresh biscuits and cornbread topped with apple butter from nearby church festivals. I even grew to like the 'gree-its' that Glenna cooked with milk in a cast-iron skillet reserved for that purpose only.

Bill and I hit it off, spending hours at that table trading stories. "You know, it got cold up on those ladders out there in the winter," he said, his eyes twinkling. "But this here helped keep me warm." He stroked his beard. "The rest of my hair fell off my head and took root on my chest."

He told me about working outdoors through oppressive heat, restoring service after thunderstorms, replacing lines downed by hurricanes, and I explained what it was like to run a printing press at the envelope plant. During one of these conversations over coffee, I happened to mention my union involvement.

"So my daughter married not only a damn Yankee, but a union man, too, did she?" Bill set down his cup.

"That's right. In fact, I got elected vice-president."

"Well, I'll be. You know, I like you, Donald, but I could never understand why anyone in his right mind would join a union." Bill tapped the table with his forefinger. "I gotta tell you, I hate unions. There used to be a big plant in town here, employed hundreds of men, three shifts, overtime. The union came in, and in a year the place shut down."

"I never trusted authority, and the union fights for our rights," I countered.

"You ain't got no rights if you ain't got no plant. They tried to unionize the power company, and I fought it all the way. Donald, they slashed my tires and smashed my windshield. All those guys do is take your money. Why should I hand over a chunk of my paycheck for dues? Rights? I could stand up for myself."

"You know how I grew up, don't you?"

"Well, I know you don't have family. Pat told me you were in some kinda state school."

"That's right." I told Bill about the power wielded by the attendants, the beatings, the verbal abuse, the forced medication and solitary confinement. I told him about Jones, what it was like to spend holidays alone, to wonder about my family, about why my mother never came to see me.

"What about your daddy? Where was he at all that time?"

"I never knew him, either. He just took off after I was born. He was in the Navy. His name was Donald, too. That's in my record...I must've been named after him. That's all I know."

Bill shook his head. "You poor bastard."

"Well, they were never married, so I guess I really *am* a bastard."

"Jesus, I'm sorry, Donald. I didn't mean it that way."

"It's okay, I know you didn't."

"Pat told us what a kind person you are, Donald, and I can see that. She's right. I'm amazed you can be that way after how you were raised." Bill rested his chin on his hand, fingers pressed against his lips. "I'll be right back." He got up from the table, and was back a minute later holding a heavy winter jacket, charcoal gray, with a red Appalachian Power logo stitched above a front pocket. "Try this on."

I stood and slipped it on.

"Fits pretty good," Bill said, adjusting the shoulders. "I want you to have that."

It was mid-summer in Virginia, but I zipped the jacket up to my neck. "Thank you," I said.

Bill looked directly at me. "Donald, if it's okay with you, I'd like to be your stand-in daddy."

And, for the first time in my life, I embraced my father.

The year that we married, Pat and I spent Christmas with her family. Two sisters, three brothers, their spouses and all their kids flocked back to the homestead for the holiday, bringing hugs, laughs, kisses, and gifts. As each sibling's family arrived, the collection of red and green packages, ribbons, and bows spread well beyond the branches of the tree in the living room. By Christmas morning, with the addition of all the ones Santa left, there had to be more than 300 presents stacked and leaning on each other around that tree.

After church the Kahle clan, more than 20 of them, crammed into the living room. Not wanting to intrude on a family tradition, I lagged behind in the kitchen. I had never seen that kind of togetherness before and it scared me. It seemed fake. I figured, with the Christmases I grew up with, I'd be better off nursing a cup of coffee.

Soon after the commotion of the gift opening began, Pat's sister Kathy stepped into the kitchen. "Donald, why are you still in here? Come on, it's time to open presents!"

"I don't know, I thought I better stay here till you guys are finished."

"What are you talking about? You're part of our family now. There are presents out there for you, too." She smiled, picked up my coffee, and led me me by the arm into the living room, which by now was a frenzy of flying wrapping paper, shouts, and happy faces.

"Set yourself down, Donald, and join the fun," Bill shouted, handing me a stack of presents. "Here, tear into these!" I squeezed in beside Pat and opened my gifts, gifts from family that no one would confiscate later.

Over the years, Bill began having problems with his balance. He grew unsteady on his feet and his fine motor skills suffered. Eating became difficult for him. He was diagnosed with a glioblastoma, the most aggressive kind of brain tumor, and soon required round-the-clock nursing care. Always pleasant and loving, Bill was now irritable and agitated, trying his wife's patience and frustrating his own children. "It's like dealing with a two-year-old drunk," Pat said. It was hard to watch. Bill fixated and suffered hallucinations. One calm day with no storms in sight, he believed the power had gone out and that people needed his help. It had been ten years since he retired, but Kathy had to drive him all over town to convince him everyone was okay.

When Pat and I visited, I tried to redirect her father, calm him down, and give Glenna a break from constantly caring for her husband. I had grown up with people whose minds didn't do what minds routinely do, and recognized his frustration. I saw that his wife and family were doing too much for him. With the best intentions, they followed him around, opened doors, turned on lights, set out his clothes. A part of him knew they were trying to help, but he was fighting the thing that was taking over his brain. He needed a sense of independence, and as much as possible near the end, I let him cope for himself with a sense of dignity.

In 2007, at the age of 79, my stand-in dad passed away. I still wear his jacket.

Stigma

"If you don't behave..."

"Listen, Dad, I need to warn you about something." Dave was calling from Tucson. "They're running security checks on me out here, and you're probably gonna get a call from the feds."

More than a dozen years had passed since Dave and I had searched out my family. When he retired as a detective on the Northampton police force, he studied computer forensics. He had a sharp mind for technology, and coupled with his police experience, this interest was a natural fit. In 2009, he and Laura moved out west to start new careers, and now he had been hired to a sensitive position with the federal government.

"Okay, I guess I can handle that. Any idea what they might ask?" It didn't register that this wasn't about me. I thought about being denied a gun permit thirty years earlier. I thought about being stopped by that trooper in North Carolina and having my vehicle ransacked, about the scrapes I had gotten into in the military. I thought about being picked up after my escapes, my being on "parole," being labeled a 4-F retarded moron.

"They might inquire about my behavior as a kid, my judgment about things like whether or not I used drugs, if I acted out, or was ever in serious trouble," Dave said. "Character stuff like that. Just answer their questions if they call. And Dad? Do us both a favor. Stay calm."

Dave knew all too well that staying calm was never one of my strong points, especially when it came to authorities, or when I felt people were pushing me around. I couldn't distinguish between times when relatives, neighbors, or co-workers were merely trying to be helpful or when I was being controlled. He realized it would be a good idea to give me advanced warning about such a phone call, particularly when the conversation would be about him.

While he was growing up, I gave him good reason to be concerned. Once, when Dave was about ten years old, I asked him to help me replace some drafty windows on our house, a father and son do-it-yourself project. We had just removed a large dining room window when a car pulled up in the driveway.

"Dad, it's Pépé!" Dave leaned out through the opening to wave.

"Looks like you're helping your dad?" his grandfather asked from below.

"Yup, we're putting in new windows! I hand him the tools he needs. Dad says I'm the gopher—I go for this, go for that."

"Great! You'll know how to do it yourself when you have a place of your own someday."

Whether it was carpentry, plumbing, or electrical, Louis knew his way around home repairs. He could've taught workshops for guys like me.

Before installing the window, I had to replace the header, a weight-bearing piece about five feet long across the top of the opening. Because Dave wasn't tall enough to hold it, the header was awkward to handle, and I was struggling to nail it in place. It had to be level.

"Need another hand?" Louis called up to me.

"Nope. Dave and I can handle it. We're doing okay."

Louis eyeballed the header. "Looks from here like it might be a little low on the right end." I could tell he was being careful with his phrasing. "Sometimes that's hard to see, you know, when you're right in front of it."

I didn't say anything.

"Hold on, I'll be right up," Louis said.

"Goddammit, Louis! You think I don't know how to put in a fuckin' window? Is that it? This ain't brain surgery!" I pounded my hammer on the side of the frame. "Don't tell me what to do!"

Just then the header came loose, dropped through the opening, and caught Louis across the shoulder, knocking him to the ground. Dave ran out to check on his grandfather while I continued to erupt. "This is my house! I can handle it! I'm not a retard!"

I had lashed out at my son's Pépé for no good reason. I can only imagine now what was going through Dave's mind, or Louis's for that matter. For eleven years at Belchertown, every day from morning till night, people had told me what to do. I wanted to be my own man, not a moron—or even a former moron. Being treated like a retard had gnawed at me so much that I couldn't accept suggestions as anything else than efforts to control my life. I had left Belchertown, but Belchertown hadn't left me.

I was defiant about everything—even simple stuff like wearing a belt—which embarrassed and irritated Susan. Except when Sergeant Nittoli forced me, I refused to wear a belt till I was in my fifties, not because Ol' Lady Howard had humiliated me by hanging me on that hook in the day hall, or the pain that it caused—but because I wasn't gonna be told what to do.

I wanted to prove I wasn't a moron, even when it wasn't an issue, and I didn't wait for people to give me an excuse. I'd intentionally work my institutional background into conversations—blurt it out to see their reactions—which, of course, made them feel uneasy. I didn't do it constantly, but often enough that it pushed people away. When neighbors heard my outbursts, they stopped dropping by, and would-be friends didn't materialize. Sometimes it was just the excuse that a narrow-minded person needed, and I willingly supplied it. I just didn't know how to socialize normally.

I drove Susan nuts. "Donald, why are you doing this?" she'd ask. "They didn't even mention Belchertown. They had no idea about your background. Why do you keep bringing it up? You wonder why we don't have friends over. Well, can you blame them? They probably feel like that's exactly what you're doing, blaming them for what happened to you." I couldn't listen to reason, and that hard-headed attitude contributed to the demise of my marriage.

I was bitter. When I was locked up at the state school, I hated kids who had visitors. It was more than jealousy, it was hate. All those people driving up in their cars, taking their kids out for the day—shopping, to a restaurant, a park with swings and no barred windows, maybe a Lone Ranger movie—I hated them, too.

It never occurred to me the pain those parents were suffering over having a retarded son or daughter, or the guilt those mothers bore when doctors told them it was their fault that their child wasn't normal. *If you had been a good mother, this wouldn't have happened*, was a common response in the medical profession. And it never occurred to me how bad those parents must have felt when the outing was over and they had to watch their son or daughter disappear again behind locked doors and barred windows. Or how those kids themselves must have felt. They had seen the world beyond their wards. They had tasted freedom, security, and affection, and had to return to a hell hole. No matter how truly handicapped they were, they could recognize the difference between hugs and beatings. But that didn't occur to me. I hated them anyway.

I know my attitude affected my kids. AnneMarie, who wanted little to do with me in later years, was a good student despite her father. Dave, on the other hand, was different. I'm not sure if defiance can be inherited, but it certainly can be learned. Dave spent fifth grade in a special education classroom with a bunch of screwed up kids. Some had legitimate development or attention issues from Down Syndrome to what today is called Attention Deficit Disorder. They couldn't focus no matter how hard they tried. But the majority were behavioral problems, perfectly intelligent kids who had disrupted regular classrooms, to the point that they were segregated from the rest, even with their own bathrooms. Instead of improving Dave's attitude, this environment made him act out even more. I felt like Belchertown had reached down another generation and grabbed my son by the neck.

One day he and a few buddies left the cafeteria and snuck back into their classroom while their teacher was at lunch. They threw every desk and chair, every textbook, pencil and piece of chalk, every scrap of paper from the closet and waste basket, into one huge pile in the corner of the room. Dave claimed the teacher had been giving him and his friends a hard time, and this was payback. To top it off, he ran outside to the parking lot and put a sizeable dent in the fender of the teacher's car. The weapon? His knee. It seemed my son was developing a problem with authority as well.

Susan and I received fifty-two disciplinary letters about Dave that year. I later found out he was keeping count because he was in a contest with two other boys to see who could accumulate the most. Dave came in second, but he was suspended six times.

My history haunted my son, and he was fighting regularly. The state school carried a stigma, and when other kids found out about my background, they goaded him unmercifully. He'd arrive home with a fat lip, ripped shirt, or some other evidence of a scuffle, and I never knew if Dave was defending himself or his dad's name.

Kids can be cruel, and when they sense a difference—somebody who doesn't fit the mold—they pounce. They learn some of this attitude from adults around them. "If you don't behave, we'll send you to Belchertown," was a threat often used by area parents to discipline their kids. Their sons and daughters had little idea of what Belchertown really was, and if the parents themselves had known, they never would have used that line. From the way kids heard adults talk, they knew it wouldn't be good. They had visions of some sort of hellish place for looneys and nutcases, that place off the road where people screamed and moaned behind barred windows, that place where bad kids went, usually never to return. And they knew that Dave's father was from that place.

The bullying extended beyond school. When Dave tried out for Pee Wee Football, he was a target. "Hey, Vitkus," the coach's son taunted. "I hear your ol' man got his education at Belchertown, the school for morons. That makes you the son of a moron!" He shoved Dave to the ground, and the coach condoned it by not addressing the situation. At the next practice, the rest of the team joined in, and Dave quit.

The same thing happened with Cub Scouts. "No wonder you're in trouble with teachers all the time," a future helpful, friendly, courteous, and kind young man said at a den meeting. Dave flew across the table at the kid. His scouting experience lasted less than a month.

Susan, a compassionate, caring mother, tried to discourage Dave from fighting in any way she could. "Don't pay any attention to them, Dave," she'd say. "Don't let them get to you. They're just plain ignorant. Don't stoop to their level." That tactic only set him up for more ridicule. Three brothers from the neighborhood, the Clark boys, harassed him daily on the way home from school. "What's the matter, Vitkus, is mama's boy too scared to fight? Do you need a pacifier?" And they would gang up on him. When I complained to their father, Mr. Clark said, "Oh, well, boys will be boys."

I thought my son was taking it on the chin because of my upbringing, so I signed Dave up for karate lessons. Susan was less than enthusiastic about it. I also gave him some fatherly advice. "Look, Dave, this is what I used to do, and it worked. Get the oldest brother when he's alone sometime—at school, outside the candy store, in his own front yard—wherever. Surprise him, Dave, and beat the shit out of him. Don't stop till the bullying stops. You'll be in trouble with me if you don't."

Not long afterwards, Mr. Clark called to complain about his boys being "ambushed" by Dave. "Oh, well, you know how it is. Boys will be boys," I said, and hung up.

A similar incident involved AnneMarie. She was about five years old when Peter, a sizeable neighborhood fourteen-year-old, started picking on her. Whenever Peter saw AnneMarie outdoors, he chased her on his bike, threatening to run her over. The kid was old enough to know better, but he was perfectly okay with terrorizing a little girl.

Peter's father was aware of where I grew up, and that might've triggered these episodes. Dave had watched me argue with Peter's dad about it, and could tell that the guy wasn't going to take any such complaints from a local moron seriously. Besides, my leg was in a cast at the time following a work accident, and Peter's father probably didn't consider me a threat.

Eventually, Peter ran his bike into AnneMarie, knocking her down. That wasn't okay with Dave. One by one, he put rocks through every window—old-fashioned, multi-paned windows—in Peter's house. Each pane had to be puttied and re-painted, and I paid a pretty penny for the repairs. But Peter stopped harassing Dave's little sister.

Dave was right about the background check. Eventually, I got a call from a federal office, which turned out to be routine. I responded calmly, and his position was secure.

Every now and then, I think back to his graduation from the police academy. I had a real problem seeing him in uniform. In fact, I disliked his becoming a cop intensely. Yes, he looked sharp, successful at becoming part of community law enforcement to protect and serve the public. The rational part of my brain told me to be proud. But the gut part saw handcuffs dangling from Dave's belt, dredging up images of Jones's ring of keys, memories of being tied down, restrained in a strait jacket, thrown into solitary. It was hard to see my son through the uniform and the authority that it represented.

When I later visited his house on weekends and holidays, Dave would often have to get ready for work. He'd come out in his uniform, and he could recognize that I was growing apprehensive. We'd each try to make jokes to ease the weird tension between us.

"Oh, there he is, my son, another no-good cop like the ones who used to drag me back to the state school when I escaped!"

"Keep it up, Dad! I'll gladly take you back."

No Longer a Moron

> THE COMMONWEALTH OF MASSACHUSETTS
> ## HOLYOKE COMMUNITY COLLEGE
> THE BOARD OF TRUSTEES, IN ACCORDANCE WITH THE RECOMMENDATION OF THE FACULTY AND THE PRESIDENT, AND WITH THE AUTHORITY CONFERRED BY THE MASSACHUSETTS BOARD OF HIGHER EDUCATION,
> HEREBY AWARDS TO
> ### DONALD E. VITKUS
> THE DEGREE OF
> ### ASSOCIATE IN SCIENCE
> IN THE CURRICULUM OF
> ### HUMAN SERVICES
> TOGETHER WITH ALL THE RIGHTS AND PRIVILEGES APPERTAINING THERETO.
> GIVEN AT HOLYOKE, MASSACHUSETTS THIS FOURTH DAY OF JUNE, 2005.

I continued my job at the plant, edging toward retirement. But the economy was shifting. Across the country, thousands of manufacturing jobs were relocating overseas for cheap labor. Then, it happened to me. U.S. Envelope was acquired by MeadWestvaco, and our work would be sent to Mexico. I was jobless after thirty years with the company.

I had always fought for decent pay, benefits, and members' rights. I hated injustice. It wasn't possible to stop the move, but I joined other union members to push for compensation. We were successful in negotiating an agreement that would provide training for new jobs.

Through the North American Free Trade Act, I became eligible to take college courses at no cost. But to study what? For a number of years, like Dave, I had tinkered with computers. Technology fascinated me, but those in charge of the funding said I wasn't qualified for the field. Maybe they thought I was too old, or not smart enough. But programs to provide care for the developmentally disabled were expanding, and there was a shortage of people to fill these positions. If I wanted training, I'd have to study human services for a job that would pay a fraction of what I'd been earning in industry. On the plus side, however, I certainly had experience with the mentally handicapped.

In September of 2003, I enrolled as a fulltime student at Holyoke Community College, a mile from the Soldiers Home where I once washed dishes while "on parole" from Belchertown.

I carried 16 credits a semester, and along with a free education, I was getting paid to attend classes. Not a bad deal. I took required courses in English, history and math, with sociology and psychology my primary focus, studying how to take care of the kind of people I had grown up with.

Surrounded by students 40 years younger, many fresh out of high school, I felt out of place. Fortunately, a psychology instructor named Bob Plasse put me at ease. He recognized I had never been exposed to this kind of atmosphere, while his other students had never been exposed to my kind of institution. Their generation had never heard of this place called Belchertown State School. It was already boarded up when they were in kindergarten.

"I'm not gonna hurt you," I said. "When you settle down, I'll let you up."

I had taken on a part-time job as one-to-one caregiver with a Springfield agency. Jim was my assignment.

Gripping his wrists behind his back, I had him pinned face down to the dining room floor in his group home. I was bigger and heavier, but he was younger and more agile. We were both breathing hard, a 65-year-old man with a weight advantage straddling a skinny guy half his age, a pair of mismatched wrestlers.

There were rules about this kind of restraint. You couldn't put your hands on a person unless he was attempting to hurt himself or others. And if you had to take him down, you had to minimize the risk of injury—to the individual, not yourself. There was a three-minute maximum.

Rules or no rules, I didn't want to hurt Jim. It had been only a minute or so since I had dropped him, but it seemed longer. He kicked and squirmed a few more seconds, then turned his head to the side.

"Okay," he said, "settle down, settle down."

I loosened my grip and eased off him. "Remember the rules. No more coffee now until this afternoon, and you have to cooperate till then."

"Settle down. Settle down now or no more coffee, no more coffee. Settle down now."

Jim continually repeated words. He might parrot phrases he had just heard, or from hours, days, even years ago. The label for this behavior is "echolalia," a common symptom of autism. To me, it was Jim telling me what he wanted.

While my courses provided the academic standing I needed to work in human services, it was my life experience that gave me the compassion to be a good direct care worker. I didn't want to be like those who paid more attention to their cell phones than the human being, failed to sit with them at meals or in vans, collecting a paycheck for ignoring the individuals in their care. I had been the recipient of that kind of "attention" on the other side of the bars.

We had a lot in common, this "client" and me, a former "moron" of Belchertown State School. Jim pushed the envelope, but so had I. We were misfits who challenged authority. We each struggled with what it meant to be human, mentally handicapped or not. Neither of us was trusted with a knife or fork, we were supervised in the bathroom, and we knew how it felt to be restrained. We both loved our coffee, and, like Jim, there was a time when I would do anything for a cigarette. I knew where he was coming from, and I wanted to teach him life skills, responsibility, and respect. When I looked at Jim, I saw potential.

He needed guidance, practical rules that would allow him choices to regulate his caffeine, sugar, and nicotine intake, modifying his behavior with consequences that he could understand, including an occasional take-down. To my way of thinking, whatever worked, worked.

Now in his thirties, Jim had grown up at home, and attended public school as a Special Ed student. When he eventually became too much for his parents to handle, they placed him in a group home. The manager had trouble keeping staff in this house, and Jim was the main reason.

He had a very short fuse. When things didn't go his way, he threw violent tantrums. He hurled furniture, smashed windows, sliced his shoes and mattress with a knife, even lit fires.

He looked physically normal, on the short side, thin with dark eyes and hair. He smiled easily. He could read, write, sign his own name, and tell time. He was, in fact, high functioning, but he had loads of behavior issues.

He had a compulsion to straighten out furniture that to him appeared askew, or to circle a chair before sitting. It wasn't uncommon for Jim to enter a room, squeeze against the wall behind a chair, do a 360, then sit down. Then he rocked, from his torso, forward and back. Sometimes he rocked standing up, one foot in front of the other for balance, forward and back, to some internal rhythm. He might twirl his wrist endlessly, or sniff his fingers.

So he drew stares in public. Some people got annoyed with him, but exasperating as they might be, I understood that these repetitive motions provided Jim comfort. They were just part of who he was. I had grown up surrounded by such behavior.

Jim was hyper, in constant motion despite the meds that were supposed to calm him. At mealtimes, his spoon never rested. He bolted his food like every meal was a pie-eating contest, and later would feel queasy. I had to come up with a way to slow him down. I didn't want to feed him like a baby—that would be demeaning. So I let him use the spoon, but after a couple of mouthfuls I took it away and said, "Take your time." When he swallowed, I waited. "See? You can actually taste it!" We passed the spoon back and forth, a relay team seeking success, not speed.

He liked using a blade razor for shaving, but was prone to cutting himself, sometimes intentionally, with his sudden, jerky movements. I tried allowing him to shave only his cheeks, while I did the up strokes under his neck. When that didn't work, I switched him to an electric. "There, you look good," I'd tell him when he was done shaving, and he smiled.

He was hooked—no, he was fixated—on coffee. In restaurants, when he finished a cup, he turned it upside down, spilled out the remaining few drops, and set it back on the table. That was his signal for a refill, and he wanted to start fresh. If it was slow in coming, he held his cup in the air, pointed to it and said, "Coffee, coffee, coffee" to the waiter—any passing waiter. If I didn't watch carefully, he'd help himself to another customer's cup.

At breakfast that morning, I heated water for instant coffee. I had been warned by my supervisor: "No brewed coffee for Jim because he'll chug down a full pot if you let him, or scald himself, or throw it at you. One cup at a time, and always use plastic."

When the water was warm enough, I filled Jim's mug at the counter and gave him a spoon to let him add his own coffee. He shoveled in three huge scoops, reached for the sugar bowl and did the same, then gulped it down and held the mug out for a refill. I poured another, but this time stirred in a single spoonful of coffee and sugar myself. He downed this as fast as the first, and held the mug out again. When I said, 'No more,' he went ballistic. Flailing his arms and screaming, he slammed the mug on the countertop and it caromed to the floor. Frustrated that it didn't smash into pieces, he kicked over his stool, ripped off his shirt, tore it in half, and threw it in my face. Then he reached for a fork. That's when I took him down.

Besides his coffee, Jim loved cigarettes. He had the yellow fingers of a chain smoker. When I first arrived, he was going through a whole pack every couple of hours, half a carton in a day. Neither of his housemates smoked, but the two other staff did. They had to be sure not to leave their cigarettes or lighters around, or they'd disappear.

Except under a doctor's orders, you can't stop an individual from smoking. That would violate his human rights. But Jim's habit was expensive, and needed to be curtailed for financial reasons if nothing else. Each morning, I gave him four loose cigarettes to keep in his shirt pocket, and locked up the rest. Those precious smokes had to last him all day. If he crushed one of them, there'd be no replacement. That was the rule, my rule.

Jim had a fascination for fire. Given an opportunity, he'd burn anything he could, paper towels, toilet paper, furniture cushions, even the clothes he was wearing. All of his shirts had burn marks. I gave him an empty matchbook and a single match at a time. He'd get another for his next cigarette an hour later. Then I extended it to two hours, eventually three. Since he could tell time, he never let me forget.

Personal hygiene was another challenge. Jim's bathroom trips were quick in-and-out events, without stopping to close the door. I had to go in with him to make sure he wiped himself and washed his hands. He didn't like taking time to bathe, either, and could build up a pretty strong scent.

"Get in that shower," I told Jim when he came out of his room later that morning. "And make sure you use soap. If you stink, we can't go to McDonald's."

"Okay, Donald. No stink, no stink." He stepped into the shower, mumbling, "Use soap. Go McDonald's. No stink."

When he was dressed, I gave him a pat on the back. "You look good, Jim. Ready to go? Get your jacket."

"Yes, ready!" He was on his toes, his hands flapping rapidly at his sides, like a baby bird trying to take off. "Buy cigarettes and coffee!"

"We'll see." More flapping. "Remember, you have to follow the rules."

"Follow rules. Cigarettes and coffee. Okay."

At the van, he slid the door open, flapped one more time like the handle was hot, climbed all the way to the back, and buckled up. I followed him in and sat down beside him, two rows behind the driver. We'd all be safer that way.

"Buy cigarettes and coffee. Cigarettes and coffee." He leaned into my face.

"What did I just tell you?"

"Follow rules."

"Right."

"Cigarettes and coffee."

McDonald's was our first stop. I picked a table away from the windows. No sense in taking chances on broken glass. Jim sat down across from me with his supersized meal. Despite my efforts, he wolfed it all down before my coffee was cool enough to drink. He gave new meaning to fast food. He let out an extended Coca-Cola belch that caused heads to turn, and began rocking. He pointed to his watch. "One-thirty, time for cigarette."

"Not in here. You can't smoke inside a restaurant."

He pulled a cigarette from his pocket and put it between his lips. "Smoke outside."

It was January, but Jim didn't mind standing in the cold, not if a cigarette was involved. Outdoors, he took out his matchbook, cupped his hands, and lit up. He was good at avoiding the wind. Rocking back and forth, he took a deep drag, then another, and another. In no time there was nothing left but the filter. He flicked it to the pavement and looked at me.

"Another?"

"Later, in two hours. That's the rule. Right now we have to go cash your check. Climb in."

The van took us to a branch office of a bank where I had helped Jim open an account for his monthly Social Security checks. I made it a point to go on Thursdays, so he could interact with the same teller whenever possible. Like most people in the system, routine was important for Jim.

"Good afternoon, Jim. How are you today?" she asked.

"Okay. I'm okay."

"Give the lady your check," I reminded him.

He took out his wallet and laid his check on the counter. The teller turned it over, glanced at me, and pointed to the line on the back. "Okay, Jim, you have to sign your name right here," she said, handing him a pen.

"Sign name right here." He concentrated, and scratched out his signature.

"Thank you, Jim." The teller processed his check and deliberately counted out his money on the counter. "That's one-hundred and seventy-two dollars. And fifty-three cents." She dropped the coins into his hand.

Jim picked up the bills. On his toes and flapping again, he turned to me. "Enough for cigarettes?"

"Yes, enough for cigarettes. Tell the lady thank you."

"Thank you. Thank you for money. Buy cigarettes."

"Before you put that away, I want *you* to count it," I said, taking him to the side. "Remember, start with the biggest, the twenties." One by one, he placed each bill on the counter, and with a little coaching, he got it right. "Way to go, Jim! Okay, now here's what you need for shopping." I let him keep fifty dollars, and took the rest. The house manager kept Jim's cash in a lock box, and doled it out to him for shopping trips. His meals, housing and care were covered by the state, but he used his own money for personal items like clothes, cigarettes, snacks, and other incidentals.

"Now cigarettes," Jim said.

"Yes, but first you need a few other things. Then cigarettes. Those are the rules."

"Those are the rules," he echoed. He wasn't happy, but I could tell he remembered what had happened that morning.

Next the van dropped us off at Wal-Mart, where Jim pushed the cart while I directed him to the men's department. I kept a list of what he needed for clothes. He hated trying things on, but today it was just T-shirts and a package of briefs, not a problem. He tossed them into the cart.

"Now cigarettes?" He was rocking.

"We'll pick them up on the way out. Right now, you need to tie that shoe." Keeping his shoes tied was another challenge. I got tired of doing it for him, so I had taught him how, squatting behind him and reaching around so he could watch from his perspective. This goal wasn't written into his service plan, but why not give it a try? Again and again, I placed one lace over the other, pulled them tight, then had him do it himself. The next day we added the loop, and so on, one step at a time, one shoe at a time, till he got it. It took a couple of weeks.

"Good job," I said when he was finished, then pointed across the aisles. "One more stop." He pushed the cart faster now, a little too fast. In the healthcare section, he grabbed toothpaste and a couple of bars of soap and threw them into the cart, harder than he had the clothes.

"Now cigarettes." This time he wasn't asking.

"Right. Now cigarettes."

At the checkout he told the cashier, "Carton of Camels." He always did this. He liked strong cigarettes. Unfiltered Camels were his favorite, but they were expensive, and without filters, he was sure to burn his fingers.

"You can't get Camels," I said. "You don't have enough money."

The rocking began. "Camels," he said again, louder.

"No, they cost too much. You can get those." I pointed to filter-tipped generics.

"Camels." He rocked faster.

I didn't want to embarrass him. I certainly didn't want to have to take him down in the checkout line of WalMart.

"Remember the rules," I said. "You can pick out one of these, or none."

He rocked without speaking.

"You'll go home without any. Your choice."

Seconds passed while he weighed his decision, then the rocking stopped. "Okay, those."

That year I took Jim to visit his brother and sister to celebrate Thanksgiving. When I was at Belchertown, I never went home for the holidays because I had no home to go to, so I was happy to accompany him. At the dinner table he ate more slowly than his siblings expected. He didn't gulp boiling hot coffee, and after the meal he went outside to smoke. Of course, I had to give him constant reminders, but his brother and sister were amazed at the improvement in his behavior. When I explained what we had been working on, they thanked me. They didn't think it was possible their brother could learn so much.

I'm proud to think I was a positive influence in Jim's life. I worked with him for almost two years. When I left for retirement, I missed work and I missed Jim. I thought about him often.

At the mall several months later, I spotted a distinctive gait. Jim was pushing a shopping cart through the aisles with another staff person. When I caught up to them, I tapped Jim on the shoulder. He turned around, and his eyes lit up.

"Donald!" he shouted.

We hugged. Then he stood on his toes, and did that bird thing.

Jim was my unofficial internship. Back in the Holyoke Community classroom, when our textbook focused on concepts like human development and behavior modification, Professor Plasse encouraged me to share my life experience. I told my classmates about the abuse and neglect, the regimentation, the dog house, the beatings. "Solitary confinement? Bars on the windows?" they asked. "No toilet paper? No talking allowed? How could that have happened?" They had no idea that *imbecile*, *idiot* and *moron* were actually clinical labels for the developmentally disabled half a century ago. They didn't realize the hurt inflicted on mentally handicapped individuals, their parents and siblings, when the word "retard" was tossed around in casual conversation, on TV, or in movies.

They elected me president of the Psychology Club, and I traveled to Cape Cod to address the annual conference of the New England Organization for Human Services Education, stressing the importance of compassion for those in their care.

Relating stories about Belchertown wasn't difficult, but writing papers at the college level was another matter. In my second year, my grades were sagging, and I needed a plan.

In 2004, Dr. Benjamin Ricci, a retired University of Massachusetts professor, published a book called *Crimes Against Humanity*, his account of a federal class action lawsuit he had led thirty years earlier in Boston. The court complaint was filed on behalf of more than two dozen Belchertown State School residents and their parents, who had united as The Friends of Belchertown. Representing more than 1,100 class members, they sued high ranking Massachusetts officials, including the Superintendent of Belchertown State School, and Milton Greenblatt, Commissioner of the Department of Mental Health.

The principal plaintiff of *Ricci v Greenblatt* was Ben's son Bobby, the F Building boy whose toy telephone I had stolen so many years ago. By the time the court proceedings began, I had been out of Belchertown for ten years, and I resented Ben and his group for not acting sooner. But now I needed to graduate. As president of the Psychology Club, hoping to win a few brownie points with my instructors, I invited Dr. Ricci to speak at HCC.

He arrived to a packed meeting room, where I sat in the audience. Dressed in a multi-colored cardigan and mismatched sport shirt, at 81 years old, he seemed more concerned with his message than his appearance. Ben stooped behind the podium and began.

"We were blessed to have two great legal minds coming together in this case, our attorney, former State Senator Beryl Cohen, and U.S. District Judge Joseph L. Tauro. Attorney Cohen was the sixteenth lawyer we approached. No one else was interested. And Judge Tauro was the fifth justice assigned to our case. In May of 1973, after he had read our complaint, he paid an unannounced visit to Belchertown, accompanied by his law clerk, Massachusetts Assistant Attorney General Terence O'Malley, and our attorney. Judge Tauro asked me to conduct the tour. We were all there to view conditions at what the Department of Mental Retardation had the audacity to call a *school!*"

Ben held up his book, his voice thin but his focus intense.

"Over nine hours on a humid day, we walked through the Nursery, the Infirmary, and the building that housed my own flesh and blood, my son Bobby. We observed overcrowding, understaffing, unsanitary and unsafe conditions. Our final stop was K Building—I call it *Dante's Purgatory*—where the 'incorrigibles' were warehoused."

He opened to a bookmark.

> "*The sound of mournful wails, howling, and animal-like grunts filled the air. Urine, feces, and food were smeared over many nude bodies, especially of persons in seclusion rooms...a female resident seeking bladder relief, awkwardly perched on the wall-mounted urinal...maggots wriggling inside or crawling out of the infected ears of several helpless, profoundly retarded persons while they lay in their crib-beds...sheets soiled with fresh as well as dried and caked vomitus...*"

When Ben finished reading, the room broke into sustained applause. And that day at Holyoke Community College, I got an autographed copy of his book.

In May of 2005 I completed the requirements for my associate's degree in human services. On a pleasant spring morning, the athletic field of Holyoke Community College filled with nearly a thousand students who would receive certificates and degrees at the graduation ceremony. Seated among them in a navy-blue cap and gown was me, a 62-year-old former retard of Belchertown State School. In the audience were my wife Pat, Dave, his wife Laura, and my grandchildren William and Helena.

Like at a previous institution, our names were called alphabetically, so I was near the end of the line. I was used to that. What I wasn't used to was thinking of myself as a college graduate. I, Donald E. Vitkus, was no longer a moron.

Beyond Belchertown

*"I'm a human services worker, and a Vietnam vet who can't own a gun.
I am an ex-husband, a husband, father, and grandfather.
And a former moron of Belchertown State School."*

"Hello, my name is Donald Vitkus," the presenter begins, holding his hands together at his waist, an apparent attempt not to fidget. He stands by an overhead projector. A bit over six feet tall and of medium weight, he is wearing a gray hoodie zipped halfway up to the neck of a navy blue T-shirt, and slightly rumpled khaki slacks. He is in his middle-sixties, his hair silvery gray and slightly receding. Beside him is a stack of transparencies, the screen behind him still dark.

"I don't remember my mother because the last time I saw her I was 27 days old. I was named after my father, but I don't remember him because he left my mother after she left me." He shifts back and forth on his feet. "They were never married, so that makes me a bastard."

Donald Vitkus is in this room at the invitation of the Massachusetts Department of Developmental Services. Seated before him around a horseshoe of conference tables are a dozen or so recently hired employees who will eventually be assigned to care for residents of group homes across the state. This session is part of their orientation.

Caring for individuals with developmental disabilities is now the speaker's occupation. Advocating for them is his mission. He is here to tell the trainees what it was like to grow up in an institution for the mentally handicapped in the middle of the twentieth century. Before his talk is over, some of them will cry.

The speaker snaps on the projector and places a transparency on the glass surface. "I lived in six different foster homes till I came here in 1949 when I was six years old." A grainy black-and-white image of an institutional brick building appears on the screen. There are bars on the windows.

"I grew up in buildings like this till I was 'paroled' at age 17."

He replaces the transparency with another. This one shows a starkly furnished room crammed with beds, maybe thirty of them, lined up so closely there doesn't appear to be room to walk between them. The room has a high ceiling, tall windows, and a radiator along one wall.

"I had my first birthday party when I turned 66. Until a few years ago, I hated Christmas, and never brushed my teeth. I sleep with the covers pulled over my head."

The next image is a document, but it is upside down. The presenter flips it over, but now it's crooked. He fumbles to straighten it, then allows time for those in the room to read what it says. It's a birth certificate with no father's name listed. Another transparency is a printed form with his mother's signature on it, turning him over to the care of the state.

These photos and records are from Belchertown State School, where Donald Vitkus grew up. The sprawling 864-acre site now lies vacant, its infrastructure crumbling, the residence halls boarded up and surrounded by overgrown bushes, weeds, and marked by 'No Trespassing' signs that warn of asbestos. Once populated by thousands of "retards," it is now the haunt of teens who explore the rotting buildings and the network of underground tunnels that connect them, with flashlights and smart phones, seeking ghostly thrills to post on Facebook.

"I'm a human services worker," Donald continues, "and a Vietnam vet who can't own a gun. I am an ex-husband, a husband, father, and grandfather. And a former moron of Belchertown State School."

He continues his stark narrative, and an hour or so later dozens of images and documents have appeared on the screen. Donald removes the final transparency and turns off the overhead projector. "Thank you for listening," he says.

For a moment, the only sound in the room is the whirring of the fan that continues in the projector. Then the clapping begins. Two women wipe their eyes. People remain seated because this is not the stuff of a standing ovation, but a long, respectful acknowledgement of what the trainees have heard for the last hour. Before they leave, several tell Donald how much they appreciate his story, and their own reasons for personal involvement—a friend, a neighbor, a relative who is afflicted with developmental disabilities.

Since earning his degree, Donald has appeared before a variety of audiences. In college classrooms he has talked to students of human services. He has spoken to high school Special Education students, self-advocates who are trying to find their way in life. When they ask questions, he answers with compassion, not condescension.

As Vice-President of Advocacy Network, Donald has traveled to Washington, D.C., to attend the annual conference of VOR (formerly Voice of the Retarded), a national organization that advocates for the care and human rights of people with intellectual and developmental disabilities. He served there on a panel discussion of "The 'R' Word" when the term "mental retardation" was transitioning to "developmental disabilities." He has visited Congressional offices to lobby for supportive legislation, making a special stop at the office of former U.S. Representative Patrick Kennedy of Rhode Island to thank the Kennedy family for their efforts on behalf of people with intellectual disabilities.

On Memorial Days, he has returned to the grounds of the former Belchertown State School for services honoring the 200 patients buried at "Turkey Hill," and members of the *Ricci Class* who have passed away since the institution closed. Through the efforts of the late Benjamin Ricci and Al Warner (the patient who peed in the paint while painting the superintendent's house), the cement markers that once identified the dead only by their patient numbers have been replaced with granite stones bearing names and dates. It is now a respectful burial ground, renamed the Warner Pine Grove Cemetery. Al Warner and his wife Agnes, also a Belchertown resident, were the last to be buried there.

Adjacent to their stone is marker #132, transferred from the site of Al's mother's grave at Worcester State Hospital.

Wherever he has spoken, Donald's focus has been on the dignity of persons with developmental disabilities, their right to be accepted, to learn and make choices to the best of their own ability. "People don't know how it used to be. They can't believe such a system existed," he says.

As a professional care giver, the person in the trenches feeding, assisting, and guiding individuals like those he grew up with—a perspective not shared by many—he has been a unique advocate. Despite the progress made in the decades since he was "Discharged from Placement" on June 13, 1963, Donald knows that abuse and neglect still exist in the system. Battles involving agencies like the Massachusetts Department of Developmental Services, privately contracted vendors, families, whistle blowers and advocates continue—often in court—across the United States.

In 2005, when Donald was a 62-year-old student at Holyoke Community College about to receive his Associate's Degree in human services, a newspaper reporter wrote: "Donald Vitkus has spent his life convincing himself that he is not a moron."

It is true. He teeters between determination and self-doubt. Despite years of therapy, despite all his accomplishments as worker, union man, Vietnam veteran, father and college student, the scars of Belchertown remain. Donald experienced the treatment of the mentally disabled as a "retard" during a dark period that many are unaware of and others would rather forget. But he cannot forget. "I never want us to return to those days," he says.

Donald Vitkus is, most definitely, not a moron.

Photos and Documents

The Commonwealth of Massachusetts
OFFICE OF THE SECRETARY
DIVISION OF VITAL STATISTICS
STANDARD CERTIFICATE OF BIRTH

PLACE OF BIRTH: Middlesex (County), Waltham (City or Town)
City or Town making this return: Waltham
Registered No. 521
No. 564 Main Street

1. **Full name of child:** Donald Everett Vitkus
2. **Sex:** m
3. **Color:** w
4. **Twin or Triplet?** one
5. **Born alive or stillborn:** alive
6. **Date of Birth:** May 12, 1943

FATHER
7. Full Name: —
8. Residence: —
9. Color or Race: —
10. Age at Time of This Birth: —
11. Place of Birth: —
12. Occupation: —

MOTHER
13. Maiden Name: Veronica Marcella Vitkus; Present Name: " " Vitkus
14. Residence, No. 564 Main Street, City or Town: Waltham, State: Mass.
15. Color or Race: W
16. Age at Time of This Birth: 20
17. Place of Birth: Cambridge, Mass.
18. Occupation: Factory worker

19. I hereby certify that I attended the birth of this child... information given was furnished by mother, related to this child as mother.

Signature of Attendant at Birth: Ludwig Kubin, M.D.
Address: Waltham
Date: —

20. Received at Office of City or Town Clerk: August 3, 1943
21. A True Copy Attest: Wm J. Laragan (Registrar)

I, the undersigned, hereby certify that I am the Registrar of Vital Records and Statistics; that as such I have custody of the records of birth, marriage and death required by law to be kept in my office; and I do hereby certify that the above is a true copy from said records. WITNESS my hand and the SEAL OF THE DEPARTMENT OF PUBLIC HEALTH at Boston on the date inscribed hereon:

MARCH 28, 1994

Elaine B. Trudeau
ELAINE B. TRUDEAU
Registrar

IT IS ILLEGAL TO ALTER OR REPRODUCE THIS DOCUMENT IN ANY MANNER

To Marion A. Joyce, Director,
    Division of Child Guardianship,
       Department of Public Welfare,
          State House, Boston.

June 8 1943

I hereby request that you receive and provide for the my } child _Donald Everett Vitkus_ who } is dependent upon public charity in accordance with the provisions of chapter 119, section 38, of the General Laws.

Veronica Vitkus { Parent

I hereby agree to pay to the Department of Public Welfare the sum of $3.00 per week, payable _____ in part reimbursement of the expense of supporting the above named child

Signed, _Veronica Vitkus_ { Parent

I desire that the above named child be brought up in the _Catholic_ faith.

Veronica Vitkus (Mother)

Accepted _June 8_ _____ 1943

Marion A. Joyce Director

5/20/43 - (MAC) Mrs. Beatty, Girls' Parole Visitor to office referring second _____ child born 5/12/43 to Veronica Vitkus. Mother returned frm her work that day and gave birth in rooming house to a child; then walked down two flights of stairs and tel'd Mrs. Quinn a former bdng mother in Waltham who arranged for ambulance to call for her and she and child were taken to the Waltham Hospital. On 5/2@ mother and child will be removed for convalescent care to TCH. She hopes to return to her defense work at the Clifford Mfg. Co. where she earns $24 a wk. Mother names Don Williams of Dracut,, a widower, 26 yrs old, without chn whom she met while living in Lowell wi mat. great aunt. He is in U.S. Navy on convoy duty. Mother expects to marry him. Mrs. Beatty also talked wi MPC re plcmnt of child. (NO)

6-8-43 - (MPC) Donald Everett received.

SUMMARY - (MPC) Donald, born 5-12-43, is the second _____ child of Veronica Vitkus, born 9-12-22 in Cambridge. Mother is to return to her job and will contribute towards the support of Donald. Donald was baptized at St. Joseph's Church, Boston, on 6-8-43. (AG)

6/30/43 - ____ JMcD reports: Boarding mother telephoned. Mother of Donald visited last Sunday. Mother apparently working and can only visit on Saturday or Sunday. If okay with Department, foster mother prefers mother visit on Sunday with permit from office as is customary. MJ approves plan providing this does not lead to any misunderstanding or complications.

10/19/43 - (EMJ) Mrs. Beatty, Visitor, Girls' Parole telephoned Veronica Vitkus is trying to decide whether she wishes to have Patricia placed to adoption. Same referred to LFM, Supervisor, AEM, visitor, and to (BAF) MPC.

                    Wrentham State School
                    Wrentham, Mass.

                                        June 6, 1946

Mrs. Marie A. Jack
Div. of Child Guardianship
Room 43, State House
Boston, Mass.

Dear Mrs. Jack:
    We wish to confirm the examination of Donald Vitkus in our Out Patient Clinic on June 5, 1946.

    In our mental examination Donald scored a mental age of 1 year and 3 months which gave him an I.Q. of .41. It is impossible to predict whether the boy is slow in starting because of some early nutritional deficiency and may pick up in later years, or whether the boy will remain on a rather low mental level with his I.Q. probably dropping still further.

    There is some indication that the child is what we call an accidental case with some possible cerebral involvement. The boy is unusually pale and frail. He walks slowly and awkwardly and has few words at this disposal. The knee jerks are active and pendulous.

    At the present time we suggest a physical examination including a blood count and an x-ray of his bones to exclude a possible anemia, or rickets. We would also suggest a check on his nutritional condition.

    In order to determine his further progress, re-examination in 2 years at this school is suggested.

                                        Very truly yours,

                                        C. Stanly Raymond
                                        Superintendent.

INFORMATION FOR CASE RECORD FOLDER

Name Vitkus Donald Everett   **Admission No.** 3394
(Name must be same throughout commitment paper)

Date of Admission July 13 1949   **Occupation:** None

Form of Commitment School   **If custodial, committed by**   Probate Court

Years in Massachusetts Life   **Years in United States**

If alien, port and date of entry

Date of Birth May 12 1943   **Birthplace** Waltham
(This is important)

Name of Father Unknown   **Birthplace** Unknown

Maiden name of Mother Veronica Vitkus   **Birthplace** Cambridge, Mass

Race Lithuanian   **Color** W   **Religion** R. Catholic   **Sex** male
(American is not a race.)   **Baptized** yes ? **1st Communion** no ?
Confirmed no ?

Grade reached in school before admission none   (If possible, give dates)

Place of last permanent residence at time of admission. (This means residence of parents if there are such. If not, then last place in community at admission.)

Roxbury , Mass .
City or Town   State

Citizenship: <u>Native-born.</u> Naturalized. Alien. Others. Unknown.

Economic Status: Dependent. Marginal. Comfortable. Unknown.
(Record family if patient is a minor.)

Use of Alcohol: <u>Abstinent.</u> Temperate. Intemperate. Unknown.

Marital Condition: Single. Married. Widowed. Divorced. Separated. Unknown.

Is patient a United States Veteran? (underline one) (a) Yes; (b) No; (c) Unknown.

Physical condition on admission: Good   **Furnished:** Home. State.

Admission Note: Donald was brought for admission by Mrs Craig O.C.G. & sent to Mrs H. He is 6 yr old I.Q. 41 Maternal grandfather said to be below par mentally & alcoholic. Mother committed to Lancaster. State furnished.

If com. paper returned for correction, we need name & address of nearest relative.

M. D. Form A-2

SOCIAL SECURITY NO. 034-32-2578

........................BELCHERTOWN STATE SCHOOL........................
NAME OF INSTITUTION

CASE RECORD FOLDER

NAME: Vitkus, Donald Everett   **ADMISSION NO.** 3394

Date of admission. July 13, 1949

Form of commitment. School   **If custodial, committed by**   **Probate Court.**
Sec. 47, Chap. 123, General Laws
Age at admission 6 yrs., 2 mos., 1 day

Years in Massachusetts. Life   **Years in United States.** Life

If alien, port and date of entry.

Date of Birth May 12, 1943   **Place of birth** Waltham, Mass.

Name of father Unknown   **Place of birth of father.** Unknown
              Don Williams (Alleged)
Maiden name of mother Veronica Witkus   **Place of birth of mother.** Cambridge, Mass.

Race. Unknown   **Color.** White   **Religion** R. Catholic   **Sex** Male
                                                            Baptized
Probable Cause.   1st Communion

  Congenital

  Acquired

Grade reached in school before admission. None

Mental Age.

7⁶   9²   12⁰
.62(7/15/55) .67(4/26/57) .80(4/3/59)

              3⁴   4⁴   5⁴   6⁶   7²   7²
Intelligence quotient. .54(7/18/49) .60(7/6/50) .65(7/16/51) .71(7/22/52) .70(7/10/53) .65(6/28/54)
                          I.Q. and date I.Q. and date I.Q. and date I.Q. and date I.Q. and date I.Q. and date

Provisional Diagnosis. Clinical: Familial (30)
Final Diagnosis. Psychological: ~~Moron (6)~~ Borderline 4/14/59 (HAT)

Discharge, date of. June 13, 1963   Mental Deficiency, Mild, Familial or
                                                                      Hereditary
  How discharged. Disc. from Placement of 6/28/60
  (Specify "on visit," "parole" "not returned" "escape," etc.)

  Condition when discharged. C.S.S.

Death, date of.

  Cause of death.

      Primary

      Contributory.

  Autopsy   Yes   No
Place of burial

PRESENTED AT STAFF MEETING JULY 20, 1949 (RAK)

D. M. D. Form A-81

28163

DESCRIPTIVE APPLICATION FOR ADMISSION TO
BELCHERTOWN STATE SCHOOL
NAME OF INSTITUTION

Application No. 3526   Admission No.

Issued 4/27/49   June 8, 1949

In order that this paper may be properly executed, it is advisable, and in most instances, necessary to consult a physician. Please answer all questions with as full details as possible.

1. Applicant's name ~~VITKUS,~~ DONALD Vitkus alley
2. Residence Glenside Ave Pinehurst
3. Date of birth May 12 1943
4. Place of birth Waltham Mass
5. Name of father Don Williams alley —   Maiden name of mother Veronica Vitkus
6. Birthplace of parents. Father unknown   Mother Cambridge Mass
7. Age of parents. Father 1917   Mother 12-12-22
8. Citizenship of parents. Father   Mother native
   (native born or naturalized) unknown
9. Have the parents a legal residence in Massachusetts? no
10. Applicant, full term or premature birth? unknown
11. Was birth prolonged, premature, instrumental or unusual in any way? mother worked this pregnancy — On day child was born mother had worked all day — returned to room house — delivered self of child — walked down two flights of stairs to tel. to former fos mother, who called ambulance and girl & baby were removed to Waltham hospital.
12. At what age was peculiarity first noticed? 1 yr.
13. In what manner did peculiarity manifest itself? Did not attempt to walk — no notice ship
14. Began to walk at what age? 1/45
15. Began to talk at what age? 8/45
16. At what age did first teeth appear? 1/44 2 teeth
17. If there is any peculiarity or defect of speech, describe. no
18. Soil or wet bed? no
19. Soil or wet day clothing? no
20. Can he dress himself? yes
21. Can he feed himself? yes

22. Is there any defect of sight or hearing? *No*
23. Is the child now, or has the child ever been subject to epilepsy (fits, convulsions, seizures or fainting spells?) *no*
24. Is there any paralysis or infirmity of extremities? *no*
25. Is the child active and vigorous, or slow and listless? *active*
26. What usual diseases of childhood has applicant had? (Measles, scarlet fever, whooping-cough, etc.) *circumcision 6/44*
27. What unusual diseases of childhood, if any? (Infant paralysis, meningitis, encephalitis, etc.) *none*
28. Has there ever been any disease, affecting general health or nutrition, such as heart disease, tuberculosis, kidney disease, etc.? *no*
29. Wasserman, plus or minus, if known. *neg*
30. What is condition of general health, at present? *good*
31. Sense of taste. Particular or does he eat without discrimination? *Particular*
32. Sight Does he recognize color and what colors? *yes*
33. Does he recognize form? Square, circle, etc. *yes*
34. Does he notice pictures and describe contents? *yes*
35. Does he comprehend and obey commands? *yes*
36. Can he do errands? *no*
37. Does he know letters? *no*
38. Does he read? Equivalent of what grade? *no*
39. Does he count? How high? *no*
40. If in school, what grade and age? *Has not attended*
41. If not in school, in what grade and at what age did he leave?

42. Mental age and intelligence quotient, if known? M.A. 1.3 J.2 41
43. Has he repeated grades? no
44. Has he attended special class, opportunity or coaching class? no
45. Has he been a behavior problem? Truant? Theft? Untruthful? Abnormal sex interest no
    or sex offences? Illegitimacy and how many? ——
    Any court record, or institutional care? no
46. Indicate any definite character traits such as being:—

    Egotistical   ✓Seclusive
    Quarrelsome   Social
    Passionate   Impulsive
    Vain   ✓Emotionally unstable
    Selfish   Ill-tempered
    Disobedient   Resentful of authority
    ✓Suggestible   ✓Over-affectionate
    Stubborn   Cruel

    (Underscore traits characteristic of child)

47. Describe any habit.
        none

48. Ever earned wages, and at what employment?
        no

49. If not a wage earner, does he assist about the work at home?
        no

50. At time of child's birth, what was the general physical condition and health of father and mother?   unknown

51. Was there any known peculiarity in the family of the applicant? That is, were any of the grandparents, parents, uncles, aunts, brothers, sisters, or cousins blind, deaf, or insane, or afflicted with any infirmity of body or mind, epilepsy, fits, convulsions, spasms, or fainting spells, alcoholism, drug addiction, syphilis or other venereal disease, chronic heart, lung or kidney disease?

mat. gra fa - excessive alcoholic - Below par mentally
mother - Com't'd to Lancaster 8/38 as shiftless child - was pregnant at time of commit - court record for stealing from stores & school truant C.A. 16.8 M.A. 11.5 J.2 84 (while at Lancaster) - Grossly immoral

D. M. D. Form A-5

BELCHERTOWN STATE SCHOOL
Name of Institution

Admitted to Nurs II

PATIENT'S WARD CARD

N. B.—THIS card must always accompany every patient in all changes from ward to ward and attendants on ward are responsible for the same. The card must be returned to the office when the patient leaves the institution. When necessary, a new one can be obtained from the medical department.

Name **Vitkus Donald Everett** No. **3394**
Admitted **2:00 P.M.** Hour **July 13** Date **1949** Age **6** Height **3' 11"**
Date of Birth **May 12, 1943**
Weight **46½ pounds** Eyes **Hazel** Hair **Blonde**

Personal peculiarities and habits. Cautions as to escape, Self-injury, Violence, etc.

Religion **R. Catholic** Baptized **yes** Confirmed **No**
First Communion ~~No~~ yes **1-1-55** How Supported **State** Clothing **State**
Remarks

R. A. Kinmonth M.D.
Admitting Physician.

DATES OF TRANSFER.

N. B.—The Ward Attendant will in every case of transfer, sign his or her name plainly in the space opposite to the date hereby certifying that patient's clothing has been transferred to the ward named, and the Attendant receiving patient will personally see that such clothing is received at the same time with patient.

Date	Ward	Date	Ward
July 13, 1949	to Ward Nurs #2 MB	Jan. 29, 1959	to Ward Camp Chesterfield
July 21, 1949	to Ward F OM	Aug 9, 1959	to Ward Voc JPS
May 19, 1955	to Ward D mmH Bldg changed	Aug 16, 1959	to Ward D ABB
July 28, 1957	to Ward Voc JPS Camp Chesterfield	June 28, 1960	to Ward Parole
Aug 4, 1957	to Ward J JPS	June 13, 1963	to Ward DIX, N.Y.
Oct 21, 1957	to Ward M RPS	193 .	to Ward
March 29, 1958	to Ward K GEB	193 .	to Ward
Nov. 3, 1958	to Ward M RM	193 .	to Ward
Jan 7, 1959	to Ward Visit (to Mercy Hosp)	193 .	to Ward
Jan. 14, 1959	to Ward M JPS	193 .	to Ward

PATIENT'S SIGNATURE	VITKUS, Donald Everett			#23-3394		
RESIDENCE	BELCHERTOWN STATE SCHOOL					
MOTHER'S MAIDEN NAME	Veronica Vitkus					
FATHER'S NAME	Don Williams (Alleged)					

Vitkus, Donald Everett   #23-3394

Date of Admission: July 13, 1949
Diagnosis: Mentally retarded
Age: 16   Date of Birth: May 12, 1943
Birthplace: Waltham, Mass.
Occupation: None
Nationality: Lithuanian
Height: 5' 11"   Weight: 160 lbs.
Hair: Blonde   Eyes: Hazel
Build: Large   Comp.: Fair
Mustache: Yes   No

INSTITUTIONAL HISTORY

August 7, 1953

NAME	Number	Institution	Date of Admission	Date of Discharge	Diagnosis
VITKUS, Donald E.	#23-3394	B.S.S.	7/13/49		

You'll Like it Here

BELCHERTOWN STATE SCHOOL
NAME OF INSTITUTION

Name Vitkus, Donald Everett   **No.** 3394   **Year No.** 1949

ADMISSION NOTE:
July 13, 1949. Donald was brought for admission by Miss Craig of the D.C.G. and was sent to Nursery II. He is 6 years old – I.Q. .41. Maternal grandfather said to be below par mentally and alcoholic. Mother committed to Lancaster. State furnished.
(Nursery II) (RAK:VMP)

FIRST STAFF NOTE:
July 20, 1949: This patient was seen at Staff Meeting today for the first time since admission to the Institution. When interviewed he was pleasant, cooperative and answered all questions courteously. Is living in Nursery II at the present time and will be transferred to "F" building shortly.
Diagnoses made today, Clinical: Mental Deficiency, Familial Type
Psychological: Moron (RAK:GIL)
Case presented by Dr. Wilson
(Nursery II)

TRANSFER NOTE:
July 21, 1949: This patient today was transferred from Nursery II to "F" building. (IMW:GIL)
(F Building)

NOTE:
August 24, 1949 Donald was chasing Edward Putala from the dayhall to the hall. Just as Donald reached the door, Edward Putala slammed it. Donald's right index finger got caught in the door and he received a ½ inch deep, ½ inch long circular cut. ½ inch below fingertip extending from volar to dorsal including nail of right index finger. Two sutures were used, and letter was sent to family and report to D. M. N.
(F Building) (IMW:JTR)

NOTE:
October 13, 1949: Donald lives in "F" Building. He is well behaved, quiet, and clean. Occasionally he has temper fits. He attends kindergarden, entertainments, and church services. He receives no mail and has no visitors.
(F Building) (IMW:BJB)

SICKNESS NOTE:
November 1, 1949: This patient has had a reaction to inoculation and is receiving treatment for a gastric upset. (IMW:GIL)
(F Building)

CORRECTION NOTE:
December 1, 1949: This boy has been posted from the Movies for being disobedient to an Attendant. (IMW:GIL)
(F Building)

SECOND STAFF NOTE:
December 28, 1949. This patient was seen at Staff Meeting today for the second time since admission to the Institution. When interviewed he was rather timid, and not too much could be gained from interrogation. Is living in "F" Building at the present time and is attending kindergarten classes at the School.
Diagnoses made today, Clinical: Familial Mental Deficiency
Psychological: Moron
Case presented by Dr. Wilson. (HAT:VMP)
(F Building)

August 22, 1951. Donald is being cared for in "F" Building and attends school classes. Hygiene - clean. Conduct - he is one of Peck's bad boys, sometimes good, sometimes bad. Does not receive mail or visitors and does not go on vacation.

August 20, 1952. Donald is being cared for in "F" Building and attends school classes. Hygiene - good. Conduct - very naughty; in need of constant supervision. Does not receive mail or visitors and does not go on vacation.

NOTE:
January 13, 1950: Donald has adjusted well in "F" Building. He is clean, quiet, and nice. He attends church, school, and entertainments. He has had no visitors.
(F Building) (IMW:BJB)

NOTE:
April 13, 1950: This quiet, clean and well behaved "F" Building boy attends school, church, and entertainments. He has had no visitors.
(F Building) (IMW:BJB)

1950 YEARLY SCHOOL REPORT: Donald is interested in Sense Training class and does rather good work. He speaks clearly and makes conversation. He is rather selfish and likes attention.
(F Building) (BSH:SAH)

BELCHERTOWN STATE SCHOOL

Name Vitkus, Donald Everett   No. 3394   Year No. 1950

YEARLY PHYSICAL EXAMINATION:
July 20, 1950. Donald is well nourished and cooperative. He is tidy. Receives no mail or visitors. Attends school classes.
Physical Examination: Age - 7 yrs. Height - 50". Weight - 61 lbs. Pupils are equal and react to light and accomodation. Deviation of the nasal septum to the left. Bilateral small palpable lymph nodes posterior triangle of neck. Heart - A2 > P2 A2 snapping quality. Quality good, sinus rythmn. No murmurs. Blood pressure 90/60 - 50. Lungs, abdomen, skin, and extremities negative. Deep reflexes equal. Patella reflexes hyperactive. No hernia or other positive findings. (RAK:JEO:VMP)
(F Building)

YEARLY PHYSICAL EXAMINATION:
August 22, 1951. Donald is being cared for in "F" Building and attends school classes. Hygiene - clean. Conduct - he is one of Peck's bad boys, sometimes good, sometimes bad. Does not receive mail or visitors and does not go on vacation.
Physical Examination: Age - 8 yrs., height - 4' 5", weight - 67 1/2 lbs. Eyes, ears, nose and throat - unremarkable. Mucosa of good color. Tonsils present. Glands - one palpable lymph node, right submaxillary area. Heart - rate 92 and regular; sounds unremarkable; P2 greater than A2; M1 split; no murmurs. Blood pressure 108/62. Lungs - clear to percussion and auscultation. Abdomen - no masses or tenderness found. Skin - clear. Extremities - unremarkable. C.N.S. - knee jerks equal and active. G.U. - testes either very small or undescended; a cord feeling like the spermatic cord could be palpated but the testis could not be identified definetely. Well nourished and well developed white boy in no evident ill health. (IMW:RGH:VMP)
(F Building)

T. B. X-RAY SURVEY:
November 2, 1951 : This patient was examined in the mass chest x-ray survey on July 24, 1951 and was found to be x-ray negative for tuberculosis.(HMT:WE)
(F Building)

YEARLY PHYSICAL EXAMINATION:
August 20, 1952. Donald is being cared for in "F" Building and attends school classes. Hygiene - good. Conduct - very naughty; in need of constant supervision. Does not receive mail or visitors and does not go on vacation.
Physical Examination: Age - 9 yrs., height - 4' 8 3/4", weight - 70 lbs. Eyes - symmetrical; EOM good; pupils react to L & A. Ears - clear; drums intact. Nose - clear; septum deviated to left. Mouth - clear; Throat - clear. Glands - lymph, none palpable; thyroid, not palpably enlarged. Heart - rate 84; heart sounds regular and normal. Blood pressure 104/56. Lungs - resonant on both sides; breath sounds and vocal resonance well transmitted. Abdomen - flat, soft, symmetrical; no palpable masses; no hernia. Skin - scalp clear; body clear; feet clear. Extremities - no deformities; gait normal. C.N.S. - deep reflexes hyperactive. G.U. - external genitalia adequately developed. Well nourished and well developed. Quiet and cooperative. (PKF:FTR:VMP)
(F Building)

HINTON TEST:
August 20, 1953. Negative. (IMW:VMP)
(F Building)

TUBERCULOSIS X-RAY SURVEY:
December 1, 1953. This patient was examined in the mass chest x-ray survey on September 9, 1953 and was found to be x-ray negative for tuberculosis. (LOF:HPM)
(F Building)

BELCHERTOWN STATE SCHOOL
Name of Institution

Name VITKUS, Donald Everett   **No.** 23-3394   **Year No.** 1955-

NOTE:
July 1, 1955. This patient was found on examination to be unfit for active sports.
(D Building)   (LOF:HPM)

1955 YEARLY SCHOOL REPORT: Donald's attitude and interest in class are both commendable. His reading and spelling are excellent and other work is very good, including handwork. He has a very good singing voice and enjoys singing class. His conduct is always excellent.   (BSH:WE)
(D Building)

NOTE:
August 4, 1955. Donald is cared for in "D" Building. Hygiene good and conduct fair. Receives no mail; has no visitors and does not go out on vacations. Is not employed.
(D Building)   (GLE:JWW:HH)

TRANSFER NOTE:
February 7, 1956. Donald received a contusion of the left side of his abdomen when he fell off a sled and bumped into a water pipe in "D" Building yard. Transferred to the Hospital for observation.
(Hospital)   (PKF:SS)

TRANSFER NOTE:
February 13, 1956. Patient this day discharged from the Hospital back to Building. Recovered. (PKF:HPM)
(D Building)

CLINICAL CONFERENCE NOTE:
March 1, 1956. This patient was admitted to the Hospital February 7, 1956. Diagnosis: Observation - trauma of abdomen. Discharged from the Hospital February 13, 1956. Case presented by Dr. Frankowski. (LOF:HPM)
(D Building)

NOTE:
July 20, 1956. Donald is cared for in "D" Building. His hygiene is very good. No mail, visitors, or vacations. (MVO:HPM)
(D Building)

1956 YEARLY SCHOOL REPORT: Donald is ready for group three in school. He is an eager interested pupil who likes to know the "Why" and "How" of things. He has done well in all classes and been well-behaved. Very rarely he shows a violent temper but his anger is short lived. (BSH:AEP)
(D Building)

SICKNESS NOTE:
March 8, 1957. This patient has developed mumps. Board of Health and ▮▮▮▮▮ notified by letter. (MVO:HPM)
(D Building)

STAFF NOTE:
July 3, 1957. This case was considered at Staff today regarding an Institutional Survey to determine the suitability of patients for community placement. It was decided that this patient is unsuitable for such a placement. (LOF:HPM)
(D Building)

1957 YEARLY SCHOOL REPORT: Donald made some progress in Group III this year. At the third grade level did good in reading and language and fair in other subjects, does well in all other activities. Behavior is good. (WJL:AMD)
(D Building)

NOTE:
July 24, 1957. Donald is cared for in "D" Building and attends school when in session. Hygiene and conduct are good. Does not receive mail, have visitors, or go on vacations.
(D Building) (MVO:AED)

ON VACATION NOTE:
July 28, 1957. Patient this day went on vacation to Camp Chesterfield. Due to return August 4, 1957. (AED)
(On Vacation)

FROM VACATION NOTE:
August 4, 1957. Patient this day returned from vacation. (HPM)
(D Building)

TRANSFER NOTE:
August 4, 1957. About 5:40 P.M. Donald thrust his left hand through a pane of glass and received two severe lacerations and several minor superficial abrasions. There were a few brisk bleeders in the lacerations. Tourniquet and sterile covering applied at the scene and boy moved to the Hospital. Bleeders checked with hemostats. Examination revealed (1) the 5th extensor tendon to be completely severed and the segments retracted, (2) nearly complete severing of the 4th extensor tendon. The Assistant Superintendent was consulted and Dr. Adolf Franz was called. Dr. Franz sutured the tendons and sheaths and closed the lacerations with sutures. One suture was placed to hold a small skin flap in place over one of the small abrasions. Demeral sedation and local novocaine infiltration used. Sterile dressing and forearm splint applied. Boy admitted to the Hospital for continued care. Correspondent, Mr. V. Leonardo, being notified by letter. (BFB:HPM)
(Hospital)

CLINICAL CONFERENCE NOTE:
September 1, 1957. This patient was admitted to the Hospital August 4, 1957. Diagnosis: Laceration of left hand. Case presented by Dr. Brown. (LOF:HPM)
(Hospital)

TRANSFER NOTE:
October 1, 1957. Patient this day was returned to D Bldg. from the Hospital. Wounds healed by first intention, complete extension and nearly complete flexion of fingers.
(D Building) (BFB:HHH)

CLINICAL CONFERENCE NOTE:
October 1, 1957. This patient was admitted to the Hospital August 4, 1957. Diagnosis: Laceration of left hand. Discharged from the Hospital October 1, 1957. Case presented by Dr. Brown. (LOF:HPM)
(D Building)

TRANSFER NOTE:
October 21, 1957. Donald was transferred to "M" Building. He is a large boy, has temper tantrums, and female employees are afriad of him when he is disturbed.
(M Building) (BFB:AED)

ACCIDENT NOTE:
January 2, 1958. Donald accidentally cut his left knee when he bumped into a bed. One stitch was required to close the wound. (JWW:AED)
(M Building)

D. M. H. Form A-61

Belchertown State School
Name of Institution

ACCIDENT AND INJURY REPORT

WARD II Bldg

NAME Donald Vitkus   HOUR 5:30 P.M.   DATE Aug. 4, '57

Give full account of accident, injury, suicide, sudden death, etc.
Name all witnesses. Pass Report to Supervisor at once. Donald Vitkus, after an argument with several other patients, left the dining hall where he was eating. In the hall, he was evidently so angry that he put his hand through a pane of glass. This resulted in several severe cuts on his hand and wrist ranging from one to two inches. Supervisor was called and patient taken to hospital.

Signed .... Attendant
David V. Reynolds   Nurse

INVESTIGATION OF SUPERVISOR

I have fully investigated the circumstances of the above ... accident ... and have examined the patient and find that Donald Vitkus had several bad gashes on his left hand. He was taken to the hospital clinic where Dr. Brown treated him.

There were no witnesses to this accident — Donald got into an argument & blows in the Dining Room. They pushed by a chair & threw it across the room — he was then put out of the Dining Room & told to stand in the Hall — a few minutes later he raised the door and [illegible] that is well [illegible]

Hour 5:45 p.m.   Date August 4, 1957   Signed Frances P. Smol, Supervisor

REPORT TO PHYSICIAN AT ONCE

This was reported to Dr. **Bessie F. Brown**
on **August 4, 1957** by **Miss Frances Smola** at about **5:40 P.M.**
    (Date)   (Time of Day)

Medical care started by Dr. **Bessie F. Brown**
on **August 4, 1957** at about **5:45 P.M.**
    (Date)   (Time of Day)

The resulting injuries were as follows: **Left hand: (1) About 1 3/4 inch laceration on dorsal metacarpal area with extensor tendon and sheath of 4th digit severed except for a small bundle of fibers. (2) About 2½ inch laceration around carpo-ulnar area with extensor tendon of 5th digit completely severed and segments retracted. (3) Few minor superficial abrasions. Several brisk venous bleeders in lacerations.**

The casualty was witnessed by **No witnesses.**

The responsibility for the injury has been placed as follows **Accidental injury resulting from outburst of temper and poor judgment.**

Action was taken by the Superintendent as follows **Tourniquet and sterile covering applied at scene and patient moved to B.S.S. Hospital. Seen by M.D. at once and bleeding checked with hemostats. Surgical Consultant, Dr. Adolf Frans was consulted and he came to the B.S.S. and operated on the boy. Ligated bleeders, sutured 4th and 5th extensor tendons and sheaths, closed the lacerations with sutures, forearm splint, sedation, antibiotics, etc. Forms - D.M.H. A61 and 36. Correspondent, a friend, notified by letter.**

Recommendations to prevent similar occurences in the future **Accidental injury.**

                                                                                    , M.D.
                                                                              Superintendent

BELCHERTOWN STATE SCHOOL
Name of Institution

Name VITKUS, Donald Everett   **No.** 23-3394   **Year No.** 1958

TRANSFER NOTE:
March 29, 1958. This patient and ▬▬▬▬▬ were transferred to "K" Building seclusion today because they ganged up on another patient and gave him a beating.
(K Building)   (JWW:AED)

TRANSFER NOTE:
March 30, 1958. Donald was returned to "M" Building at 4:00 P.M. today and will be continued on post.
(M Building)   (JWW:AED)

1958 YEARLY SCHOOL REPORT: Donald made very good progress in group IV this year. Has good comprehension of his work and is interested in gaining general knowledge. Reading comprehension is good at a fifth grade level. Did well in other subjects at a fourth grade level. Does fairly well in music, bym, and manual training classes. Shows little mechanical aptitude. Did well in other subjects, in cooking class. Conduct is very good.
(M Building)   (WJL:HHH)

NOTE:
July 17, 1958. Donald is cared for in "M" Building and goes to school classes. Hygiene clean. Conduct, has a few bad temper moments, but of late very good. No visitors, no vacations. Age 15 yrs. Height 5'11½". Weight 160 lbs.   (HJL:HHH)
(M Building)

CORRECTION NOTE:
September 11, 1958. This "M" Building patient was caught smoking in bed. He refused to answer any questions regarding where he got the match or cigarette. Placed in strong room. Posted for one month. Later threatened suicide and was banging his head against the wall. To prevent self-injury, he was given Thorazine, 50 mgm., I.M.   (LJL:AED)
(M Building)

TRANSFER NOTE:
December 21, 1958. This patient transferred to the Hospital with a diagnosis of effusion into left knee joint caused by trauma. His condition was complicated by an allergic reaction to merthiolate manifested by a morbilliform rash, measle-like in type, not involving foot, soles, hands and not presenting the picture which is characteristic for scarlet fever. There was albumen in his urine, the temperatures are still spiking up to 103. Radiological examination of both knee joints in different planes revealed a massive effusion into the left knee joint and a partly lifted tubercle of the tibia probably due to pull from the tendon leading to the patella. Since both sides give almost an identical picture where the tuberosity of the tibias are concerned we should consider a condition which is known as Schlatter characteristically appearing in juveniles bilateral often asymptomatic and brought to attention by trauma or infection. This skin condition has cleared up and patient was taken off all medication until it was definitely known that the merthiolate was the offender. The knee condition is still causing spiking temperatures. The entire left knee has been immobilized by a long splint. Elastic bandages have been carefully applied, ice packs to knee.   (HJL:RBC)
(Hospital)

CLINICAL CONFERENCE NOTE:
January 6, 1959. This patient was admitted to the Hospital December 21, 1958. This boy fell, apparently on the ice while skating, and showed a swelling of the prepatellar fat pad and bursa which became acute, inflamed, and swollen. He showed a spiking temperature. Four ounces of thick, creamy pus were aspirated. X-ray showed a lifting of the tuberosity of the tibia, but an x-ray of the other knee joint showed the same condition. This boy also showed a skin allergy, apparently to merthiolate, with a morbilliform rash resembling measles. (EJF:HPM)
(Hospital)

ON VISIT NOTE:
January 7, 1959. Patient this day went out on visit to Mercy Hospital, Springfield. No relatives to be notified. (HAT:HPM)
(On Visit)

NOTE:
January 8, 1959. Written operative permission sent to Mercy Hospital today. (HAT:HPM)
(On Visit)

FROM VISIT NOTE:
January 14, 1959. Patient was returned from Mercy Hospital in Springfield with a wide open incision extending over the lateral area of the knee joint. Iodoform one half inch strip packing was removed; fresh granulation tissue is appearing; the lesion was again packed with iodoform strip and Balsam of Peru was added, the surrounding skin area of the entire knee covered with Baciguent ointment, sterile dressing and elastic bandage applied. Patient still on Panmycin 250 mg. every six hours, multivitamins, and diet rich in calories especially proteins.

This patient has not had visits from his relatives (foster parents) for the past nine years and the Social Worker (Miss Meyer) has been consulted.

Another evaluation of his mental and intelligence status has been requested.
(Hospital) (HJL:HPM)

NOTE:
January 29, 1959. Patient this day statistically transferred to "D" Building in order to screen low grades from relatively bright patients. Presently in Hospital.
(Hospital) (HJL:SS)

CLINICAL CONFERENCE NOTE:
February 3, 1959. Donald was admitted to the Hospital December 21, 1958. As reported previously, patient was hospitalized for suppurative arthritis of the left knee which started with a bursitis. This patient was removed to Mercy Hospital, Springfield, Mass. and the wound was drained by Dr. LaMarche. He was then returned one week later to our Hospital for convalescence. A rash developed, before he went to Mercy Hospital. Since the culture from the wound showed Beta-hemolytic streptococci, Dr. Ludwig thinks that this patient had scarlatina even before the operation. Patient is improving on treatment. Case presented by Dr. Ludwig. (EJF:HPM)
(Hospital)

TRANSFER NOTE:
March 26, 1959. Patient has been discharged from the Hospital and transferred to "D" Building after completed secondary healing of the wide incision at the left lateral knee.

The pyodermia was secondary and most likely contracted on the ward. Sterile dressing technique and Vioform ointment resulted in a spontaneous subsidence.

The function of the knee is satisfactory and will probably regain full capacity within a few weeks. (HJL:HPM)
(D Building)

CLINICAL CONFERENCE NOTE:
April 7, 1959. The surgical scar has healed and the skin condition was under control. Patient discharged from the Hospital to his dormitory March 26, 1959. Case presented by Dr. Ludwig. (EJF:HPM)
(D Building)

ON VACATION NOTE:
August 9, 1959. Patient this day went on vacation to Camp Chesterfield. Due to return August 16, 1959. (HHH)
(On Vacation)

NOTE:
July 15, 1959. Donald is cared for in D Building. No mail or visitors. Goes on vacation to Camp Chesterfield. He is employed. Age 16 yrs.
(D Building) (HJL:FVS)

PHYSICAL EXAMINATION:
June 23, 1960. This patient, Donald Vitkus, is so far in excellent general physical condition. He is suffering from a mild case of acne vulgaris, primarily involving the chestwall - Acnomel Cream should control this condition. He is, however, at present time being treated for Pediculosis pubis and therefore not fit for parole, to go out, Monday 27, 1960. The social worker, Miss Johnson, was notified.
(D Building) (HJL:FVS)

This patient has not had visits from his relatives (foster parents) for the past nine years and the Social Worker (Miss Meyer) has been consulted.
Another evaluation of his mental and intelligence status has been requested.
(Hospital) (HJL:HPM)

NOTE:
January 29, 1959. Patient this day statistically transferred to "D" Building in order to screen low grades from relatively bright patients. Presently in Hospital.
(Hospital) (HJL:SS)

NOTE:
July 15, 1959. Donald is cared for in D Building. No mail or visitors. Goes on vacation to Camp Chesterfield. He is employed. Age 16 yrs.
(D Building) (HJL:FVS)

PHYSICAL EXAMINATION:
June 23, 1960. This patient, Donald Vitkus, is so far in excellent general physical condition. He is suffering from a mild case of acne vulgaris, primarily involving the chestwall - Acnomel Cream should control this condition. He is, however, at present time being treated for Pediculosis pubis and therefore not fit for parole, to go out, Monday 27, 1960. The social worker, Miss Johnson, was notified.
(D Building) (HJL:FVS)

BELCHERTOWN STATE SCHOOL
Name of Institution

Name VITKUS, Donald Everett   **No.** 23-3394   **Year No.** 1959

FROM VACATION NOTE:
August 16, 1959. Patient this day returned from Camp Chesterfield - only an absence period of 7 days. (SS)
(D Building)

1959 YEARLY SCHOOL REPORT: Donald did very well in Group IV this year. Has shown much interest in his school work and his academic work is at a fifth and sixth grade level. While he was in the hospital several weeks he did exceptionally well in keeping up with his studies. Has good general knowledge and is alert to the current news. Comprehends new work easily and shows reasoning ability. Does well in music class. Follows directions well and displays good sportsmanship in "Gym" class. Work is only fair in manual training. He is in his glory in cooking class. Neat and clean about his work and follows directions well. Recently joined the printing class and shows much interest in the work. Conduct is very good. Has an agreeable disposition.
(D Building)   (WJL:JAC)

NOTE:
June 15, 1960. Dormitory physician brought up problem that this boy, recently graduated from school, has an I.Q. of .80. He is, however, only 17. Social Service have been considering problem; they can hardly place him before he is 18. They state the best placement for a boy like this would be a hospital bus boy. Our Supervisor of Nurses will therefore place him to work in the Infirmary that he may receive this type of training. (EJF:HPM)
(D Building)

ON PAROLE NOTE:
June 28, 1960. Patient placed on parole today with - Sister Superior, Our Lady of Providence Home for Children, Riverdale Road, West Springfield, Mass.
(On Parole)   (LOF:SS)

1960 YEARLY SCHOOL REPORT: Donald made good academic progress in Group IV this year. His rate of progress was not as fast this year as it was during the previous school year. Has good general knowledge and fairly good reasoning ability. Likes to sing and did well in music class. Made satisfactory progress in beginners piano lessons. Showed much interest and made good progress in printing class. Does fairly well using hand tools in manual training class. His conduct in school has been very good. Has an agreeable disposition. He is in the graduation class of 1960. (WJL:JAC)
(D Building)(Now on Parole)

DISCHARGE NOTE:
June 13, 1963. Donald was today discharged from Placement. (LPB:SMcD)
(Discharged)

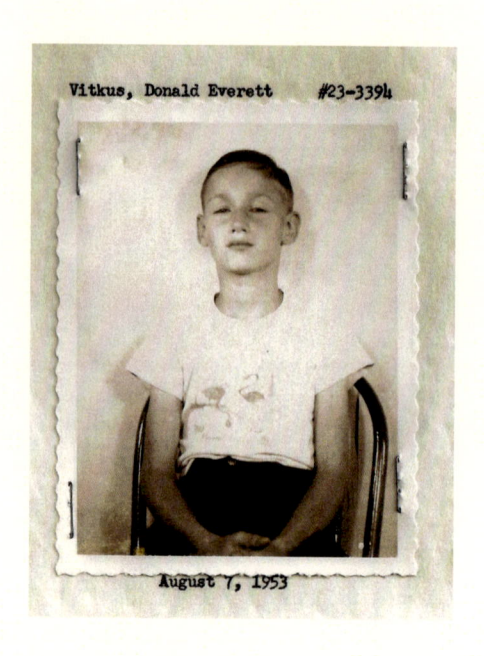

These "runaway shots" from Donald's Belchertown file, provided to police to track down escaped patients, show him at ages 10, 14, and 17.

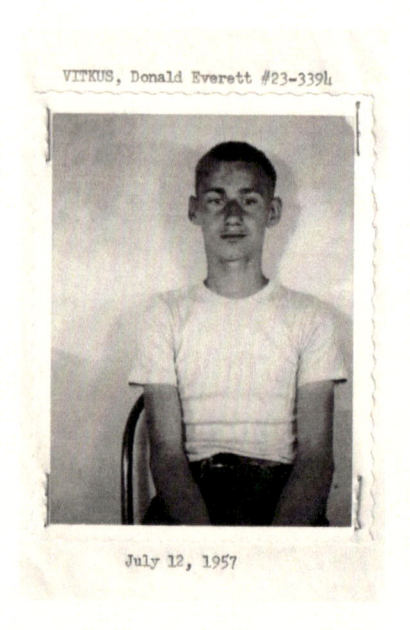

Donald climbed the stairs of the Administration Building to be admitted to Belchertown State School on July 13, 1949. He was six years old.

The cupola clock on the top of the Administration Building stopped, frozen in time, after Belchertown State School closed in 1992.

The remaining ward buildings are boarded up and posted with No Trespassing *and* Danger Asbestos *warning signs.*

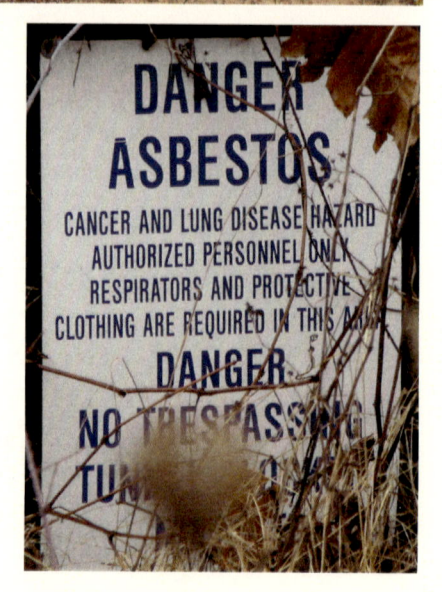

Boarded up cottages where some former attendants and employees resided on the grounds. Female patients were required to do the housekeeping in these homes.

Giant key rings and locked doors are common at Belchertown.

Attendants controlled the movement of patients with their rings of keys. Keys meant authority.

Courtesy Springfield Newspapers

Donald and his "Escape Committee" friends arranged their getaways through first floor windows like this one on a ward building. Visible on the brickwork to the left side of the window frame are brackets that held the exterior jail-like bars. As a patient, Donald believed that the brackets were never removed as a reminder that "... they could put the bars back at any time."

SCHOOL DAYS — This file photo shows a typical classroom in the School Building. It was probably taken in the early 1930s.

As everywhere on the grounds, students in the school building were separated by sex. This photo, dated from the 1930's, shows a girls' classroom. Courtesy Springfield Newspapers

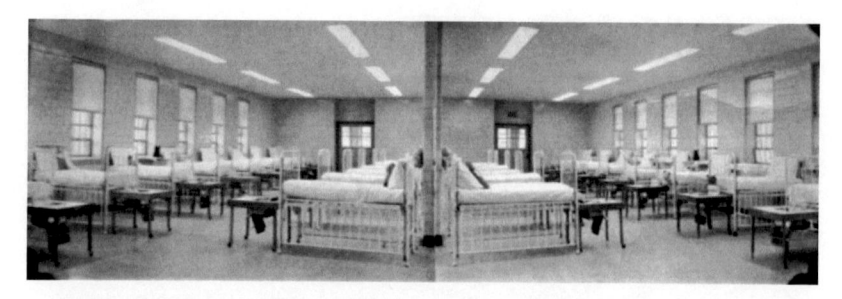

This undated photo, possibly taken before the Infirmary opened, shows a ward divided by a central partition. Courtesy Springfield Newspapers

A network of tunnels conveyed heat from the central power plant and utilities to all the buildings on the grounds. Patients used the tunnels for forbidden meetings with members of the opposite sex. Photo courtesy Jeret Ledger Facebook page: Belchertown State School for the Feeble-Minded

Patients at Belchertown ate their pureed food with utensils like these. No knives or forks were allowed.

Wards were crammed with beds with little or no space between them, often with no pillows. Courtesy Springfield Newspapers

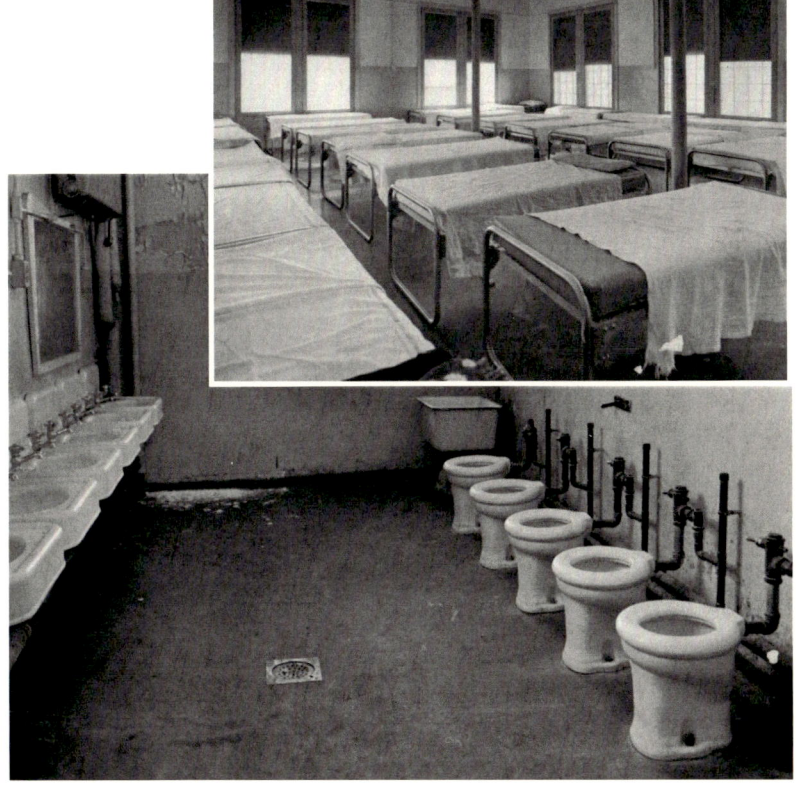

Privacy was non-existent, even in the bathrooms. This same room was used for showering, with a singled showerhead in the ceiling above the floor drain, out of camera range in this photograph. Often the water line to the sinks was turned off, making them unusable for patients. There was no toilet paper. Courtesy Springfield Newspapers

Residents of Belchertown State School enjoy the carousel ride on its opening day, October 17, 1948. Archive photo courtesy Massachusetts Dept. of Developmental Services.

Boy Scout Troop 509, seated on stage for a ceremony in the Belchertown State School auditorium. Archive photo [circa 1955] courtesy Massachusetts Dept. of Developmental Services.

Donald's Honorable Discharge (above)
May 23, 1966

Donald's service photo (right), Fort Dix,
New Jersey 1964

In 2005 at Holyoke Community College (above), Donald got to meet Dr. Benjamin Ricci (left), the father of Bobby Ricci, who was a patient at Belchertown during some of the same years as Donald. As president of the Psychology Club, Donald had invited Ben to speak to students about his own book, Crimes Against Humanity, *an account of the 1973 class action lawsuit that ultimately led to improvements at Belchertown and similar institutions.*

As vice-president of Advocacy Network, Inc., in 2008 Donald attended the annual VOR conference, in Washington, D.C., visiting the office of Congressman Patrick Kennedy of Rhode Island to thank the Kennedy family for their support for the rights of the developmentally disabled (left).

Donald speaks at the annual Memorial Day Ceremony in May 2010, the site once referred to by Belchertown State School patients and attendants as "Turkey Hill."

The original marker for Celia Warner, mother of former patient Al Warner, displayed on Memorial Day 2010 at Warner-Pine Grove Cemetery, and the headstone of Al and his wife Agnes, both former residents of Belchertown State School. Celia Warner was patient #132 at the former Worcester State Hospital. Her marker was moved to the Belchertown site to be where Al and his wife Agnes are buried, the last to be interred at Warner-Pine Grove.

> THE COMMONWEALTH OF MASSACHUSETTS
> ## HOLYOKE COMMUNITY COLLEGE
> THE BOARD OF TRUSTEES, IN ACCORDANCE WITH THE RECOMMENDATION OF THE FACULTY AND THE PRESIDENT, AND WITH THE AUTHORITY CONFERRED BY THE MASSACHUSETTS BOARD OF HIGHER EDUCATION,
> HEREBY AWARDS TO
> ### DONALD E. VITKUS
> THE DEGREE OF
> **ASSOCIATE IN SCIENCE**
> IN THE CURRICULUM OF
> **HUMAN SERVICES**
> TOGETHER WITH ALL THE RIGHTS AND PRIVILEGES APPERTAINING THERETO.
> GIVEN AT HOLYOKE, MASSACHUSETTS THIS FOURTH DAY OF JUNE, 2005.

After obtaining his associate's degree in human services, Donald was invited to address new employees of the Department of Development Services in Northampton, Massachusetts, as part of their orientation training, in the hopes that "...conditons never go back to what they once were."

Donald hugs his wife Pat at his graduation ceremony at Holyoke Community College where he received his degree in Human Services in June, 2005.

Author's Bio

*E*d Orzechowski *is a writer whose features and columns have appeared in* The Republican, The Daily Hampshire Gazette, Early American Life *and other publications. A retired high school English teacher and radio newsperson, Ed lives with his wife Gail in Northampton, Massachusetts.*